650

LAWRENCE AND THE WOMEN

Also by Elaine Feinstein

NOVELS

The Crystal Garden
The Shadow Master
The Border
Mother's Girl
All You Need

BIOGRAPHIES

Bessie Smith
A Captive Lion: The Life of Marina Tzvetayeva

POETRY

Some Unease and Angels: Selected Poems

LAWRENCE

and the

WOMEN

The Intimate Life of D. H. Lawrence

ELAINE FEINSTEIN

HarperCollins*Publishers*

Library of Congress Cataloging-in-Publication Data

Feinstein, Elaine.
    Lawrence and the women : the intimate life of D. H. Lawrence / Elaine Feinstein. — 1st U.S. ed.
      p.   cm.
    ISBN 0-06-016226-0
    1. Lawrence, D. H. (David Herbert), 1885–1930—Relations with women.   2. Women and literature—England—History—20th century.   3. Authors, English—20th century—Biography.
4. Women—Great Britain—Biography.   I. Title.
    PR6023.A93Z6283   1993
    823′.912—dc20
    [B]   92-53378

93   94   95   96   97   RRD   10 9 8 7 6 5 4 3 2 1

CONTENTS

Acknowledgements		7
List of Illustrations		8
Introduction		9
Chapter 1	*Mother*	13
Chapter 2	*Bonds*	21
Chapter 3	*Jessie*	29
Chapter 4	*Schoolteachers*	44
Chapter 5	*Son and Lover*	60
Chapter 6	*Frieda*	72
Chapter 7	*The Wanderers*	83
Chapter 8	*Gargnano*	90
Chapter 9	*The Widening Circle*	97
Chapter 10	*Passionate Friends*	107
Chapter 11	*The War*	119
Chapter 12	*Cornwall*	137
Chapter 13	*Infidelities*	145
Chapter 14	*Capri and Taormina*	161
Chapter 15	*Travelling*	169
Chapter 16	*New Mexico*	181
Chapter 17	*Old Mexico*	191
Chapter 18	*Frieda and Murry*	196
Chapter 19	*Once Again in the New World*	204
Chapter 20	*The Return*	213
Chapter 21	*The Villa Mirenda*	219
Chapter 22	*Last Things*	227
Chapter 23	*Aftermaths*	240

CONTENTS

Source Notes   253
Select Bibliography   267
Index   269

ACKNOWLEDGEMENTS

I should particularly like to thank Stanley Middleton for his hospitality and for guiding me about Nottingham and Eastwood so knowledgeably; the Nottinghamshire County Library for allowing me to listen to their tapes of interviews with D. H. Lawrence's family and friends; Bridget Pugh, who made several helpful suggestions; Miranda Seymour, who made the manuscript of her forthcoming book about Lady Ottoline Morrell available to me; Francis Wyndham, who shared his memories of Lady Cynthia Asquith; Barbara Weekley Barr, for allowing me to record many hours of her reminiscences of Lawrence and Frieda; Saki Karavas, who talked to me about his memories of Frieda, Brett and Angelo Ravagli in Taos, and showed me Lawrence's paintings which he keeps in the office of La Fonda hotel there; Robert Lacey, for his detailed editing of this manuscript; Jane Wynbourne who so generously typed many amendments without complaint; the London Library, and Rick Gekoski, who was able to find me the few books that were not available therein; Cambridge University Press for making available James T. Boulton's six volumes of Lawrence's letters.

Copyright material is reproduced by permission of Laurence Pollinger Ltd and the Estate of Frieda Lawrence Ravagli.

ILLUSTRATIONS

The Lawrence family   *Nottinghamshire County Library Service*
Ernest Lawrence   *George Hardy*
Gypsy Dennis   *George Hardy*
Ada Lawrence   *George Hardy*
The Chambers family   *University of Nottingham Library*
Jessie Chambers   *George Hardy*
Lawrence, 1908   *Nottinghamshire County Library Service*
Alice Dax and her daughter   *George Hardy*
Helen Corke   *Photography Collection, Harry Ransom Humanities Research Center,*
   The University of Texas at Austin
Lydia Lawrence   *George Hardy*
Louisa Burrows   *Professor J. T. Boulton*
The young Frieda von Richthofen   *Photography Collection, Harry Ransom*
   Humanities Research Center, The University of Texas at Austin
Katherine Mansfield   *Peter Day*
John Middleton Murry   *Alexander Turnbull Library, Wellington, New Zealand*
Lady Cynthia Asquith, photograph by Bassano   *National Portrait Gallery,*
   London
Lady Ottoline Morrell, portrait by Augustus John   *National Portrait Gallery,*
   London
Lady Ottoline Morrell, photograph by Cecil Beaton   *National Portrait Gallery,*
   London
Catherine Carswell   *John Carswell*
Lawrence's wedding day   *Nottinghamshire County Library Service*
Amy Lowell   *The Hulton Picture Company*
Mary Cannan   *Chatto & Windus*
Aldous Huxley, Dorothy Brett and Mark Gertler, photograph by Lady Ottoline
   Morrell   *The Estate of the late Mrs. J. Vinogradoff*
Mabel Dodge   *Goldberg/Private Collection*
Lawrence and Frieda, Mexico, 1923   *Photography Collection, Harry Ransom*
   Humanities Research Center, The University of Texas at Austin
Lawrence and Frieda leaving America   *Private Collection*
Angelo Ravagli with his family   *Photography Collection, Harry Ransom*
   Humanities Research Center, The University of Texas at Austin

INTRODUCTION

To approach D. H. Lawrence through an account of his relations with the women in his life does not reduce his stature as an artist. Relations between the sexes was a major theme in his work, and indeed he intended to be a spokesman for women. In December 1912 he wrote to an Eastwood neighbour, Sallie Hopkin, that as a writer he wanted to 'do my work for women, better than the suffrage', and many highly intelligent women knew and respected his insights into their problems. In recent years, feminist critics have been angered by Lawrence because he increasingly came to see liberation for women entirely in terms of a saving sexual relationship, and his writings show a mounting rage against women's desires to use their minds and express their individuality. It is my intention to explore the way this transformation in his attitudes came directly out of his own experience.

In part Lawrence was a creature of his times. The reaction against Victorian attitudes to sexuality ran alongside the demand for greater equality for women, and did not appear to conflict with it. As his story unfolds, however, it becomes clear how far Lawrence's fear of powerful women, and his uncertain idea of masculinity, have a biographical source. I shall avoid any attempt to impose a psychoanalytic interpretation,[1] and will look instead at what can be established about the personalities of the women in his life, beginning with his formidable mother.

A number of the women Lawrence knew well, including his mother, were involved in the movement for women's emancipation. All his early girlfriends were schoolteachers, and that is the profession his mother would have chosen had she had been more fortunate. Many of his most loyal women friends were writers and artists. It was part of his wife Frieda's very considerable charm for Lawrence, however, that she was not intellectual in the sense of wishing to enter into economic or artistic competition with men. Her candour and high spirits convinced Harry Moore, Lawrence's biographer, that she was the ideal consort for Lawrence, and I'm inclined to agree with him.

Yet it is after their marriage, from about 1915 onward, that the need to break away from female domination becomes a central theme in Lawrence's writing. Both his interest in love between men and his dabbling in political thought connect to this theme, and the source seems clear: Frieda had become what Lawrence called a 'Magna Mater' in his life, and Lawrence experienced a degree of dependency on her which 'made it difficult to get the sexual relationship right'.[2] In *Women in Love*, the schoolteacher Ursula Brangwen has this threatening power quite as much as the imperious literary hostess Hermione Roddice: 'She too was the awful, arrogant queen of life, as if she were the queen bee on whom all the rest depended . . . she was so certain of her man that she could worship him as a woman worships her own infant, with a worship of perfect possession.'[3] Later, in Lawrence and Frieda's joint wanderings about the American continent, his wish to change Kate Leslie in *The Plumed Serpent* into a self-effacing and supportive wife has an equally clear biographical source.

Lawrence and Frieda's quarrels are famous. There were friends who saw them as a kind of sexual foreplay; I think myself they often had a sadder origin, since for all the passionate love that bound them together, Frieda did not find Lawrence the most satisfying of her lovers. What attached her to him was the tenderness which she identi-fied in the first weeks of their relationship as he bent over paper boats with her children. Lawrence was the one child she could not leave.

Almost every woman who made an impression on Lawrence found her way significantly into his fiction, from his childhood love Jessie Chambers, whom he called 'the anvil on which I forged myself', onwards. Some of his most generous friends, such as Lady Ottoline Morrell, found themselves portrayed pitilessly; the American heiress Mabel Luhan found her fictional counterpart ritually sacrificed by an Indian tribe. Yet the portrait of Bertha Coutts in *Lady Chatterley's Lover*, with her 'beaky' demand for clitoral stimulation, sits uneasily in Mellors' autobiography. His account so closely resembles Lawrence's own life that his detailed horror at Bertha's sexual behaviour is a puzzle. There is no obvious model for Bertha. Jessie Chambers was too passive to push at Lawrence aggressively, and Alice Dax too afraid of losing him even to risk a quarrel. Only one woman had the confidence to persist in a form of behaviour Lawrence said he disliked, and that was Frieda. One may guess at the need.

Frieda was surely right to laugh when people called Lawrence brutal; she describes him as 'tender and generous and fierce'. Their long, battling marriage is almost unequalled in its intensity, and Lawrence knew he could not live without her. His sexual fidelity after his marriage is unusual in a man who attracted the many personable and unconventional women who became an important part of his story. His dislike of promiscuity may be attributed to his upbringing (he had to accept notably different rules for Frieda), but we may assume he experienced little genuine temptation. His impulse towards homosexuality, which he mainly repressed, may have been stronger. With women, he had a bright-eyed, intense genius for friendship, just as Frieda's readiness for sexual involvement attracted men to her even in her middle age.

Most of Lawrence's biographers have been men, and the most brilliant of the feminist attacks (such as Kate Millett's) have been more concerned with establishing Lawrence's viciousness than understanding the man himself. His essential spirit is perhaps best reached through his poetry, in which the intensity of his response to the world around him, even in his last years, continues to move us with the music of its courage.

Tolstoy, writing enviously of the succour offered to Dostoevsky by his second wife, said, 'Life would have been quite different for Russian writers if they had had wives like Anna Grigoryevna.'[4] It is tempting to speculate how Lawrence might have developed if he had not set up his life with Frieda. If he had married his first love, Jessie Chambers, he might never have lived in Europe, or thrown off his Midland puritanism. Her gentle compliance might have rendered his insistence on male supremacy unnecessary. On the other hand, he would have had to argue his theories about natural aristocracy and the wisdom of the blood with a woman whose education was wide enough to allow her to question them cogently. He would certainly have found it harder to write as he did in *Lady Chatterley's Lover*: 'The supreme pleasure of the mind! And what is that to a woman?'[5] Yet it is hard to feel that Jessie would have enjoyed a lifetime of Lawrence's energies as Frieda did. For all the fury of their life together, it was only in his relationship with Frieda that Lawrence found himself; even when she behaved with some selfishness in the last years of his illness, it was in her presence, as in no other, that he came to life.

Elaine Feinstein
March 1992

Chapter 1

MOTHER

All the images we have of Lawrence's mother, Lydia, suggest a small, determined woman, dressed very correctly in dark colours, who carried herself with pride and assessed the world shrewdly. She spoke with self-confidence, had no trace of the local Nottinghamshire dialect, and pointed up her observations with an ironic sniff to indicate amusement or disapproval. Her neighbours in the Nottinghamshire village of Eastwood disliked her superior airs, but they respected her domestic competence and her dedication to the welfare of her family. What gave her situation some poignancy was the frustration of her own aspirations; these she transmuted into a passion for the education and social betterment of her children. She was the most powerful figure in the Lawrence household, and her perception of events dominated her son David Herbert's thinking for the first half of his life.

Lydia liked her children to believe she had married beneath her, but the facts do not altogether support this. By Lydia's time both her father's family, the Beardsalls, and her mother's, the Newtons, were as much part of the working classes as the Lawrences, and rather less prosperous. The Beardsalls had once been comparatively well off, and had even owned land, until they were ruined by the crash of the lace industry, probably during the depression of 1837. On her mother's side of the family, Lydia could look back to the composer John Newton and, a generation earlier, the famous writer of Methodist hymns, another John Newton, who had been a friend of the poet William Cowper. There was, however, a genuine polarity in the aspirations of the Beardsall and Lawrence families. Lydia's family could take some pride in their superior education; the Lawrences had little interest in it: they had a Midland scepticism about anything that did not relate to material wellbeing.

Lydia's father, George, had been a skilled engineer: he worked in the cotton mills, then as a fitter on the railway and the docks at Sheerness in Kent. The quality of the family's accommodation was often beyond their means, and they sometimes coped by taking in a lodger. In 1870, however, their situation worsened dramatically. George Beardsall was lamed by an accident which left him unable to work, and by 1871, when Lydia was nineteen, she and her two sisters were working at home as sweated labour for the Nottingham lace industry. In material terms, a family of miners in work, like the Lawrences, was decidedly more comfortable. George Beardsall became a disappointed, quarrelsome man whose only solace was his religion. Lydia once told a friend that her father made them all wait on him hand and foot. The experience left her determined 'not to dance attention' on any man.[1] Nor did she.

Lydia liked to think of herself as a woman who had been a school-teacher, and indeed, at thirteen, while still living in Sheerness, she had tried to become one by working briefly as a pupil-teacher. When she did not succeed in that apprenticeship, she actually tried to start a school of her own. This enterprise failed altogether, but no member of the Lawrence family would have been able to entertain such a scheme. Lydia could write in a fine Italian hand and, according to Lawrence, could compose 'a clever and amusing letter when she felt like it'.[2] She read widely, wrote verse which appeared in local magazines, and loved intellectual discussions. Her other sisters married well; indeed the husband of her younger sister Ada became an international Arabic expert: Fritz Krenkow was born in Germany, lived in Leicester, and was to become a Professor of Islamic Studies at the Muslim University in Aligarh, India, from 1929–30, and Professor of Arabic at the University of Bonn from 1931–35. Lydia must have found her sister's good fortune rather a contrast with her own fate.

Before meeting Arthur Lawrence, Lydia had walked home from chapel in Nottingham with the son of a well-off tradesman, who gave her a Bible she treasured all her life. Although he never entered the ministry as he wanted, or offered to marry Lydia as she hoped, he became the image of the kind of man she felt she ought to have married.

Arthur Lawrence resembled this ideal husband in no respect. Born in 1846, he left school before he could read or write, went into the colliery aged seven, and seems to have experienced no pangs of regret for any opportunities he may have thereby lost. His three brothers also went into the mines. The Lawrences and the Beardsalls were related by marriage, and Arthur Lawrence's grandmother was also the daughter of a lace manufacturer. Arthur's father had a shop that supplied pit trousers to the colliery. He was an athlete, a giant of a man who loved sport and was an excellent oarsman; Lawrence remembered the great rolls of flannel for vests, the old sewing machines in his grandfather's shop and the physical ease with which he dealt with them.

Arthur was twenty-seven when he met Lydia at his aunt's home; he was smartly dressed, red-cheeked, and he laughed a great deal. In *Sons and Lovers* Lawrence imagines Lydia as Mrs Morel, seeing Arthur's good humour as 'soft, non-intellectual, warm, a kind of gambolling'.[3] Lydia was also very pleased to give up the drudgery of her father's house, although Lawrence does not mention this in the novel. She and Arthur were married on 27 December 1875, when he was twenty-nine and she twenty-four, and Lawrence repeats what was probably her own claim: 'For three months she was perfectly happy; for six months she was very happy.'[4]

Lydia had married Arthur for his good-natured gaiety. Sadly, everything she later objected to in him arose from precisely that carefree spirit, which was so unlike her own. He liked animals, got on well with his workmates in the pit, and never pretended to have a moral, religious nature. Her disappointment in her marriage and her husband was intense. She had not realised that the phrase 'mining contractor', with which Arthur had described his trade on their marriage certificate, meant he went down the mines himself. He was a 'butty': a sub-contractor who negotiated with the company to mine a certain area of coal and then hired his own day-men. He could earn £5 a week in the winter and, though the pits would go slack in the summer, on average his wage throughout the year would be fifty or fifty-five shillings a week. Out of this he was supposed to give Lydia thirty shillings to pay for the rent, food, clothes, insurance and doctors. When he did have spare cash, he didn't save it, and Lydia couldn't have saved much out of her allowance. On the other hand, Arthur was helpful in the house. He got up sometimes before five and enjoyed making his own breakfast; he didn't expect his wife to look after him as many husbands did. He raked up the fire, boiled the kettle, enjoyed his bacon toasted on a fork and his doorstep slice of bread. Lawrence's younger sister Ada remembers their father sitting like a tailor on the mat and hammering away happily, mending kettles or fixing the eight-day clock, carefully putting the screws and spare parts in saucers and boiling the works in a big saucepan to clean them thoroughly. He didn't understand or sympathise with his wife's love of books and refinement. Still, he was an affectionate man, and Willie Hopkin, an Eastwood shopkeeper and antiquarian, reflects that if Lydia had taken even a part of the same trouble to understand her husband as she lavished on her children, the family might have been a happy one.

Lydia had not anticipated the rigours of being a miner's wife; the coal dust Arthur returned home covered in every evening, and the lack of fastidiousness which made it possible for him to eat ravenously before he had washed any more than his hands. But she made the best of it, and didn't sulk. She put all her energy into raising her children as well as she could, hoping to increase their chance of living with self-respect. That too became a source of quarrels with her husband.

It is easy to see why Lydia was idolised by her children. She managed the complicated domestic arrangements and the struggle to feed and clothe them with bustling cheerfulness. She was a good mother: the children always went to school scrupulously clean; she taught them to read and struggled in every way she could to brighten the family's poverty. She baked bread, bought crockery that was as pretty as she could find, and loved flowers with an intensity that matched her son's. An attempt to open a shop selling baby clothes and ribbons in the bay-windowed front room did not work out, because Lydia lacked the easy-going affability necessary in a successful shopkeeper.

It is equally easy to see why other Eastwood wives might have wondered what Lydia had to complain about. She was relatively well off; for a time at least she had a washerwoman coming in. The houses she lived in were miners' cottages, small and inconvenient by modern standards, but every move the family made was up the social ladder.

The Lawrences began married life in Sutton-in-Ashfield, about eight miles north of Eastwood, then lived for a time in a cottage in Brinsley, where their first child, George, was born. Ernest and Emily were born in New Cross in 1878 and 1882, and soon after this the family moved to Victoria Street, in Eastwood. Their small red-brick house, at a sharp angle to the steeply falling road, was surprisingly roomy and substantial. Cooking facilities and hot water were provided by a cast-iron kitchen range, and the fire kept the room warm as well. The furniture was solid and attractive, and there was a large rectangular window in the front room. Any immigrant family crushed together in London's East End would have regarded the situation as luxurious. It was in Victoria Street that David Herbert Lawrence was born on 11 September 1885. Two years later the family moved again, to The Breach, which was part of a tenement block built for colliers' families. An extra sixpence a week had secured the Lawrences a slightly larger garden, but it was a scrubby affair, separated only by wooden palings from the ashpits where women gossiped and children played. The Breach's front rooms and front gardens, though kept very clean, were hardly used. Lydia, who had a very firm sense of her own intrinsic worth, didn't like the situation, and for that reason her neighbours drew back from her. She insisted on her own pew in the Methodist chapel, according to the son of her eldest child George, who claimed that no one else would sit in it for fear of her.

A studio photograph of the whole family taken in about 1897 shows Lydia looking a good deal older than her husband, though she was in fact five years his junior. Many biographers have assumed she was by then worn down with work and childbearing. Her firm bones suggest a pretty face, if little animation. She sits with her hands clasped, looking tired, though there is some sweetness in the mouth. A much later photograph, taken when she was in a wheelchair and already suffering from the cancer that was to kill her, shows a face with some of the humour in it that made her such an attractive personality.

Arthur, by contrast, even in that studio portrait, has a jaunty white flower in his buttonhole. His health and good looks are unmistakable. It is easy to imagine him enjoying himself, singing in a choir, as he did, with a melodious voice. He hardly looks an oppressive villain. Yet Lawrence, as he vividly puts it, 'was born hating his father'.[5] He entered into a family in which the father was thought of as both contemptible and frightening.

The enmity between Lydia and Arthur was palpable. They quarrelled nightly, and the children upstairs could hear the rows. All through his childhood Lawrence saw his mother as the victim of a brutal husband, though Arthur remained faithful to his wife and continued to love her passionately.

The causes of their battles changed over the years. Early in the marriage Lydia disapproved of Arthur's drinking. He had signed the pledge to impress her, but had soon broken it; he wasn't a drunk, although he enjoyed drinking with his friends in a public house. There was always financial pressure, and Lydia complained because Arthur let money slip through his fingers. Yet he was a good provider; he never neglected his work, and always brought his paypacket home. At first Lydia may have resented being left alone in the evenings; then she came to feel that Arthur's money was being wasted on drink. Her dislike of his behaviour engendered a violence in him which grew more brutal with the years. Ada remembers her father arriving home fuddled, but amiable and apologetic. It was Lydia's rage and the flood of biting truths she unleashed which made him lash out physically in his turn.

Another factor in their quarrelling was Lydia's interest in the Eastwood branch of the Women's Co-operative Guild, which discussed social questions and tried to make women realise the unfairness of their conditions. Lydia occasionally wrote a paper of her own. As the children grew, there were other arguments. Arthur thought his sons should be like himself; he wanted them to belong to the community in which he felt he had thrived, and would have been delighted to have them work at his side in the pit. Lydia, on the contrary, was determined this should never happen. She wanted her children to leave Eastwood, which she never liked, and recover what she had lost in economic and social independence.

Arthur began to feel his children were being privileged at his expense. He could see that they were given attention he was not, and his jealousy caused many arguments. In Lawrence's play *A Collier's Friday Night*, it is the children for whom the mother buys tinned fruit and grapes, and on whose behalf she warns her husband not to eat too many. This draws a cry more of anguish than anger: 'Nothing's got for me. You can get things for them but you begrudge me every bit I put in my mouth.'[6]

Arthur was further isolated from the rest of the household by his hours of work. When he was on night shift he would come home just as the children were having breakfast; then he slept through the day, and left home again at around 8.30 in the evening. When on day shift, he would get up at 4.45 a.m. and be out of the house by 5.30. No doubt that suited Lydia well enough; as Mabel Collishaw, a childhood friend of Lawrence observed: 'Arthur had no company at home. The mother used to isolate the children from him.'[7]

There was always another element in Lydia and Arthur's quarrels; they were about power. Lydia had little hope of doing anything with her own life except protecting and serving her children; that is why she needed the centre of the family for herself. Yet Arthur's needs were equally pressing. A character in Lawrence's story 'Jimmy and the Desperate Woman' makes the point: 'If I give in to the coal face, and go down the mine every day to eight hours' slavery more or less, somebody's got to give in to me.'[8]

Lydia never gave in to her husband's opinions, and she wasn't frightened of him either, though he hit her on several occasions, and threw things at her when he was drunk. Lawrence remembers his father shouting, 'I'll make you tremble at the sound of my footsteps,' and Lydia giving a peculiar and amused laugh and asking, 'Which boots will you wear?'[9] But the most important way in which Lydia made sure of winning the battle with her husband was by making her story known to the children she was working so hard to bring up. They always saw her as the heroic victim of an insensitive and unjust tyrant.

Lawrence in particular felt gratitude and indignation on his mother's behalf. And well he might. He drew from her a love of books, the wish to work with his mind, and a notion of how to keep house, so that wherever he lived he made a home. Nevertheless, it was from his father that he learnt, without even noticing it, his love of nature and animals, his pleasure in being alive and his rejection of conventional values.

The scene in *Sons and Lovers* in which Mrs Morel is shut out in the garden by her drunken husband is modelled on an incident which took place before Lawrence was born; it had passed, as had so much else, into the family mythology. The novel however is less unjust than the myths. Walter Morel, like Arthur himself, has a real capacity for tenderness and a vivid turn of phrase, for all his lack of interest in books. When he first meets his future wife, he enjoys her quick wit: 'Tha'rt not long in taking the curl out of me.'[10] And, for all Lawrence's intentions, he cannot help showing that Mrs Morel's resentment is unrelenting. When Morel takes her a cup of tea in bed, she replies grudgingly, 'Well, you needn't, for you know I don't like it.'[11] The novel depicts a man dismissed to the periphery of his family who becomes more brutally intransigent as a result. He is also as needy as he is angry, which is why, though his children are inconsolable at the thought that he might abandon them, Mrs Morel knows he could never leave her. Lawrence could not fail to observe that, like Walter Morel, his father was dependent, 'almost like a child', on his wife and that, for all his physical strength and occasional violence, he backed down whenever his wife seriously challenged him.

It was the pattern Lawrence was to take for the most important relationship of his life. The terrifying parental quarrels of his childhood gave him a conviction of a necessarily violent opposition between men and women, and led him to feel most at home when at war in his marriage to Frieda: he insisted their relationship was healthy just because they quarrelled so ferociously. 'If a woman's husband gets on her nerves she should fly at him,'[12] he declared in *Fantasia of the Unconscious*.

Chapter 2

BONDS

D avid Herbert Lawrence was Lydia's youngest and frailest son, and she was afraid he would not survive. She hadn't wanted another child, and his delicacy meant she had to look after him more than any of her other children. A thin child, for all his mother's coddling, his older brother George remembers carrying him around on his shoulders with ease. He was ill throughout his childhood, and whereas the other children went to school at five, he only began at seven. He was a 'snuffy-nosed little beggar, seldom without a cold';[1] a moody child, teased for crying and being 'mardy', and so often sunk in this moping and tearful state that even his mother dealt with him coldly, although she prevented his father from smacking him.

The child's passionate attachment to his mother arose from the unusual attention he required. Nevertheless, he was not Lydia's favourite son. That was her third child, Ernest, a handsome, confident boy with his father's twinkling eyes and thick brown hair, who was very clever at school in an easy way that Lawrence never equalled. Nor was he to be her last child. Of his two sisters, the elder, Emily, was tomboyish enough as a girl, but grew into a priggish young woman, while his younger sister Ada had a livelier interest in intellectual matters.

When Lawrence was six the family moved again, this time to a roomier house in Walker Street. It had a view of the whole Erewash valley and an ash tree close at hand which the wind caught and made howl. In a memorable poem, 'Discord in Childhood', this became an image for his parents' quarrels.

He was called Bert at this time, or Bertie, which he much disliked.

When he went to the Beauvale Board School at seven, he found it difficult to hold his own in playground games and preferred playing with the girls, often going off blackberrying with them after school, for which he was teased as cowardly and effeminate by the other boys. He does not seem to have attracted much attention from the teachers, or to have excelled at lessons, though he was praised for his tidiness. Mabel Collishaw, a year older than him, acted as his protector. She found him crying at a stile one morning in his first week of school and had to drag him there against his will. When she came out of class that afternoon, he was waiting for her; on the way home she and her friend Gertrude Cooper escorted him while boys knocked his cap off from behind, calling out insults. A few weeks later he suggested to Mabel that they skip school, hide in a meadow and gather flowers. They made a hole in a hedge to creep through so they could reach some fallen apples. Mabel remembered he selected the rosiest for his mother.

At nine, Lawrence wrote a poem for Mabel and called her sweetheart. Mabel was not particularly impressed, but she kept the poem until the paper fell to pieces. She never forgave him, though, for saying he was going to marry a pretty lady when he grew up, adding unkindly, 'not like you'.[2]

In later years Lawrence liked to identify with the colliers' children, who hated having to learn to read and write and were eager to escape to the adult world of the pit. He would complain that the schoolmasters tried to tame honest, decent lads with their threats of thrashing. But it is clear that boys of this kind shunned him, and frequently tormented him. Quite early on he began to retaliate with words, essentially his mother's weapon. His brother George recalled that he was 'sharp as a needle'.

He enjoyed helping his mother in the house and shared her wish for gentility. According to Mabel Collishaw, he didn't mind doing 'women's jobs' such as black-leading the grate or scrubbing floors; he had joined his mother's world. Away from school more than most children because of his poor health, he entered intelligently into his mother's daily life, acquiring many skills conventionally thought of as female, and he would amaze shopkeepers by his ability to talk knowledgeably about groceries. He had a fastidious sense of household pride, and minded when curtains had to be hung on tapes rather

22

than a proper bamboo pole. When he imagined growing up, it was to earn money and buy his mother a pretty bonnet.

Lydia decided everything. Lawrence remembered wondering as a child why God was a man and not a woman, since on earth women always knew best, and men didn't care. More than any of the other children, Lawrence burnt with hatred of his father (his elder brother George was fond of him, although he too thought his mother a wonderful woman). Lawrence's hatred was not based on his own ill treatment. Arthur was only rarely violent to his children, and even when Lawrence was very rude to him as a child he was never smacked, except by his mother. May Chambers, a sister of Lawrence's boyhood love Jessie, recalls him confessing: 'I have to hate him for Mother's sake'.[3] When his father was taken off to hospital after an accident, Lawrence was openly delighted at what he saw as the departure of his mother's oppressor.

Lawrence grew up in a household dominated by women and girls. As a young child George, nine years older than Bert, was sent away from home to live with Lydia's Newton relations in Nottingham for a year to ease the strain on the family finances; at the age of ten he left home altogether to live in Nottingham where he was apprenticed to one of his uncles. Ernest, though closer to the rest of the family than George, much preferred playing out of the house with his friends. Lawrence was mothered by his older sister Emily, who often read aloud to him when Lydia was busy, but his closest companion was his younger sister Ada. In that 1897 group studio photograph she looks an innocently pliant little girl, with charming ringlets. All through their childhood she idolised her brother. He was always the leader in their games, whether making illicit toffee in their mother's absence or going for country walks; he enjoyed teaching her the names of plants, and liked to point out baby rabbits or cock pheasants for her. Ada learnt to play the piano, which Lawrence never succeeded in doing, although he sat at her side for hours encouraging her to practise, and they often sang together.

On one matter he saw things differently from his mother. Lydia didn't like pets, which made the house untidy. But Lawrence loved animals; when some rats set up house in a box prepared to receive a promised rabbit he became very attached to them, and he had the tenderest feelings towards a terrier that a Beardsall uncle once asked the family to board for him. When he heard the animal crying piteously downstairs, he brought it up to his own bedroom – indeed, all the children treated the animal with such kindness that the uncle found it spoilt and soft when he returned to claim it.

Lawrence enjoyed other activities more than school: a travelling theatre, or readings – often from Dickens – at the British School on Albert Street, in a building adjoining the Congregational chapel. He loved the Bible and hymns, and was much influenced by the Congregational religion, even sneaking into revivalist meetings, which his mother thought common. This was a very small rebellion. He never laid claim to an independent life of his own like his brother Ernest, who played billiards, danced at the local hop (Arthur had been an excellent dancer) and was popular with girls. Ernest did everything well; he was top of his form and won prizes for sports as well as for good conduct. Nevertheless, like his older brother George, Ernest left school at fourteen to help the family with his earnings. He got a job as a clerk, first near Eastwood and then at Shipley colliery nearby in Derbyshire. In his spare time he not only learnt shorthand and typing but taught himself French and German by correspondence. His charm was considerable; a number of girls – some of them from wealthy families – wrote him love letters. It is easy to understand Lydia's unhappiness when this brightest child set off for London. She had taken a particular pride in him, and his laughter and fun were much needed at home, but the wage of £120 a year offered by the shipping underwriters John Holroyd & Co. was too attractive to refuse. She had enjoyed looking after him, and had shown her love in small acts such as putting out tea when he wanted it, or ironing the collars of which he was so proud. But Ernest himself took the parting less painfully. It would seem that – perhaps because he was the favourite child – Ernest was much less obsessed with his mother than was Lawrence.

Nor was he as dutiful as his younger brother. Lydia had hoped that Ernest would contribute to the family's expenses, but Ernest seems to have been dilatory about such payments. In fact, both her elder sons were of less help to Lydia than she expected. George, who had once promised to stay at home and take care of Lydia when he grew up, started going out with a local girl at the age of seventeen instead, and signed up for the army soon afterwards (Lydia somehow managed to

find the £18 to buy him out again). Then he got his girlfriend pregnant, and married her in May 1897. According to Lawrence's schoolfriend George Neville, George was more like Arthur Lawrence than
any of the other children.

In London Ernest fell in love with a girl called Gypsy Dennis, a
stenographer who loved parties and silver slippers, and of whom
Lydia disapproved. Lawrence talks about Ernest 'giving his love to a
fribble'[4] when he became engaged to his Gypsy in 1901, and in *Sons
and Lovers* there are revealing conversations in which William, the
character who corresponds to Ernest, describes his girlfriend to his
mother as a frivolous creature. Both in life and in the novel, however,
Ernest continued to do exactly what he wanted. Lawrence has Wil-
liam/Ernest declaring, 'Oh well, I've gone too far to break off now,'[5]
and proceeding with his wedding plans despite Mrs Morel's disapproval. In his synopsis of *Sons and Lovers* written in 1912 for Edward
Garnett, who was then advising him on his literary affairs, Lawrence
said of the character modelled on Ernest that he had given his sex to
a girl, while 'his mother holds his soul. But the split kills him.'[6] This
accords neither with the eventual narrative of *Sons and Lovers* nor with
Lawrence's own life. The terrible, paralysing dependence of Paul
Morel on his mother is clearly of another order.

Meanwhile, Lawrence continued his education. Because Ernest had
been so intellectually able, Lawrence did not credit himself with
superior intelligence, though it was clear once he got down to school
work that he had a formidable brain. What he did identify as his
especial quality was a consciousness of how other people felt, particularly his mother. Nevertheless, in 1897 he won a scholarship to Nottingham High School, a grammar school which dated back to the
thirteenth century. The scholarship was worth only £14 a year, and
there were clothes and a season ticket costing £1.11d to buy, but
Lydia was adamant that he should go anyway, and Lawrence was
enrolled at the school in September 1898. In Eastwood he now felt
more isolated than ever, but he had always felt different. He had hated
collecting his father's wages from the colliery offices, and had to be
pushed forward by Mabel Collishaw to do so.

Lawrence was well taught at the high school and, though Willie
Hopkin says he suffered because he couldn't bear to be criticised, he
learnt a measure of spiritual resilience there. Colliers' sons were not

looked on favourably by bourgeois parents, and Harry Moore tells of the parents of one boy forcing their son to break off a friendship with Lawrence. But whatever else, Lydia had instilled sufficient self-esteem in her children for them not to regard that type of rejection as personal.

At first Lawrence was a model pupil, even though he had an exhausting two-hour daily journey to and from Nottingham, and in spite of the glaring difference in social class between himself and the other pupils. But his marks started to fall off in 1900. No doubt there were many possible reasons for this. On 18 March of that year, however, Arthur's brother Walter threw a carving blade at his fifteen-year-old son which penetrated his brain; the boy died a few days later. Newspaper reports suggested that the quarrel had been about money; it was well known that Walter Lawrence's earnings suffered because he drank too much. If it had already been a little shameful to be a miner's son, it must have felt much worse to be a murderer's nephew. Whether or not Lawrence felt ashamed of it at school, the brutal tragedy can only have increased the turmoil in the Lawrence household.

When Lawrence left Nottingham High School in July 1901, at the age of fifteen, he drafted a letter with the help of his brother Ernest, stressing his skill in modern languages, and succeeded in getting a clerical job at Haywood's Surgical Garments factory in Nottingham, where he had to copy letters, make parcels and write addresses. We know a great deal more of his life at Haywood's than we do about his time at Nottingham High School. He hated the work, and found it difficult to relate to the people he was working alongside. He might, to entertain his friends the Chambers family, who lived on a nearby farm, make fun of a few kind old women who tried to help him, but he couldn't deal with the young working girls, who found his politeness made him an ideal butt for their teasing. As George Neville describes it: 'They were perfect beasts, they were little devils. They were filthier than anybody he had ever conceived, and they *would* persist in thrusting their filth upon him.'[7] Lawrence didn't like his new life, but he knew his mother needed the money it brought in, and so he set off every morning by train at 7 a.m., taking his midday meal in a basket, and tried to adjust to the new world around him.

Long before he could do so, the whole family structure was altered by the tragedy of Ernest's death.

In October 1901, Ernest returned from London with a small patch of inflammation on his throat. This marked the beginning of an infectious disease called St Antony's Fire, or erysipelas, and led to acute blood poisoning. Nevertheless, he took the first train back to London on Monday morning and went to work as usual that day. The following day he could not move from his bed; he had contracted pneumonia, and his temperature rose to 104. For the next three days he lay unattended in his room. The first warning Lydia had of his illness was a telegram from his landlady. She rushed down to London to be with him, but by the time she arrived Ernest's face was horribly red and swollen and he was too delirious to recognise her. No doctor could do anything to save him. And so on Friday 11 October Lydia lost her most loved son. She returned to Eastwood bowed, tearless and so stunned with grief she was almost incapable of moving about the house. She dealt with all the practical matters of undertakers and officials, and arranged for the body to be brought to Eastwood and buried. It was a matter of further grudge to her that Arthur Lawrence did not help her with any of this. After the funeral she sat with her face blank and her mouth tight shut. She never really recovered; never took part in singing again, or took any interest in family games. She had placed all her hopes in seeing Ernest succeed. He had been the pride of her difficult life. Now he was gone.

Lawrence's emotions may be guessed at. Alongside the sense of loss would have been more uncomfortable feelings of resentment as he observed that his mother's utter depression was unrelieved by his own love. He continued his work at Haywood's until one day he too fell ill with pneumonia. It would be a simplification to claim that this illness was induced by his wish to re-establish a connection with his mother, but the attention he now needed woke her from her stupor of misery and brought her back to life. And so a terrible seal was placed on their intimacy, as Lydia redirected all her love towards another son. From this point onwards there was a reciprocal bond between them. Lydia had needed Ernest far more than he needed her after he reached manhood; Lawrence had needed his mother with an intensity she did not share while her hope of happiness lay in Ernest. Now they clung to one another with an equal desperation.

Lawrence came through the crisis of pneumonia, but his lungs remained delicate for the rest of his life. His voice broke during his illness, and when he recovered he was so much taller he had grown out of all his clothes. He was sixteen.

In a letter to the Scottish poet Rachel Annand Taylor written in 1910, Lawrence described the intensity of the bond to his mother: 'We have loved each other almost with a husband and wife love, as well as filial and maternal. It has been rather terrible and has made me, in some respects, abnormal.'[8] This knowledge did not stop Lawrence from recollecting the perfection of their tenderness for one another for the rest of his life, and setting up a pattern of the kind of relationship he wished he might enjoy with other women. He was to describe this in *Fantasia of the Unconscious*: 'If you want to see the real desirable wife-spirit, look at the mother with her boy of eighteen. Look how she serves him, how she stimulates him, how her true female self is his, is wife submissive to him as never, never it could be to a husband.'[9]

Nevertheless, he decisively rejected just such a relationship when he turned against the first love of his life, his childhood sweetheart Jessie Chambers.

Chapter 3

えん

JESSIE

It was through his mother that Lawrence met Jessie Chambers.
Lydia and Jessie's mother Ann attended the same chapel, and the
two women took to one another; Mrs Chambers was impressed by Lydia's difference from the other miners' wives, while Lydia
liked Mrs Chambers' submissive, quiet manner and the evident sin-
cerity of her religious feeling. Both were outsiders in the colliery
community.

Ann Chambers was the wife of a tenant farmer, Edmund Chambers.
Lydia never regarded a farmer's wife as superior in status to herself;
indeed, Jessie always heard a faint note of patronage in her voice
when Lydia spoke to her mother. The Chambers family were fairly
poor. Edmund Chambers had to do a milk round to make ends meet,
and his wife had to help on the farm as well as look after the house.
Nevertheless, there were social differences. While Arthur Lawrence
could barely make out a newspaper, Edmund Chambers read Hardy's
Tess of the D'Urbervilles to his wife as soon as it came out. Lydia was
not given to thinking of her own worth as being defined by her
husband, however, and felt she had more spirit than Ann Chambers;
certainly she enjoyed much greater autonomy within her own
household.

Haggs Farm, where the Chambers family lived, was about three
miles from Eastwood, a lovely walk over the fields past Moorgreen
reservoir. Lawrence still remembered it with love when writing from
France to Jessie's younger brother two years before his death. His
first visit came when he was fifteen, and thereafter he took delight in
helping with the work in the fields, including the haymaking. He
relished the whole variety of natural life outside and the liveliness of

29

the Chambers family: teas with stewed figs in winter, and stewed apples in August.

Lawrence's first impression of Jessie was of a dark-eyed, curly-haired girl with a vivid face. He observed that her brown eyes resembled her mother's, and that both women were constrained by the need to please the men in the household. Jessie resented her domestic chores, and was often clumsy in doing them (in *Sons and Lovers* Miriam, who is based on Jessie, allows the potatoes to burn). Lawrence's sister Ada, who was jealous of Lawrence's attachment, unkindly remembers Jessie as generally ungainly in body, 'as she walked with her head and shoulders bent forward'.[1] Yet even Ada admitted that Jessie had a beautiful face. The one dissenting voice is that of Mabel Collishaw, who may have been a little jealous of Jessie, although photographs support her opinion to a modern eye: 'Jessie was not pretty. She had a lot of character in her face but she wasn't what you could call a pretty girl.'[2]

Much more important to Lawrence was that Jessie's intelligence was eagerly sensitive to language and feeling. If she seemed hurt and moody sometimes, it was largely because she had been forced to leave school when she was ten, and her daily life offered little more than drudgery. In her feeling of being different from those with commoner sensibilities she resembled Lawrence's mother. He sympathised with her sense of being a princess forced into an uncongenial servitude, and once, when her brothers' mockery made her particularly unhappy, scribbled 'Nil desperandum' on the stable door for her. She was determined not to be just a skivvy for her brothers, and retaliated fiercely when they pulled her hair. In her determination to instil Christian values, Mrs Chambers rebuked her for this, and did what she could to lead Jessie towards self-denial and meekness. It was a lesson which left Jessie sadly easy to manipulate by the young Lawrence.

Lawrence was in his last term at Nottingham High School when he first began to visit the Chambers family, and they were impressed by his school clothes, which resembled those worn at Eton: the elder daughter, May, rather expected him to find their old house and plain furniture 'very countrified'. For his part, he found it easier to relax with them than he did at home. 'You Haggites see the best of me,'[3] he once remarked. Lawrence's own self-assurance probably developed at Haggs Farm. The Chambers children found him fun. He was no longer shy, and he had always been excellent at charades and all kinds of mimicry. He taught the children whist, chess, dancing and singing, and they began to feel that something exciting would happen whenever he came round. He was no longer so well-behaved either, though he was still not physically sturdy; he sometimes lost his temper, once even giving one of the Chambers brothers a blow in the face.

The eldest brother, Alan, was three years older than Lawrence, and became his first close friend. They wandered over the farm together and often lay looking up at the stars. There was some gently homosexual element in the attachment, and those passages in *The White Peacock* in which Lawrence records the narrator Cyril's excitement at the beauty of the male body, the bathing scenes and the pleasure he takes in being rubbed dry and held close after swimming, relate to Alan Chambers. Compton Mackenzie claimed in his autobiography *My Life and Times* that Lawrence once told him: 'I believe the nearest I've come to perfect love was with a young coalminer when I was about sixteen.'[4] Alan Chambers was a farm boy, not a miner, which undercuts the likelihood of his being the young man in question, but strong homosexual feelings between young men of that age are not uncommon, and *The White Peacock* suggests unusual intimacy:

> *He saw I had forgotten to continue my rubbing, and laughing he took hold of me and began to rub me briskly, as if I were a child, or rather, a woman he loved and did not fear. I left myself quite limply in his hands, and, to get a better grip of me, he put his arms round me and pressed me against him, and the sweetness of the touch of our naked bodies one against the other was superb. It satisfied in some measure the vague, indecipherable yearning of my soul; and it was the same with him. When he had rubbed me all warm, he let me go, and we looked at each other with eyes of still laughter, and our love was perfect for a moment, more perfect than any love I have known since, either for man or woman.[5]*

Even if this does not bear on controversy about Lawrence's later homosexuality, it points up the difficulties he was to have in finding a similar erotic excitement with women.

The girls in the Chambers family treated Lawrence as if he were one of them, and loved to show him their new hats and frocks. Jessie noticed that Lawrence imitated his mother's voice. This is a possible explanation for the high pitch that characterised his own for the rest of his life, though Harry Moore suggests it may have been due to that adolescent bout of pneumonia.

It is easy to see why Jessie attracted Lawrence; she was so very earnest, and became so deeply involved in the books he brought her. It was her older sister May who first made contact with Lawrence and who brought back the news of his recovery to the family after his illness, but quite soon it was to Jessie alone he was writing his letters. She was the one to whom he revealed all his early ideas and who led him to believe in himself.

She certainly believed in him; he changed her life. He had a knack of making people feel that whatever was happening was enormously worthwhile. With him she learnt to recognise the flowers: Lawrence had picked up a wide knowledge of their names from books. In the fields he read poems to her, especially Shelley, Wordsworth and Keats. They shared books he introduced into the household, beginning with *Little Women*, in which they identified themselves as Jo and Laurie. They loved Dickens, especially *David Copperfield*, with whose hero Lawrence felt much affinity. More surprisingly, he also responded to George Eliot's *The Mill on the Floss*, and thought Maggie Tulliver was too vital to marry the crippled Philip Wakem. It is interesting that in his adolescence Lawrence regarded Maggie with such enthusiasm, when she is just the kind of intelligent woman whose aspirations he was later to find both misplaced and menacing. At the time he knew Jessie, Maggie was his favourite heroine.

Lawrence took the leading role in everything, which was natural enough, since unlike the Chambers children he had been educated at a grammar school. He was surprised to find that Jessie wanted to learn maths and French, and though he taught her what he knew, her younger brother David (who went on to become a professor of economics at the University of Nottingham) remembers that he became very impatient with her. Lawrence had something of a talent for mathematics, and bullied Jessie mercilessly when she found his cursory introduction to algebra hard to follow. Jessie's submissiveness and gentleness, induced in part by her mother's Christian teaching, served her ill as the relationship developed. When she made errors, Lawrence had a vituperative and cruel temper. And she was altogether too eager to please. On one occasion she invited him to a Literary Society social, and when he found nothing but banal games in progress, she was as ashamed as if it were her fault.

Jessie's tender acceptance of Lawrence's view of things may have been damaging to her, but it was marvellously helpful to him. He winkled out of Jessie her wish to be a writer, confessed his own, and began the habit of showing her his manuscripts which continued long after their first break-up as adolescent lovers.

Lawrence had already begun to articulate the idea that a man's greatness was founded in a woman. As far as his writing was concerned, Jessie was the woman he was founded in. No wonder Lydia became jealous of his attachment. This jealousy came long before sexual involvement between Lawrence and Jessie could have been feared. Jessie Chambers remembers Lawrence reporting as early as 1902 his mother's complaint that 'he might as well pack his things and come and live with us'.[6] In the same year her sister May felt there was gossip about the amount of time Lawrence was spending away from home, as if 'we as a family are stealing him from his mother'.[7]

Lydia had other worries, however. As Lawrence was still recovering from his pneumonia, Arthur was providing the only money now coming into the family. There were bills to pay; for Ernest's headstone and Lawrence's doctor. Lawrence could not enjoy his convalescence forever; the family needed his financial contribution, but he was not strong enough to go back to work in a factory. At length it was decided that he should train as a pupil-teacher in the Boys' Section of Albert Street School, Eastwood. He would only be paid a shilling a week, and it was far from an easy life; he had to arrive each morning an hour before the teaching day began for a lesson from the headmaster. May Chambers, who was a teacher in the Girls' Section of the school, reflected: 'The sort of boy he was not strong enough to play with he was now to try to teach.'[8]

Even as Lawrence now assumed that teaching was to be his career, in his first year at Albert Street – some time in 1905 or 1906 – he began to take his first tentative steps at writing. In this he was sustained and helped by Jessie Chambers more than anyone else. When Lawrence confessed to Jessie his fear of being thought absurd – 'A collier's son a poet!'[9] – she at once encouraged him to think his desire was possible.

Jessie's faith in Lawrence was all the more important since Lydia clearly did not share it. She herself had once had writing ambitions of her own; at the age of thirteen, Lawrence had discovered an exercise book of her poems. Her first comments on the early draft pages of *The White Peacock* were withering, and not only because she found the idea of an abandoned pregnant woman shocking. She was surprised and, perhaps worse, amused, to think that a son of hers should have written such a story.

Lydia was decidedly anxious at the prospect of her son considering a literary career: then, as now, its rewards were uncertain, and it was altogether easier for Jessie than Lydia to respond eagerly with the belief that Lawrence might do anything he set his mind to. If Lawrence needed Jessie behind him at this stage, however, it was important that she should be perceived as being several steps behind. He did not encourage her own longing for education. When he began to attend the Teachers' Training Course at Nottingham University College in September 1906, he advised Mr Chambers not to send Jessie there, giving his own experience as the reason. He claimed that the teachers would simply put her through a grind that would make her the same as everybody else. In part it was his own disillusionment with college courses that made him say so; but only in part. When Jessie discovered she was not to go to college, she said she wanted to study for the matriculation examination of the University of London, but Lawrence opposed this on the grounds that she might not pass, which would disappoint her. His final argument against her education – that she might become a bluestocking – hardly seems very convincing, and it is difficult not to reach the conclusion that he preferred her not to share in his educational advantage.

Lawrence himself did not fully understand this; he was not yet aware of all the pressures upon him, and entertained the fantasy that all the people he loved might live happily together in the same house, which Jessie perceived would not be likely to work out well. She saw more clearly than he did the tensions in the Lawrence household, between mother and son as well as between wife and husband, and had no illusions about the relative importance of the love Lawrence felt for his mother and for herself: in recording Lawrence's interest in *Coriolanus*, she observed that the play had significance for him because it was the mother who counted in it and the wife hardly at all.

Lawrence's relationship to Jessie was intellectual, companionable

34

and entirely sexless until he was about twenty-one. He appears to have developed late, both physically and mentally. Once, reading a passage from Schopenhauer to Jessie in which the philosopher declares: 'Everyone in the first place will prefer and ardently desire those who are most beautiful,' he looked up and expressed his own discomfiture: 'I *don't* ardently desire.'[10]

Both Jessie and Lawrence were conditioned to fear sexual feelings, though Lawrence's inability to feel sexually attracted to her was not only caused by that. He was still altogether inexperienced in sexual matters. George Neville, one of Lawrence's friends when he was a student teacher, records Lawrence's shocked incredulity when he added pubic and armpit hair to a drawing of a nude. Lawrence related to women conversationally with ease, but physical encounters were another matter. In a letter to Blanche Jennings, the socialist suffragette, to whom he liked to confide his affairs of the heart, he was still writing of how impossible he would find it to kiss a girl on the mouth in 1908, when he was twenty-three.

Lawrence's sexual feelings, as they began to trouble him, led him to turn on Jessie with savagery. He upbraided her for almost every gesture she made: even her way of cuddling her younger brother or her liking to touch the flowers she loved. In her memoir, written after Lawrence's death, Jessie recalls many such incidents with painful sharpness. She remembers being accused of resembling Emily Brontë because she was too intense and introspective, and being condemned for not having a strong intellect.

However innocent their relationship, Lawrence and Jessie were indeed talked about in Eastwood as Lydia and Ada claimed. There was nothing scandalous in the gossip; it was simply assumed that they would marry. Lydia could not accept this. For all his physical weakness and emotional dependence, Lawrence attracted many other girls apart from Jessie. They drifted in and out of the Lawrence kitchen looking for him; Lydia thought there was safety in numbers, but she disliked Jessie even though she was no 'fribble' like Ernest's Gipsy. Her fear that Jessie would leave no room for herself in her son's heart may have played a part, but Ada, too, resented her brother's attachment to Jessie. The family as a whole did not take to her.

There may well have been another element, something akin to snobbery. Lydia was very aware of social position, and must have seen Jessie as a disappointing choice. She regarded Jessie's determination with anxiety, thinking her son was less involved with the girl than she was with him. In a letter to her sister Lettie four years later she was still saying of Jessie that 'she will not let him slip if she can help it'; and suggesting 'though he is fond of her it does not seem like the real love he ought to have if he intends to marry her'.[11] By 'real love' Lydia must have meant a serious emotional commitment; she had no respect for animal lust. The 'want of common sensuality' with which her son was to charge Jessie would have been a meaningless accusation to Lydia. She was as puritanical on such matters as Jessie's own mother. Nor could Jessie's craving for an intellectual life be what she feared, since the desire resembled her own.

In spring 1906, when it was clear that Lawrence was going to college, Lydia asked him to make up his mind about Jessie, as it was unfair to the girl's marriage prospects not to do so. This induced an indecision that could have only one outcome. It is described in *Sons and Lovers* and in Jessie's own poignant memoir. In both accounts Lawrence tells Jessie that he has looked into his heart and cannot find that he loves her 'as a husband should love a wife'.[12] Five years later Lawrence described the breaking of the growing love between himself and Jessie as 'the slaughter of the foetus in the womb'.[13]

If the relationship of the two young people had ended there and then, it might have been better for Jessie. But Lawrence did not want to discontinue their friendship, which he rightly saw was the only one in his life that had ripened. The next evening he was at Haggs Farm as usual, and was quite angry when Jessie barely looked up from her book to acknowledge him. In the course of the evening he suggested that he was eager to marry if it were possible, and added with some pathos, 'I'd marry you if only I could.'[14]

Lawrence was well aware of the hurt he had inflicted and the way Jessie was likely to brood over their lost love, but he still needed her help. So he neither abandoned his friendship with her nor changed his tone towards her. The reproaches increased cruelly. Moreover, when she was invited to tea at the Lawrences' house, Jessie continued to feel the fixed hostility of Lydia and Ada. In the August before Lawrence entered college, Jessie was one of a party which included the Lawrences who spent a fortnight at Mablethorpe on the Lincolnshire coast. Lawrence was the centre of the party, much as Paul, in

Sons and Lovers, arranged a holiday for his mother because his 'father was no good'.[15] In the novel, Mrs Morel takes charge of the house, and Paul 'stuck with her as if he were *her* man'.[16] The tension between Lydia and Jessie on that holiday led to torrents of new and angry accusations from Lawrence. Their rivalry continued, even though Lawrence was known to have spelled out the limits of his affection. When Jessie tied her hat under her chin with a broad silk scarf on a Sunday morning, Lawrence asked his mother to share his admiration and received a bitter glance in response. That evening Lawrence and Jessie went for a walk together during which he reproached her violently. She was bewildered by his incoherence, and by a mounting sense that his unhappiness was all her fault. As recounted in *Sons and Lovers*, during their walk on the sands Paul is overwhelmed with sexual desire, while Miriam stares intently at the beauty of the moon.

Jessie and Lawrence's father travelled home together from Mablethorpe after a week. Jessie was not far from tears on the way, and responded gratefully to Arthur's kindliness. She may also have sensed him as an ally against Lydia. If so, he was powerless.

From this point onward Lawrence's criticism of Jessie became brutal. He gibed casually, 'It isn't as if you had a strong intellect,' and some time in 1907 he reflected 'It comes to this, you know. You have no sexual attraction at all, none whatever.'[17] Jessie could never put the cruelty of those words out of her mind, and her younger brother David found this section of her memoir so painful that he could not bear to read it a second time.

No doubt Lawrence's outpourings of cruelty were partly caused by sexual frustration, but the cruelty itself took many forms. He was unable to leave the question of their relationship alone, and worried away obsessively at what he felt was wrong, convinced there were two men inside him: one who loved Jessie, and another who never could. As he pressed on the sore place and puzzled at why that should be, he undermined all Jessie's self-esteem:

> *'Very few people* like *you, do they?'*
> *'I don't know* very *many people,' I replied . . .*
> *'That's just it,' he declared. 'At the bottom you don't really care whether people like you or not.'*
> *'Why should I care? I can't help it either way.'*

> *'No, but you see,' he said, with sudden gentleness, 'there must be some*
> *fault in you if nobody likes you. The others can't all be wrong.'*
> *'But they do like me, those who know me properly,' I protested.*[18]

Almost every conversation recorded in Jessie's memoir takes the same shape. Jessie twists and turns, while Lawrence is determined to analyse all the ways in which she cannot give him what he needs. This process of 'internal dismemberment', as Jessie called it, he thought of as an attempt to understand. She was surely right to see it as destructive.

In *Sons and Lovers* Lawrence articulates Paul's dislike of Miriam's submissive qualities and wishes she could laugh at him, but it is hard to see how, once such a sado-masochistic relationship had been set up, she could be expected to escape without help.

Lawrence was clear only about the help he needed himself. In an incident in the novel which overlaps with Jessie's memoirs, she gently advises him about the brakes on his bicycle. According to Jessie's version, he is touched by her pleading concern for his safety. As Lawrence tells it in *Sons and Lovers*, his recognition of her affection is mingled with resentment: 'She did not seem to realise *him* in all this ... she never realised the male he was.'[19] An almost vengeful recklessness crept into his cycling as a result, and verbally he took another kind of vengeance for this refusal to acknowledge his maleness.

The Chambers family gave Lawrence a set of watercolours for his twenty-first birthday, and at Christmas he gave Jessie a selection of Shelley's poems. It was on Jessie's twenty-first birthday in January 1908 that Lawrence sent her a long letter which included this key paragraph:

> *When I look at you, what I see is not the kissable and embraceable part*
> *of you, although it is so fine to look at with the silken toss of hair curling*
> *over your ears. What I see is the deep spirit within. That I love and can*
> *go on loving all my life ... Look, you are a nun, I give you what I*
> *would give a holy nun. So you must let me marry a woman I can kiss*
> *and embrace and make the mother of my children.*[20]

Jessie saw his problem differently. She believed it had nothing to do with her, but that the polarity he described came from a split in himself, the source of which lay in his relationship to his mother, and the position she occupied in the Lawrence household. As she put it, 'Mrs Lawrence . . . ruled by a sort of divine right of motherhood, the priestess rather than the mother. Her prestige was unchallenged; it would have seemed like sacrilege to question her authority.'[21] Jessie concluded that all her problems with Lawrence arose from Lydia's unassailable belief in her own rightness.

It was not, however, only Lydia's opposition that troubled Lawrence. He had transferred enough of his love for his mother to Jessie to make sexual relations with her difficult to imagine; this accounts for his insistence on Jessie's resemblance to a nun. At the same time he still could not do without her, and insisted that his writing and 'all that side of his life' would continue to belong to her. Lydia offered no help to his literary aspirations; her ambitions for him were much more practical. It was only from Jessie that he received encouragement and constructive criticism of his first draft of 'Laetitia', which was to become *The White Peacock*. He brought his writing to her for assessment and sometimes followed her around as she did the housework in the evening in order to talk to her. As the novel took shape in his mind, he became introspective and gloomy; he had a fear of his own ambitions. Jessie does not make absolutely clear when it was he read Balzac's *Le Peau de chagrin*, which he admired very much, but she remembers that he dwelt upon the progressive diminishing of the hero's life that followed every wish he was granted. It seemed a personal matter, as if he feared his own aspirations, rather as the ancient Greeks feared hubris.

Jessie not only saw Lawrence's ability, she enhanced it with her insights. All the time he was criticising her lack of spirit and intelligence, he depended on both. It is true that Lawrence also encouraged Jessie to write herself, as she had always wanted, but she was unable to do so. She attributed her failure to poor education, though she had read more widely than many a student at academic institutions. It was not her lack of knowledge so much as her lack of self-esteem which prevented her. This is hardly surprising. Apart from conversations with Lawrence which stimulated all her self-doubt, Jessie was aware of his family's dislike of her, and her own family's mounting disapproval. Soon she also had to accept not only Lawrence's relationships with other women, but intimate conversations about them.

The Chambers family did not wish their daughter to marry Lawrence, who in their view belonged to a mother who would never give him up. Jessie was by now so unhappy she began to think of moving away from the area; but this upset her own mother, and in any case it was clear that Lawrence planned to find a job away from home quite soon. Jessie was understandably impatient with Lawrence's insistence that their 'strands would remain entwined together' even if he married someone else.

At twenty-three, Lawrence was still a virgin. Some time in his twenty-fourth year, however, he was introduced to the 'great experiment of sex' by a friend he had known for a number of years: Alice Dax.

Alice Dax was a woman of about thirty who worked in the post office. An active member of the Congregational Literary Society and the Eastwood Debating Society, Lawrence knew her as a frequent contributor to discussions in both circles. She was married to a pharmacist, though when she grew close to Lawrence she was estranged from her husband. Born in Liverpool, she was one of a family of seven children of a Harbour Board clerk, and her childhood poverty had a pinched gentility not so different from Lydia's. Appearances were cripplingly important. Alice felt shut in 'behind clean faces and gloved hands'. Her suffragette convictions arose from observing the self-sacrifice of her mother, who was for years the breadwinner of the family, and hating her father for his silk hat and frock coat, even though the insistence on linen and doileys when there weren't enough cakes to go round may well have been her mother's.

In Eastwood, Alice was seen as an outsider. She was thought a little eccentric for refusing to have Nottingham lace curtains in her windows, and she shocked the milkman by wearing sandals without stockings. The Daxes' chemist shop was bought out by Boots in the summer of 1910 and the family moved to Shirebrook, ten miles north of Eastwood. Enid Hilton, Willie Hopkin's daughter, describes Alice as completely uninhibited and 'advanced' in dress and thought. Her clear, clean house was uncluttered with knick-knacks and reflected her own directness. She was widely read, a committed socialist suffragette, and most of the men she knew were afraid of her – she often contradicted what they said. Enid observed that her father feared Alice's influence on his own wife. Yet, for all her forthrightness, Enid

Hilton recalled that people turned to Alice in trouble, because she was one of the kindest women she had ever met.

Lawrence wrote mockingly to other friends, notably Blanche Jennings, a socialist he had met through Alice, suggesting that Alice's suffragette opinions were no more than the result of her unhappiness; occasionally he wished she would come to her senses and be an 'ordinary woman' rather than an aspiring intellectual, but he valued her opinion. He showed her the manuscript of four chapters of 'Laetitia', and the completed manuscript soon after Jessie had read it. At the time, Alice was recovering from the birth of her first child, and Lawrence was apprehensive about her response: when it came, in June 1908, there was no more than 'half a dozen laughing lines of amused scoffing'. Alice thought the novel 'too full of moods' and expressed an uncompromising scepticism about whether the people in it could actually exist. If Lawrence found her criticism useful, he was also impatient with her schoolteacherly attitude to flaws in his command of English. In a letter to Blanche Jennings, he indignantly rejected what Alice had said: 'Mrs Dax told me her opinion – she is wrong – she is no judge of style.'

Alice was a very large woman, with disordered blonde hair. The photographs we have suggest she was not as pretty as Lawrence's later girlfriends. More importantly, Alice had always perceived herself as plain: as a child she had been told that no man would ever marry her, and she had accordingly married the first man who proposed. Yet she it was who seduced Lawrence. How exactly this came about is recounted more than once by Willie Hopkin, who told a journalist friend that Lawrence had called on Alice one morning.

'There's a poem I want to write.'
'Well,' says the lady, 'there's pen and ink and paper in the next room. Go and write your poem and then perhaps you'll be a bit more sociable.'
Lawrence went on walking about the room as he said, 'That's just the trouble. I can never work until after I have had sexual intercourse.'
'Too bad,' says the lady, disappearing from the room. Ten minutes later she reappeared in a dressing gown, saying, 'All right, Bert. You can use me.'[22]

The source of Hopkin's information would presumably have been his wife Sallie, who was a friend of Alice, but there are some implausibilities in the story. Lawrence might have wanted Alice to think that he was accustomed to regular sexual intercourse, but this was not the case. The crude facts however are not in dispute. Another version has it that Alice told Sallie Hopkin, 'I gave Bert sex. I had to. He was over at our house, struggling with a poem he couldn't finish, so I took him upstairs and gave him sex.'[23]

It is difficult to establish exactly when this initiation took place. On balance, it seems that it was some time in the first half of 1909; in May of that year Lawrence wrote approvingly to Blanche Jennings about Alice's increased womanliness, and announced cryptically that he himself was now 'tremendously grown up'.[24] According to Jessie Chambers, on the other hand, Alice Dax had 'given Lawrence plenty of provocation of which he had taken no advantage' until 1910. The miracle of sexual release was something for which Lawrence was extremely grateful, and he found it easy to like Alice, but he was never in love with her. For all her habitual directness, Alice was too afraid of losing Lawrence to quarrel with him and, although she was older than he was, and in most respects more worldly, she acknowledged him as altogether her superior. The affair went on for many months, and was a topic of scandal in Eastwood, though Alice categorically denied the rumours of it to Jessie: given Alice's independent and defiant spirit, that lie must have been an act of the purest kindness, as Jessie very much wished to believe that Lawrence's involvement with Alice did not precede her own sexual commitment. Alice was reluctant to hurt Jessie, and when she had read *Sons and Lovers* she specifically wrote to reassure her that the affair between Paul Morel and Clara Dawes (who was clearly based in part on herself) was entirely fictional. 'I have read *Sons and Lovers* and I *swear* it is untrue.'[25]

Whenever the affair began, it continued alongside Lawrence's affair with Jessie; and it was at least possible for Alice to hope that the child she bore in October 1912 could have been fathered by Lawrence. Alice and Lawrence were still close when Lawrence met Frieda von Richthofen in March 1912, and he told Alice about the meeting the very next day.

Alice never felt up to Lawrence, and when she wrote to Frieda in January 1935 after reading *Not I, But the Wind*, the memoirs Frieda published after his death, she touchingly confessed as much. As frankly as Tatyana scorning to pretend she no longer loves Onegin,

Alice Dax confessed, 'Alas, I loved him,'[26] and admitted how bitterly envious she had been when she read, in a card Lawrence wrote from Lake Garda in September 1912, of his happiness with Frieda. Alice had a self-knowledge and an ability to assess her own situation and feelings that anyone might have envied and respected. When she gave Lawrence up she went through a kind of hell.

There is just a hint that her emotions might have been a little less noble than her letter to Frieda suggests, as she refers to her resentment of Lawrence's snobbery. She remembered Lawrence saying he would have liked to introduce her to Frieda, and saw in his face that he was imagining a meeting which could not go well. Alice knew she had never become the woman she might have been. She had been brought up in a family that had no thought of books or culture, and saw that in going off with Frieda, Lawrence had escaped, while she had not.

None of Lawrence's correspondence with Alice survives, apart from the postcard from Lake Garda. In it he hopes Alice is 'going on decently'[27] with her pregnancy. All through that summer, pregnant and ill, Alice faced up to her loss, and brooded on her own inadequacies. As she wrote to Frieda in 1935: 'I fear he never even enjoyed "morphia" with me – always it carried an irritant. We were never, except for one short memorable hour, whole; it was from that one hour that I began to see the light of life.'[28] It was surely with Alice Dax that Lawrence had his earliest experience of happy sexuality, and this is what Alice meant by 'morphia'. Back with her husband, Alice found herself living a life bounded by women's expectations, and quite as wasted by the society in which she found herself as Jessie's. In 1913 Jessie, writing of Alice's egoism and melancholy, nevertheless reflected: 'How can she help it? I should think she has more of what Alan [Chambers] used to call "superfluous" sense than anybody in Shirebrook, and all powers that run to waste raise a crop of weeds.'[29]

Chapter 4

SCHOOLTEACHERS

In October 1908, having passed his examinations at Nottingham University College, Lawrence was offered a job as assistant master teaching all subjects at Davidson Road School, Croydon, south London, at £95 a year. He set off into a completely unknown world. Apart from day-trips, he knew little of England. At first he felt the uprooting from everyone he had known was unbearable; he wrote Jessie a letter she described as 'like a howl of terror'. He took lodgings with a family close to the school, and his mother was glad to hear there was a baby in the house, which she was sure would keep her son pure. She would have been less pleased to know that his landlord, Mr Jones, pointed out likely prostitutes to him, and was willing to supply him with condoms, or that Mrs Jones, who often quarrelled with her husband, had a flirtatious manner. For the moment, Lawrence was too conscious of his displacement to be tempted by such adventures, but his Croydon years are the only time in his life during which he pursued a number of women sexually at the same time.

Teaching in Croydon was difficult. It was a poor neighbourhood, the forty-five boys in his class were rough and insolent, and Lawrence found the effort of imposing discipline was like trying to tame wild animals. The boys were far poorer than the colliers' children in Eastwood, and a number of them came from the Gordon Home for Waifs and Strays. Some of the sense of violation he felt in the next two years is given to the schoolteacher Ursula Brangwen in the last section of *The Rainbow*. He went on reading and finding out about the world with enthusiasm, however, discovering both Wagner and Nietzsche in his first year at Croydon. Nietzsche was very popular with writers and artists of the time; Lawrence had read of him in H. G. Wells and George Bernard Shaw, and his books were to be found in Croydon Public Library. It is possible that Helen Corke, a Croydon school-teacher who was to become an important friend of Lawrence, and who encouraged his love for Wagner, was the one to put Nietzsche into his hands; she had begun to read him in 1908. Lawrence was to find Nietzsche useful in formulating what he disliked about characters such as the well-bred Leslie Tempest in the manuscript of his novel, now called 'Nethermere'.

Lawrence's loneliness in Croydon was apparent to everyone, and he had no illusions about the significance of the only recognition his writing had so far received. In August 1907 he had entered three of his stories in a competition run by the *Nottinghamshire Guardian*, one under his own name, one under Jessie's and the third under the name of Louie Burrows, a beautiful young girl also training as a teacher, and a member of a group of friends in Eastwood who shared literary interests. The story entered under his own name, an early version of what was to become 'A Fragment of Stained Glass' called 'Ruby Glass', was given an honourable mention. Winning the competition with 'A Prelude', entered under Jessie's name, an intensely literary portrait of the Chambers family, was pleasant, but the prize money of £3 hardly changed Lawrence's situation.

He wrote home to Louie as well as Jessie, and even suggested that they collaborate on some of her stories, which he offered to try and get published. He had not attempted as much for his own work. Although he had finished the first draft of his novel by the end of 1907, he went on revising it throughout his first year at Croydon, and continued to send poems to Jessie.

In the spring of 1908 Lawrence had sent some of his work to G. K. Chesterton, whose writing he had admired in the *Daily News*. He was bitterly disappointed when some months later it was returned by the author's wife with perfunctory apologies. Her husband had been too busy to comment. Lawrence felt he had tried, been turned down, and would try no more.

It was Jessie Chambers who took the next step for him. She had the idea of sending some of his poems to the *English Review*, a literary magazine under the editorship of Ford Madox Hueffer (later Ford Madox Ford), which they had read together with excitement.

Lawrence agreed, though he pretended not to care what happened to his work. Jessie gathered together the poems Lawrence had been sending her over the winter of 1908, selected those she thought most striking, and sent them to the *English Review* under the pseudonym 'Richard Greaseley'. Early in August 1909 she had a letter from Hueffer promising that he would do something with them, and when Lawrence returned from a holiday on the Isle of Wight with his family, she was able to put Hueffer's letter triumphantly into his hand and hear him saying '*You* are my luck!'[1] The sweetness of that appreciation did not last long, however, for he took away the letter proudly to show to his mother, and Jessie never saw it again. In 1929 Lawrence bore witness to his gratitude to Jessie in a lovely metaphor: she had 'launched me so easily on my literary career, like a princess cutting a thread, launching a ship'.[2]

In November 1909 four poems – 'Still Afternoon', 'Baby Movements', 'Discipline' and 'Dreams Old and Nascent' (the last appropriately enough written to Jessie) – appeared in the magazine. Lawrence had not yet begun his affair with Jessie, though it is probable that he had already become involved with Alice Dax. Around this time he began to make sexual advances to several young women, as if he had been given a sudden access of confidence.

The first of these was Agnes Holt, a fellow teacher at the Davidson Road School. She was tall, with grey eyes and auburn hair, and Lawrence told Jessie that he was seriously attracted to her. Jessie observed an awkwardness about Agnes, and claimed she often spoke to Lawrence like an elder sister, but she is hardly an impartial witness. All we know about Agnes Holt suggests she was alert, smart and independent in manner; she was impressed by Lawrence as a published writer, and was eager to help him. To mark the publication of his work in the *English Review*, for instance, she copied poems out for him into a notebook he kept for his poetry. She also helped him to prepare a clean copy of the beginning of the manuscript of 'Nethermere' for Hueffer.

It is less clear how they related sexually. Lawrence wanted a relationship without any kind of emotional commitment, and Agnes was probably interested in a conventional marriage. Lawrence wanted her to see their relationship as an exciting game, and Agnes might have been willing to do so if he had made the playing of it more flattering, but he was incapable of offering her what he scathingly called 'the woolly fluff of romance'.[3] Even so, he did consider marrying her for a time, and it was as a possible fiancée that he introduced her to Jessie when she came on a visit to Croydon in 1909. It was also to Jessie that he most fully explained his problem: he couldn't see how to commit himself to a life supporting a family, and he needed a woman who would love him enough to sleep with him without that commitment. Agnes Holt was an unlikely candidate for such a role. She had mid-Victorian standards, a tendency to lapse into sticky sentimentality, and little understanding of what Lawrence could mean by 'naked life'. Lawrence knew Agnes was ignorant and old-fashioned, and probably not as fond of him as she pretended to be, and it is not surprising that by Christmas 1909 he had decided that the idea of marrying her was a mistake, and told her as much. She left Croydon soon after and married another teacher.

Lawrence's problems with Agnes Holt resulted in his hinting to Jessie that he needed her to sleep with him. On Jessie's visit in November 1909, after seeing a play, they returned to Lawrence's lodgings, where Lawrence cooked supper. At one in the morning he begged her to stay and talk. Jessie was tired, since she had set out from home at six the previous morning, but was incapable of not trying to please him. When he asked her what she wanted from life, she had to hide her tears. Lawrence, however, was preoccupied with his own sexual desperation. He had an overpowering need for 'that' without marriage, he explained. Jessie understood the euphemism and, exhausted as she was, actually remained to discuss with him whether it was possible for him to ask for such a thing. Would a girl find it wrong? Jessie replied that it would depend on whether the girl loved him enough. Impatient with this evasion, Lawrence then made the enquiry personal, as indeed it must have been all along. Would Jessie herself find it wrong? Jessie's thoughts ran on Christian texts of giving out of love and charity, and she said that she would not think it wrong, but difficult.

To make such a request in such a way may seem brutal and callous, but Lawrence had no idea of how to woo Jessie towards sensuality. When they were younger he had lent her French novels and read Baudelaire to her in a throaty voice; now he simply stated his own needs baldly. After Jessie retired to bed that night she was surprised to hear a tentative knock on the door, to which she did not respond. Yet very soon afterwards she became Lawrence's mistress.

Meanwhile, Lawrence was drawing closer to a woman who attracted him much more: Helen Corke, a teacher at another Croydon school. A photograph of her taken in about 1912 shows a young woman with a pleasant face, straight nose and humorous mouth. This does not convey the feature which most attracted Lawrence, however; in all his descriptions of her as Helena, the central figure in his second novel *The Trespasser*, which he began in 1910, it is the deep blue of her eyes that he singles out for praise.

For her part, Helen valued her mind more than her physical beauty, and her sexuality was ambivalent. She was emotionally attached both to her cousin Evelyn and to Agnes Mason, the colleague at the Davidson School who had introduced her to Lawrence, and later she was much attracted to Jessie Chambers. She was born in Hastings, Sussex, in 1882, into a family well enough off to have a maid, with a mother who had time to read to her, and a father who bought her books. Their prosperity came from a small grocer's shop; a move to larger premises, intended to better their chances, failed to do so, and bailiffs seized the family chattels. From then on the most obvious life for Helen, like Lawrence's other girlfriends, was that of a pupil-teacher. She entered the profession unwillingly; she had already published poems in the local paper, and had secret aspirations to become a writer.

Helen was a natural rebel with no desire to marry or have children. She had become the mistress of her violin teacher, Herbert MacCartney, who was unhappily married but unable to break away from his wife. Her love for a married man pleased her in part because it risked no conventional outcome; she was unafraid of going away with her lover to the Isle of Wight, but had little understanding of the urgency of the sexual drive, which she thought of as peculiarly male. After five days with Helen, MacCartney went back to his wife, and soon afterwards committed suicide. This tragedy became the subject of a novel of her own, *Neutral Ground* which was published in 1933, and it was also to form the basis of *The Trespasser*. After MacCartney's death, it was her friendship with Lawrence that helped Helen to find a purpose in living – not because she was attracted to him, but because he was a writer, which was what she had always wanted to become.

Helen and Lawrence developed a habit of taking walks together on Saturdays. They would meet at the railway terminus at Purley, then go on to the North Downs. Sometimes they would visit a cottage where a woman would make them a cup of tea or give them a newly-laid egg.

Lawrence asked for Helen's help in editing the manuscript of 'Nethermere', rather as he had asked Jessie. Helen had never seen a writer's manuscript before, and it made her look at Lawrence with new interest. She had already observed his ability to write even with his landlady's baby on his knee, and now she was much impressed by the ease and fluency of his writing. She read the manuscript with fascination, and was particularly taken with the portrait of Emily of Strelley Farm, based on Jessie Chambers. When she expressed that interest, he showed her a letter from Jessie, told her his mother did not like her, and spoke of the conflicts within himself.

It was natural then that when Jessie came to spend a weekend in Croydon, Lawrence introduced the two women. Helen was impressed by the beauty of Jessie's soft, fine hair and dark eyes, and the grace of her movements as she prepared the tea while Lawrence sprawled on the hearthrug. After seeing Jessie off at the station, Lawrence eagerly asked Helen her opinion of her. Rather to his surprise, Helen expressed emphatic approval. She seemed to have found a warmth and strength of personality in Jessie which had been missing in Lawrence's description of her; indeed, she found her extremely attractive. Later Helen admitted she had been much more in love with Jessie than with Lawrence.

While he was at college, Lawrence would have found it impossible to ask a girl he respected to satisfy his sexual needs; aroused by his pursuit of Helen Corke, who was at least in principle unafraid of sexual experience, he changed his mind. He still had no idea that Jessie had a sensuality of her own, nor any idea of how it could be aroused. In the short story 'A Modern Lover', written in January 1910, the central character admits he would have preferred a bolder woman to Muriel, the sensitive Jessie figure. Nevertheless, at Christmas 1909 Lawrence asked Jessie straight out to become his mistress, and she agreed.

Lawrence's desperation was understandable. Helen Corke was seemingly indifferent to him sexually, and Agnes Holt had rebuffed him. On his salary from the Davidson Road School he could barely have afforded marriage to anyone, and marriage would have meant being trapped in a teaching job for life. For all her tough mind and independent spirit, Alice Dax failed to answer his romantic and spiritual needs. And she did not encourage his writing as Jessie had; she had been scathing about *The White Peacock* when he had shown her part of in 1908, and her judgements intimidated Lawrence because they were delivered with brutal frankness.

Jessie knew none of this. Indeed, for all the Eastwood gossip, she had never believed that there was anything much between Lawrence and Alice Dax, only that Alice had given Lawrence a good deal of encouragement. For her part, Alice remained staunch in her denials to Jessie of any physical relationship with Lawrence.

So it was that on Christmas Eve 1909 Lawrence went up to Haggs Farm determined to ask Jessie to sleep with him. Jessie saw something was different from the first moment their eyes met. Soon she was hearing words she had stopped hoping to hear. It was not Agnes he loved but her, and from now on he belonged to her. They kissed passionately. There had not been many kisses in their relationship up till that evening (Lawrence had a reluctance to kiss which continued for the rest of his life, even in the most sexually intimate moments). Jessie agreed to take him as her lover. Lawrence assured her that she need not worry about pregnancy, as he would take precautions against it. His landlord had supplied him with contraceptives.

Jessie's courage can hardly be understood by those women of the same period whose class and education led them to find such actions liberating. Jessie had no such belief. Her good reputation was essential to her continued employment as a teacher, and she could not have counted on the support of her family if Lawrence's precautions had failed. She must surely have also doubted his protestations of love, which never included fidelity, and fell short of matrimony unless she became pregnant.

In turning to Jessie after Agnes, Lawrence was making use of her in a way it is impossible not to condemn as exploitative. Even worse, he was going to a woman he had for the past three years stressed held no sexual attraction for him. She went into the relationship with everything he'd ever said about her sexual nature inhibiting her. That is the background to those few occasions – not more than five, Jessie tells us – whose lack of exuberance Lawrence describes in *Sons and Lovers*:

> *He never forgot seeing her as she lay on the bed, when he was unfastening his collar. First he saw only her beauty, and was blind with it. She had the most beautiful body he had ever imagined . . . And then he wanted her, but as he went forward to her, her hands lifted in a little pleading movement, and he looked at her face, and stopped. Her big brown eyes were watching him, still and resigned and loving; she lay as if she had given herself up to the sacrifice: there was her body for him; but the look at the back of her eyes, like a creature waiting immolation, arrested him, and all his blood fell back.*
>
> *'You are sure you want me?' he asked, as if a cold shadow had come over him.*
>
> *'Yes, quite sure.'*
>
> *She was very quiet, very calm. She only realised that she was doing something for him. He could hardly bear it. She lay to be sacrificed for him because she loved him so much. And he had to sacrifice her. For a second, he wished he were sexless or dead. Then he shut his eyes again to her, and his blood beat back again.*[4]

Lawrence had previously declared that he could not love Jessie as a husband should love his wife, and on one occasion he had wondered if they would not have been closer if Jessie had been a man. His old schoolfriend George Neville, who guessed something of what had happened, gave his opinion that Lawrence was trading on someone's regard for him instead of 'getting away and buying yourself a woman'.[5] Lawrence's letters to Jessie the following week speak of the 'great good' she had done him,[6] but it seems likely that it was a profoundly disappointing experience for both of them, and Lawrence was soon criticising Jessie for her part in the experiment.

Jessie and he managed a weekend together at the end of March 1910, perhaps in a hotel, since Jessie felt it was no longer honourable to take advantage of the hospitality of his landlady. They also spent some time together at Easter, though it is not clear whether they had a chance to make love; and a few days at Whitsuntide, making love in the open air, as two of Lawrence's poems ('Scent of Irises' and 'Lilies in the Fire') record. It was a rainy Whitsun, and the experience was intensely depressing to both of them. 'Lilies in the Fire' tries to console a lover with the hope that perhaps it is the chill of the earth underneath that is responsible:

> *You hold yourself all hard, as if my kisses*
> *Hurt as I gave them; you put me away –*

but the third section states baldly:

> *I am ashamed, you wanted me not to-night –*
> *Nay, it is always so, you sigh against me.*
> *Your brightness dims when I draw too near, and my free*
> *Fire enters you like frost, like a cruel blight.*[7]

Lawrence felt more degraded than simply disappointed by the experience. It was not in the least as he had imagined; Jessie did not want him as he had hoped.

Even more worryingly, he did not want her. Since Christmas he had become increasingly attracted to Helen Corke. In her own novel, *Neutral Ground*, Helen describes a kindly schoolteacher based on Lawrence, who works to revive her interest in life after the painful experience of the death of her violin teacher, called Siegmund in the novel. Lawrence visited her frequently and tried to draw her out of her depression. He brought everything he had read to bear on her situation, and for four months she shared with Lawrence her memories of the brief affair, her lover's unhappy marriage, his inability to break away, and the horror of learning that he had hanged himself on returning to his wife. For this support Helen was grateful, but she had no desire to become Lawrence's mistress.

Lawrence probably began to write 'The Saga of Siegmund', which became *The Trespasser*, after he read 'The Freshwater Diary', a detailed account of Helen's five days with MacCartney on the Isle of Wight in February and March 1910. Helen's reason for lending Lawrence the diary, as she wrote two years later, was to have him make some literary use of it; she wanted 'clothing for the soul of Siegmund, and voice for his silence'.[8] This Lawrence was able to do the more readily, since he had begun to share Siegmund's desire. Helen, however, refused his sexual advances, and some of his best early poems dealt with his frustration. He listens to her playing the violin in 'The Return', and in 'Repulsed' describes a night on which he feels 'insect small' as they sit on the side of a hill together:

> *How we hate each other, tonight, hate, you and I,*
> *To numbness and nothingness; I dead, she refusing to die,*
> *The female, whose venom can more than kill, can numb and*
> *then nullify.*[9]

In 'Excursion Train', Lawrence imagines a woman (whom he calls Helen) stripping him naked, and touching him, while he lies unable to move:

> *And strip me naked, touch me light*
> *Light, light all over.*
> *For I ache most earnestly for your touch,*
> *Yet I cannot move, however much*
> *I would be your lover.*[10]

He longs for her to take the initiative sexually while he remains passive. Passivity is the eroticism of dreams, in which there is no guilt; it was how Alice Dax had wooed him, but Helen was disinclined to do any such thing, and felt no more than affection for him. In an interview given when she was eighty-six, Helen Corke was emphatic that she felt no desire for Lawrence as a lover: moreover, she made it clear that she had had no intention of being a wife to him or anyone else. This, together with her admission that she put herself in the middle of the spectrum between masculine and feminine, makes it all the more fascinating that Lawrence should have found her so compellingly attractive. When pondering the attributes that made for an ideal wife, he sometimes selected the caring and nurturing qualities of a mother; none of these were on offer from Helen Corke. Jessie, on the other hand, offered them in abundance. Lawrence's infatuation with Helen Corke shows how he was sexually drawn to exactly the kind of woman he was later to declare most destructive. He had already felt some intimations of the danger when he and Jessie had seen the sixty-four-year-old Sarah Bernhardt in *La Dame aux Camélias* in Nottingham in June 1908. Lawrence had experienced such horror

53

at the power of the actress's presence that he had had to rush from the theatre, alarmed at the possibility that a 'woman could enslave him', [11] but this fear of powerful women did not prevent him from pursuing Helen Corke, whose continued refusal to consider him as a lover affected Lawrence badly. By July 1911 he was ready to declare that he would 'never ask for the sex relationship again unless I can give the dirty coin of marriage; unless it be to a prostitute, whom I can love because I am sorry for her'.[12] He and Helen Corke only stopped seeing each other in 1912, when Lawrence invited her to stay with him at Edward Garnett's cottage, saying Garnett was 'beautifully free of the world's conventions',[13] and Helen refused coldly.

Lawrence was never averse to the acquisition of other people's experience, and Helen's responses were soon incorporated into his work. In Seaford, where they took separate rooms in a boarding house in October 1910 after walking from Brighton over the cliffs, Helen woke in a state of terror and wrote a poem about a sea fog. When she showed it to Lawrence he remarked, 'I always feel, when you give me an idea, how much better I could work it out myself.' Lawrence's 'Coldness in Love' is a reworking of some of the emotions Helen records in her poem 'Fantasy', and is a much more remarkable poem:

> ... And I slept till dawn as the window blew in like dust
> Like a linty, raw-cold dust disturbed from the floor
> Of the unswept sea; a grey pale light like must
> That settled upon my face and hands till it seemed
> To flourish there, as pale mould blooms on a crust.

> And I rose in fear, needing you fearfully,
> For I thought you were warm as a sudden jet of blood.
> I thought I could plunge in your living hotness, and be
> Clean of the cold and the must. With my hand on the latch
> I heard you in your sleep speak strangely to me.

> And I dared not enter, feeling suddenly dismayed.
> So I went and washed my deadened flesh in the sea
> And came back tingling clean, but worn and frayed
> With cold, like the shell of the moon; and strange it seems
> That my love can dawn in warmth again, unafraid.[14]

Lawrence made good use of the experience of all the important women in his life, and in future years he would frequently turn to his wife Frieda to fill out his understanding of female response. In *Sons and Lovers* he used an incident first described by Jessie of a boy looking at a broken umbrella with anguish because it had belonged to his dead brother. *The Trespasser*, which takes as its subject the tragedy of the suicide of Helen's lover, is the most extreme example of Lawrence's appropriation of the experience of a woman friend. He used the landscapes of the Isle of Wight, where he had been with his mother, his sister Ada and a few friends in the happy and untroubled summer of 1909, and set against them the story of Helen and her married lover who have gone away for a holiday and make one another wretched.

Like Jessie, Helen had vivid and often surprising responses, and Lawrence's relationship with her resembled that with Jessie, as both depended on shared and companionable interests. A visit to the Tate Gallery led to Lawrence's poems 'Corot' and 'Michelangelo'; they loved walking together and talking about what they saw. This helped Helen as she struggled to overcome her unhappiness and guilt about her former lover's suicide.

Lawrence was a little devious in concealing from Jessie the attraction he continued to feel towards Helen Corke, and he was also far from open about Alice Dax. Some time after Easter, Alice visited him in London, and they went to the opera together. Soon afterwards, Lawrence wrote to Jessie that he had been so aroused by the music as nearly to be unfaithful to her. Since Alice and he were probably already lovers, there is something disingenuous in this confession. Whatever happened, the mature woman's sensually arousing behaviour contrasted very strongly with that of the inexperienced Jessie, and Lawrence felt himself exonerated from his failure with Jessie by the success of his encounter with Alice. From then onwards, Lawrence was always urging Jessie not to feel he was bound to her.

Lawrence's poems of the time are pervaded with the failure of his and Jessie's lovemaking, for which he blamed her: 'I am ashamed, you wanted me not tonight'. As it seems unlikely that he ever made any physical move to arouse her, or offered her any avowal of commitment, he was asking her to desire the naked act itself as he did. Or as he wished he could.

In spring 1911, Lawrence confessed to Jessie that he had had a relationship with Alice Dax, though he insisted it was now 'all finished', but he was always reluctant to admit to the strength of the feelings he had for Helen Corke. Helen herself was careful not to hurt Jessie, though in talking intimately with her Jessie was aware of Helen's closeness to Lawrence, and that awareness coloured their own friendship.

In failing to admit to Jessie the feelings he had for Helen Lawrence felt deceitful, but he was also afraid of the pain such knowledge would give her. He wanted to end the relationship. Early in the summer of 1910 he had written 'Sigh No More', exhorting himself to be brave and lamenting the pain he gave her 'mournful, constant heart'.[15]

For all his exhortation, Lawrence was incapable of ending the relationship cleanly. He found himself telling Jessie that he would always return to her, even as he insisted that she must leave him free. Faced by the knowledge that he needed Helen Corke – for the book, he claimed – it was Jessie who began once again to suggest a complete break, but all through July Lawrence resisted it. He and Jessie saw each other again when she came to London, and once more briefly in Nottingham after term ended.

Lawrence and Jessie had arranged to go and stay at the Chambers family's new farm in Arno Vale in August 1910, but the holiday never took place. The day before he was to meet Jessie Lawrence had written to Helen Corke explaining how treacherous he felt himself to be: 'If I have courage, I shall not stay. I must tell her that we ought definitely and finally to part; if I have the heart to tell her.'[16] Jessie, who had been looking forward to the holiday, met Lawrence as they had arranged, but, as she puts it in her memoir, 'instead of returning with me as he had planned to do, he broke off our engagement completely'.[17] Lawrence knew he had wronged her. In 1935, when she came to write about these events, Jessie put the blame for Lawrence's decision on his mother's interference. Lydia may have been pleased, of course, but she was hardly responsible.

When Jessie read *Women in Love* after Lawrence's death (without the benefit of the still unpublished prologue, which made clear the connection with her) she recognised aspects of herself in Hermione Roddice, although the physical descriptions of Hermione do not resemble her, because of the account of Hermione and Rupert Birkin's lovemaking, in which Lawrence depicts a man with little desire for a woman using her to find sexual release. It is possible that it had been difficult for Lawrence to achieve even that.

Lawrence had found his inability to give Jessie any sexual pleasure a disappointing and humiliating experience. After Whitsun he renewed his suit to Helen, but to no avail. Alice Dax remained as solace. Her attachment to Lawrence deepened, and she told a friend that he had asked her to go away with him, but that she had refused to leave her husband and child.

After Lawrence's death, Jessie discussed her sexual encounters with Lawrence in a letter to the French critic Emile Delavenay, who was writing about Lawrence: 'The times of our coming together, and with Lawrence's most earnest injunctions to me not to try to hold him, would not exhaust the fingers of one hand.' Jessie told Delavenay that on that flimsy foundation he 'judged and condemned me without stopping to inquire whether his own attitude was beyond reproach'.[18]

Lawrence always insisted that Jessie's inability to attract him sexually was due to some fault in her. These are imponderable matters, yet her yielding, which Lawrence writes about with such disdain in *Sons and Lovers* as scared and sacrificial, was at the least an act of love. It is hardly surprising that an inexperienced, rather frightened but tenderly loving girl was unable to help Lawrence feel what he wanted. Long, probing conversations continued instead. Jessie endured Lawrence's onslaughts meekly, but the cruelty of his accusations went into her very soul. It was not her frigidity, but her tenderness and gentle nature that unfitted her to be a partner in the battleground which was Lawrence's idea of a marriage.

Lawrence's entry into the London literary world was meanwhile being made possible by the influential Ford Madox Hueffer, whose interest had been aroused by Jessie's intervention the previous year. Hueffer's account of how he came across Lawrence's work is a little different from that of Jessie and Lawrence. He says that he was sent prose as well as poetry, and mentions recognising the first paragraphs of the story 'Odour of Chrysanthemums' as so clearly talented that he put the manuscript into his tray of accepted work without reading further. As was his habit, he began mentioning Lawrence as a genius he had discovered, and so it was that Lawrence's name became known to writers like G. K. Chesterton and H. G. Wells before he himself knew that Jessie's attempt to secure publication for him had been successful. Certainly Lawrence owed a great deal to Hueffer. To appear in a journal like the *English Review*, which also published such writers as Joseph Conrad, Henry James, Thomas Hardy and John Galsworthy, ensured that his work would receive attention.

During Jessie's visit to London in November 1909, she and Lawrence were invited to Sunday luncheon with Hueffer and his mistress Violet Hunt in Holland Park, together with Ezra Pound (who, like Wyndham Lewis, Hueffer had also 'discovered' that year). The invitation rested on the tacit and mistaken assumption that Jessie and Lawrence were to be married. Violet greeted Jessie with praise as someone who had found a genius, and Hueffer treated her with great courtesy. His enquiries about her political beliefs confirmed her sense of herself as a suffragette and a socialist, and he even encouraged her to think of herself as a writer. He had been shown a little sketch Jessie had written, and suggested she write more. Lawrence immediately put in: 'It wouldn't be any good. She's incommunicable.' The odd choice of word is recorded in Jessie's memoir; she felt the remark was a put-down, but it made a kind of sense to her, implying that it was impossible for Lawrence to communicate with her himself. Hueffer reacted to Lawrence's attempt to reduce Jessie with some sympathy, saying lightly, 'There you are, you see: labelled, put on the shelf and done with.'[19]

Jessie's nervousness made an unfavourable impression on Violet Hunt. At one point she asked in a whisper whether she should keep her gloves on during the meal; whereas Lawrence, who must have been as socially uncertain as she was about forks, knives and proprieties generally, solved the problem with little fuss. He loved the glitter of such occasions, as Jessie did not. And he enjoyed talking to the young Ezra Pound, whom he had visited in his Kensington attic ten days earlier.

The metropolitan literary world had opened to welcome him. Hueffer advised Lawrence to send the manuscript of his first novel, which Helen Corke had helped to edit, to Heinemann, to whom he wrote recommending it. On 21 January 1910 Lawrence was called to see William Heinemann in person and told the novel had been accepted, though Sidney Pawling, one of the editors, thought it should be shorter. The title had also been disliked, and Lawrence discussed various alternatives over the next few months, among them 'Tendrils' and 'Crab-apples', which suggest that his publishers were right to overrule Lawrence's uneasiness about the final title, *The White Peacock*.

Chapter 5

SON AND LOVER

In the summer of 1910, as Lawrence struggled to find a woman he could love and relate to with all of himself, his mother, who was fifty-eight and had always seemed healthy despite her fragility, was diagnosed as having a tumour in her abdomen. Her condition was too advanced for treatment. In *Sons and Lovers* Mrs Morel's dying is made to seem unbearably slow, but Lydia's cancer was to kill her in little more than three months. As Lawrence faced her suffering and impending death, he viewed her stoicism bitterly: an account of his pain is given poignantly in both *Sons and Lovers* and poems of the period, notably 'Sorrow':

> *Why does the thin grey strand*
> *Floating up from the forgotten*
> *Cigarette between my fingers*
> *Why does it trouble me?*
>
> *Ah, you will understand*
> *When I carried my mother downstairs*
> *A few times only at the beginning*
> *Of her soft-foot malady,*
>
> *I should find, for a reprimand*
> *To my gaiety, a few long grey hairs*
> *On the breast of my coat; and one by one*
> *I watched them float up the dark chimney.*[1]

Lawrence travelled up to Eastwood on alternate weekends to visit her. The sight of her courage and her pain was overwhelming for him. In her often illuminating essay on D. H. Lawrence in *Sexual Politics*, the feminist critic Kate Millett, while well aware of the tenderness between Paul and his mother, states that 'when his mother ceased to be of use, he quietly murders her'. This hardly accords with the novel, still less with Lawrence's own feelings. Far from finding that he had taken all he needed from her, as Millett maintains, Lawrence's mother still held the emotional centre of his life. Thoughts of her suffering filled his anxious weeks of teaching at Croydon. Lawrence described his bitterness at seeing her suffering in a letter written from Eastwood to his Croydon friend Arthur McLeod on 5 December 1910:

> *She has had a bloody hard life, and has always been bright; but now her face has fallen like a mask of bitter suffering . . . and sometimes I turn to look out of the window at the bright wet cabbages in the garden, and the horses in the field beyond, and the church tower small as a black dice on the hill at the back a long way off, and I find myself apostrophising the landscape: 'So that's what you mean, is it?'*[2]

On one occasion, Helen Corke was invited to Eastwood to stay at Haggs Farm with Jessie, and she travelled back to London on the same train as Lawrence. He had been devastated by the weekend with his mother, and sat in the corner of the carriage with a dead-white face, looking hardly sane. She felt powerless to help him.

He went on grimly correcting the proofs of his novel through the months of his mother's illness on the weekends when he was in Eastwood. Lawrence wrote to one of his Heinemann editors in November 1910 to ask if he might have an early copy of the book to show his mother. It was a natural impulse. As a boy he had always brought her his successes. Now her approaching death made it difficult for him to take much pleasure in his transformation into a published writer.

When he brought the early copy to her she had only weeks to live, and it did not have the effect he must have hoped for. Lydia was in great pain, and showed no sense of the magnitude of his achievement. Some fourteen years later he recorded his disappointment: 'She looked at the outside, and then at the title page, and then at me, with darkening eyes . . . It was put aside and I never wanted to see it again.'[3] If he had entertained the hope that becoming a writer would fulfil his mother's ambitions for him, this was a severe rejection. He thought it was because she could not believe anyone as unimportant as himself had written an important book.

May Chambers gives an account of his brooding on his mother's response a day or so after her death:

> *'Well, she saw your book,' I offered. 'It must comfort you to have achieved that while she could have pride in it.'*
>
> *'No, she didn't like it.'*
>
> *'Why?' I demanded.*
>
> *He shook his head sadly.*
>
> *'I don't know. She didn't like it. Even disliked it.'*
>
> *'Still,' I protested, 'she must be proud of you, of your ability to write a book. You've given her that. It can't help but be a source of pride.'*
>
> *'No,' he insisted miserably. 'She doesn't like what I write. Perhaps if it had been romance . . . But I couldn't write that.'*[4]

That death-bed glance at *The White Peacock* was by no means the only sight Lydia had had of the novel. Some part of the first version had been shown to her as early as 1907. Her comment had been withering: 'To think that my son should have written such a story.'[5] Jessie Chambers believed it was Lettie's flirting games with Leslie and George, and the omnipresence of sexual desire, which so shocked her. In 1908 Lawrence reported Lydia's disapproval: 'Laetitia, of whom my mother will say nothing except "I wish you had written on another line"',[6] and gave a wounded account of her amused scepticism when she came upon a later chapter of the book: 'But, my boy, how do you know it was like that?'[7] Lydia was quite well-informed about the progress of her son's writing; she knew of his novel's acceptance by Heinemann, and understood he was working on revisions to the manuscript. She also knew enough of his work on 'The Saga of Siegmund' to disapprove of the adulterous theme.

As a reader, Lydia felt her intelligence was equal to anyone's, but she had no experience of someone from her own class daring to make a contribution of their own. She had never wanted her son to try anything so unusual, and perhaps without Jessie Chambers he might never have believed it was possible. His reluctance to look again at *The White Peacock*, of which he had been so proud, is understandable; a lesser talent might well have ceased to write altogether.

The incident is retold in an essay in *Phoenix*, with an interesting addition in the shape of Arthur Lawrence's response – a mixture of puzzlement at the book itself (which he could hardly read), and impressed astonishment that a £50 advance could be paid to a son who had never done a day of what he himself thought of as work in his life.

Lydia's pain was unbearable to watch. The question arises of whether Lawrence hastened the death of his mother as Paul Morel did in *Sons and Lovers*. It is plausible that he could have added morphine to her milk in order to ease his mother's pain, knowing there was a risk it might cause her to die, but Paul's murderous intent seems less likely to have a basis in Lawrence's own life. The only evidence adduced for the literal truth of the account in *Sons and Lovers* comes from Lina Waterfield, the wife of the painter Aubrey Waterfield, who knew Lawrence in Italy in 1913–14. In a letter of 8 June 1914, her husband claimed that Lawrence told her then that every word of the narrative was literally true, and that they found this particularly shocking because 'I felt in the book that they did not kill her to put her out of her misery, but because he and his sister could not bear it.'[8]

Lina Waterfield republished this letter in her autobiography, and added an account of her conversation with Lawrence in which she told him that, much as she admired the novel, she found Paul's act of euthanasia out of keeping with his character and his adoration of his mother. Making the point that the selfishness of Paul's behaviour – since his mother continued to want to live – struck a false note, she was horrified when Lawrence countered her criticism by emphatically declaring: 'You're wrong!', and claiming that he had behaved in that way himself.

Lina Waterfield was a working journalist and kept a daily diary, so at the very least this conversation suggests what Lawrence believed then; but his vehemence was mainly intended to rebut her assertion about the falseness of his novel.

Whatever the truth of Lawrence's behaviour, his mother's death on 9 December 1910 left him haggard and wretched. His father's distress, too, was evident, but Lawrence continued to speak of him savagely: 'He is disgusting, irritating and selfish as a maggot.'[9] Lawrence turned to whoever could comfort him. To Jessie, the day before Lydia's funeral, he declared that he had always loved his mother 'like a lover. That's why I could never love you.'[10] When Lydia was put to rest in the same grave as her beloved son Ernest, Lawrence was desolate. His life was left without direction. In a spirit of utter misery, however, he had entered into an engagement with Louisa Burrows a few days before Lydia's death.

There is a plaque now on the pleasant cottage near Eastwood where Louisa Burrows once lived with her parents. It announces that this was the home of a girl D. H. Lawrence had been going to marry. Like Jessie Chambers, Louie had allowed Lawrence to use her name as a pseudonym when he entered the *Nottinghamshire Guardian* short story competition in August 1907. She was a radiantly beautiful girl, to judge from photographs, 'a glorious girl . . . swarthy and ruddy as a pomegranate, and bright and vital as a pitcher of wine',[11] as Lawrence wrote in a letter to Arthur McLeod; she had a kind nature, according to Lawrence's brother George, and used to visit Lydia when she was ill. Helen Corke always thought of Louie as part of Lydia's world, and Lydia had approved of her.

Louie was born in Ilkeston, near Eastwood, in 1888, and first met Lawrence when she was about twelve. She studied with him at the Ilkeston Pupil-Teacher Centre, and was a fellow student at Nottingham University College. Lawrence gives his own account of how he came to propose to Louie in a letter to Arthur McLeod. He had been to Leicester to visit an old college girlfriend and was returning by train towards Quorn, where Louie was living. Louie, who was on the train, asked him what he was going to do after Christmas. He replied apparently on impulse, thinking she looked wistful, that he would like to get married. ' "Should you?" I added. She looked out of the window and murmured huskily, "What?" "Like to marry me," I said. She turned to me quickly and her face shone like a luminous thing. "Later," she said. I was very glad.'[12] When they reached the station where Louie should have got off, she put her hand on Lawrence's and leaned against him, and they looked out of the window together at the flooded winter fields in an enchantment of mutual attraction.

By the time Lawrence saw Jessie later in the week, his mother was dead. He was no longer sure that he wanted to marry Louie, but he declared boldly enough that since she had accepted him he would stick to it. Jessie saw this as one more move in the continuing battle between them, and even ventured the opinion that Louie should not have been involved in their affairs. Nevertheless, Lawrence wrote to Louie's father explaining his intentions. Louie's parents were unenthusiastic about Lawrence as a son-in-law. In a letter to the Scottish poet Rachel Annand Taylor (to whom Ernest Rhys, the editor of the Everyman Library, had introduced him in 1910), Lawrence gives a revealing account of his motivation which ties in with Jessie's beliefs:

Nobody can have the soul of me. My mother has had it, and nobody can have it again. Nobody can come into my very self again, and breathe me like an atmosphere . . . Louie – whom I wish I would marry the day after the funeral – she would never demand to drink me up and have me. She loves me – but it is a fine, warm, healthy, natural love – not like Jane Eyre, who is Muriel [Jessie], but like, say, Rhoda Fleming or Anna Karenina. She will never plunge her hands through my blood and feel for my soul, and make me set my teeth and shiver and fight away.[13]

Lawrence was not made happy by his engagement to Louie, for all his assertion that he had made a good choice. Louie appealed to everything lively and carefree in him, as neither Helen nor Jessie had, but she was also conventional and materialistic; she wanted a well-furnished home (hankering particularly after black furniture), and would have liked to plan and save to achieve it. When Lawrence received £10 from the *English Review* for 'Odour of Chrysanthemums', he wrote to tell Louie he had bought some shoes and shirts and sent some money to his sister Ada. Louie was not pleased, and wrote by return of post accusing him of not even trying to save for their marriage. He was much irritated by this. The money was over and above his ordinary earnings and it seemed petty of her to scold him. A fundamental disagreement between them on the subject of home-making soon emerged. Lawrence was to travel remarkably light all his life, attaching himself to few material objects; indeed, he wanted none from his family home when Ada offered him his pick.

There were other difficulties. Louie was passionate, as several of Lawrence's love poems, notably 'Snap-Dragon', witness, but she had a strict code of manners which kept that passion in check. She may have been 'big, swarthy and passionate as a gypsy' as Lawrence described her, but she was also 'good, awfully good, churchy'. And

Lawrence had not yet abandoned hope that he might persuade Helen Corke to go to bed with him.

Jessie Chambers believed that Helen Corke acceded to Lawrence's demands some time in the autumn of 1910, even as his relationship with Louie Burrows was developing. Helen Corke always denied this, but there is no question that Lawrence vehemently urged his suit upon her all through 1911. Her letters often enough rebuked him for his importunacy. It is impossible to miss the electricity of her sexual attraction for him: in a letter of 12 July 1911 he declares: 'What is between you and me is sex.'[14] One may guess that it is just the kind of sexual attraction he was later to condemn as destructive; the lust of Hardy's Jude Fawley for a Sue Bridehead, so much more dangerous than the desire he felt for the healthy animality of Arabella Donn; as such it was probably unrequited. After he left Helen the night after writing that letter, Lawrence threw two condoms procured from his landlord Mr Jones over a railway bridge.

Louie and Lawrence (suitably chaperoned by George Neville and Lawrence's sister Ada) had a fortnight's holiday together in North Wales and Snowdonia in August 1911. But by the next month Lawrence was telling Helen Corke that 'as for Louie's claim on me, it is I who discount it, not you',[15] while being altogether less frank in his dealings with Louie. He even reflected in a letter to his sister Ada, 'I'm afraid she's the one I shan't tell things to.'[16]

Louie wanted the engagement to proceed like those of her local friends. Insofar as she thought of Lawrence as in any way different from the other young teachers of her acquaintance, it was only as something she could be vain about. He was a little embarrassed by her snobbish pride in his success as an author: in her memoir Jessie describes Louie handing *The White Peacock* round to her acquaintances as the work of the clever young man to whom she was engaged. *The White Peacock* had come out from Heinemann on 20 January 1911, to fairly favourable reviews. The *English Review* spoke out enthusiastically of 'a new writer, one most certainly to be reckoned with', and other friendly reviews appeared in the *Daily Chronicle* and the *Glasgow Herald*.

Through 1911 grief for his mother made Lawrence profoundly

unhappy. Ada, too, was in ill spirits: after her mother's death she had begun to lose faith in Christianity. Lawrence observed querulously that she nagged him rather as his mother had, and was shocked to discover him kissing a girl after a dance. Jessie was given an account of Lawrence's state by his brother George, who reported that on his visits to Nottingham he called out in his sleep and showed a degree of depression that would now be regarded as clinical. Asked by Jessie when Lawrence and Louie's marriage was likely to take place, George declared that they would never get married, and added his personal conviction that Lawrence had the wrong girl.

Writing to Helen Corke early in 1912 Lawrence admitted that although the common everyday man inside him really loved Louie, he was aware of another 'open-eyed, sad' person who did not. Louie Burrows had none of Jessie Chambers' or Helen Corke's intuitive sensitivity, and Lawrence was faintly bored without it.

Lawrence's uncertainty was to be resolved in part by illness. When he wrote to Louie in December 1911 he was propped up in bed in Croydon. He had been caught in the rain on the way down to stay in Kent with Edward Garnett – who read books for Duckworths and was the discoverer and close friend of both Conrad and Galsworthy – and suffered an attack of pneumonia which very nearly killed him. Ada nursed him through the crisis. In his delirium his cries betrayed his uncertainty about marrying Louie. As he recovered, Louie joined in the nursing. A sputum test had proved negative; he did not have tuberculosis, but it was clear that he was not well enough to return to teaching. He would have to convalesce and think again about his employment. It was at this juncture that Lawrence's writing career was suddenly given enormous encouragement by Edward Garnett. Lawrence had lent Hueffer an early manuscript of *The Trespasser* and was disappointed with his response: 'a rotten work of genius, one fourth of which is the stuff of a masterpiece . . . It has no construction or form – it is execrably bad art . . . Also it is erotic.'[17] William Heinemann, too, had disliked it. But now Garnett wrote excitedly to say that he was going to suggest Duckworths should publish the novel.

Garnett's encouragement may have been decisive. On 4 February 1912 Lawrence broke his engagement to Louie, giving poor health and poverty as his reasons. He had explained his straitened circumstances to Louie on that first, magical train journey; now he said he could not undertake marriage without his income from the Davidson Road School, from which he had no choice but to resign. The thought of committing himself to literature had begun to take hold of him, and he knew that Louie would hardly have accepted such a risky life. And by now, as he also admitted, he knew they were not well suited.

On 13 February 1912, a few days after Louie's twenty-fourth birthday, they met for the last time in Nottingham. At first Louie put on a show of indifference, in a pathetic attempt to safeguard her pride; she had taken the rejection much harder than she wanted him to know. As they walked round Nottingham Castle, she displayed passionate interest in an art exhibition there, and even made fun of Lawrence for his description of the town's shadow appearing faintly coloured through the fog. Her manner was convenient for Lawrence, who would have found it harder to go through with the break if she had been wistful and tender. There was only an awkward moment or two of emotion. She giggled, and then cried, and he was free. On the fifteenth he was able to write and say he was glad they would remain friends.

Louie herself was far from free; sadly, for someone with such enormous physical magnetism, she grew into a rather sombre and dispirited woman. No more than Jessie was she able to overcome the sense that she had been ill treated. She continued to work as a teacher, and did not marry until 1940, when she was fifty-two. After Lawrence's death she visited his grave in Vence, in the south of France, on at least two occasions; she was once observed there by Frieda's daughter Barbara, and once by the poet and critic Sir Herbert Read.

It was in 1911, as Jessie began to consider the paradoxes of Lawrence's involvement with Louie Burrows, and remembered how he had said to her as a boy of twenty that he could not love her as a husband should, that she began to write down her own recollections. She sent them to Lawrence in the form of a short story.

He declared the story too subtle to publish, but it seems to have germinated in his mind, and in the same year he began to work on his own autobiographical novel. Jessie did not hear this from Lawrence himself, but from Helen Corke, who remained a close friend. In

October of that year he sent Jessie the first draft of 'Paul Morel', which was to become *Sons and Lovers*. He had then written about two thirds of the story, and Jessie found it disappointing. Not even the treatment of his mother's married life was fresh, and the character he called Miriam, based on herself, had been displaced to a bourgeois household as a foundling. Jessie characterised this first draft, as she had that of *The White Peacock*, as 'storybookish'. Nevertheless, she could not but be fascinated by Lawrence's treatment of Paul Morel's love for Miriam and the conflict with Mrs Morel: 'What was it he [Paul] wanted of her [Miriam]? Did he want her to break his mother down in him?'[18]

Jessie had her own painful sense of that conflict, and felt that what had happened in reality was far more poignant and interesting than the story Lawrence had invented. She suggested he incorporate the story of Ernest's death, and keep the whole story closer to the events he had experienced. She even hoped that by encouraging him to proceed he might free himself of his psychological bondage to his dead mother. Lawrence asked Jessie to send him all the recollections she had of their early days together. He had already found this way of working helpful in writing *The Trespasser*, using the memories of Helen Corke; but this was a rather different situation, since Jessie and he shared the crucial memories. For Jessie it was the most important story of her life; she continued working on it even when she heard Lawrence had fallen seriously ill with pneumonia.

He convalesced in Bournemouth with Ada, and by Christmas, when Jessie was able to give him all her notes, she had a sense that their relationship was beginning again. Lawrence, still weakened by his illness, had to remain at home in Eastwood, but he continued writing a new version of 'Paul Morel', and took the sheets of it to show Jessie as he finished them. She loved the description of Mrs Morel spitting on the iron, and in all the early chapters of the book she could see Lawrence coming into his own as a creative artist.

The engagement with Louie Burrows was over, his mother was dead, but, whatever Jessie might imagine, Lawrence still had no intention of marrying her. He continued to bring her pages of the novel, now called *Sons and Lovers*, which was written in about six weeks in a kind of frenzy. He had taken Jessie's advice to write directly out of his own experience, and the book's subject was now not only the conflict between Jessie and Lydia, but also an exploration of the reasons Lawrence could not wish to marry Jessie.

As Jessie read his account of their relationship she saw how often she was found wanting. It is not surprising that these descriptions were hurtful to her. Lawrence knew they were, and stopped bringing her his work in person, sending it by post instead. Jessie marvelled at the injustice of his completely omitting what they had shared and everything she had done to help him. She knew exactly how he would excuse himself – as writers always have – claiming that 'It isn't what I think of you, you know it isn't.' Naturally, she saw the book as a betrayal of their shared intellectual awakening. Lawrence was perfectly well aware of what he had done; nevertheless, he expected their friendship to continue.

Jessie was staying with her married sister May on a farm near Eastwood, and one Sunday Lawrence was to come for a midday meal. He reached them only at tea time. His nerves were frayed by his fear of what Jessie might say about the novel, though he kept up an appearance of cheerfulness. She said nothing.

The following afternoon he came to see her again, still apprehensive, and looking as if he had not slept. They went for a walk, and he asked her rather wistfully if she had anything to say about the book. She did not take the opportunity to discuss the matter, and said only that she had put some notes in with the manuscript. Her inability to challenge Lawrence directly was clearly a relief to him, and at tea he seemed released from his tension, though he was still conscious enough of what he had done to ask May if Jessie had said anything to her about her anger. In writing the tale of his and Jessie's love Lawrence had been less concerned with the conflict between Lydia and Jessie, and more with the conflict within himself. To solve that, and to prove that his inability to love Jessie sexually lay not in himself but in her, he depicted Miriam as being unsuitable as an object of sexual desire because of her wrongfully developed mind. In order to make Paul's behaviour appear reasonable, Jessie is made to seem unwomanly. The significance of her failure to attract would soon be used against other female characters in Lawrence's writing who have intellectual aspirations, and are suspected of having more vitality in their heads than in their wombs. Far from being a vindication of Lydia's view of the world, as Jessie complained in her memoir, *Sons and Lovers* was an outright rejection of the hopes shared by a whole generation of women like Lydia, who had begun to imagine a freedom of intellectual enquiry for themselves.

As if to conceal that point, Lawrence makes the fictional Clara Dawes a suffragette, deliberately gives her some of the frank sexuality of Alice Dax and the voluptuousness of Louie Burrows, and establishes triumphantly that Paul has no sexual problems with her. But Clara has a subservient position in the factory where his hero works, and there is no sign in her portrait of the eager life of the mind that animates Miriam. Indeed, Clara's life with her husband Baxter closely resembles Lydia's with Arthur Lawrence, and at the end of the novel Paul restores her to her husband.

When Jessie next saw Lawrence, with his sister Ada and her fiancé Eddie Clarke on Easter Monday in the booking hall of a railway station, he looked miserable, and seemed to have difficulty finding the right words to say to her. He drove part of the way home with the Chambers family and said that he was going to Germany in the next few days. Jessie was right about his extreme anxiety, but she could not have guessed the reason for it. Lawrence had recently met Frieda von Richthofen, the wife of Ernest Weekley, a Professor of German literature at Nottingham University. It was surely her he was thinking of later that afternoon when he said to Jessie's sister and her husband: 'I like a *gushing* woman.'[19]

Chapter 6

FRIEDA

In March 1912, Lawrence went to lunch with Ernest Weekley, who had once taught him and had shown some interest in his talent. Correspondence with Professor Fritz Krenkow, the German husband of his mother's sister Ada, had encouraged Lawrence to think of a job as a lector in a German university, and he knew Weekley had many German connections. So it was that he came to meet Weekley's German wife Frieda, who was to be the most important woman in his life.

Frieda always claimed to be surprised that Lawrence fell in love with her. She was six years older than he was, and the mother of three children. But she was exceptionally good looking – tall, with a full figure, high cheekbones and green eyes – and Lawrence responded instantly to her forthright manner and her way of looking directly into his eyes when she talked. After that first meeting, Lawrence wrote a note to her declaring she was the most wonderful woman in England. Frieda's response was a teasing enquiry into the number of women he knew, but she markedly failed to rebuke him for writing to a married woman in that way.

Frieda came from the German aristocracy. The nobility of her family went back two and a half centuries; there were notable diplomats among her relations and she was a baroness in her own right. But her branch of the family was already impoverished even before her father Friedrich gambled away their remaining resources. He had begun his career in the army in 1862, serving with distinction in the Franco–Prussian war, but an injury to his hand led him to resign his commission. His subsequent gambling, and his wife's angry disapproval, made for a family pattern not so very different from Lawrence's own.

Frieda had two sisters. Else, five years older, was a brilliant woman who wrote her doctoral thesis at Heidelberg under the direction of the celebrated Professor of Sociology Max Weber. She married Dr Edgar Jaffe, a Professor of Political Economy at the University of Heidelberg, and later became Weber's mistress. Johanna (or 'Nusch') was three years younger than Frieda, and was the beauty of the family.

Frieda had a happy childhood in a pleasant house in Sablon, a suburb of Metz. Although the family was Protestant, Frieda and Johanna were educated at a convent. Neither of them had the social conscience or the drive to study of their elder sister Else. The two sisters shared a bedroom and laughed over pillowfights and dramatised readings of the classics, and the gentle nuns could not tame Frieda's exuberance.

She adored her father, although she was well aware of his irresponsibility. He was a passionate sportsman and always faultlessly dressed, from his highly polished shoes to his handkerchief embroidered with a coronet. He was affectionately indulgent of her early wildness, and in return she saw him as a hero; though clearly his handsome, authoritative appearance disguised an inner lack of confidence. There were occasional violent scenes with Frieda's mother, who once stayed up all night waiting for him to come home, and then sent servants into town to see what might have happened to him. Frieda remembered her father's return, pale and humiliated, and the discovery that he had spent the night gambling with friends in the officers' mess. This episode made it necessary to take out a mortgage on the family's house, and from that day forward there was a hostility between her parents which they did not attempt to conceal. Friedrich turned for tenderness to his daughters, saying he did not mind whom they married, as long as it wasn't 'a Jew, an Englishman or a gambler'.[1] He was to be disappointed on every count.

Metz was a town full of handsome officers in uniform, and there were many young men willing to admire the beautiful young von Richthofen sisters. At sixteen, Frieda fell briefly in love with a distant cousin, Kurt von Richthofen, who had been sent to Metz to study in the military school, and they exchanged innocent kisses. Two years later there was a more serious attachment with a Lieutenant Karl von

Marbahr. But a young lieutenant could only afford marriage to a girl with money of her own, and the von Richthofen girls had no such expectation. Forty years later Marbahr recalled their love affair with pain, saying sadly that he had not dared to kiss Frieda, still less ask her to marry him, as he knew he would have to wait ten years for a captaincy.

Ernest Weekley was nearly fifteen years older than Frieda. He was the second of nine children brought up in London by a thrifty schoolteacher mother and a poorly paid alms official. He worked hard for an external degree at London University, and went on to study modern languages at Cambridge and the Sorbonne. After a brief period at the University of Freiburg as a lecturer in English, he was offered a chair in the Modern Languages department at University College, Nottingham. When he met Frieda on holiday in the Black Forest in 1898 he was enjoying his first prospect of security. He was soon overwhelmingly in love.

Frieda was then twenty. Ernest was no longer in his first youth, but she was moved by the way he had fallen head over heels in love with her. He was good looking, clearly distinguished, and filled with a moral earnestness which she found attractive. Certainly he was no aristocrat – the baroness who accompanied Frieda to England on a trip to meet Ernest's parents was in no doubt of that – but no objections were made.

Ernest and Frieda were married on 29 August 1899 in Freiburg. On their wedding night in Lucerne Ernest went off nervously to have a drink to give him courage. Frieda climbed on top of a wardrobe, and sat there wondering what he would do if he could not see her on his return. When he came in she threw herself naked into his arms. Their marriage never recovered from the prudishness with which he told her to put on her nightdress. This first sexual encounter was so far from the bliss she had imagined that for a time she hated him.

Once established in a fine solid house in the Nottingham suburb of Mapperley, there was little for Frieda to do. She was far from skilled at housework, and was happy to let the cook run the kitchen. A nanny was brought from Germany to look after the children – a boy and two girls. Ernest, however, had little free time; in addition to his duties as head of the Modern Languages Department, he taught at a Workers' Institute three evenings a week, lectured in Cambridge on

Saturdays, and wrote books. He encouraged Frieda to edit a small volume of Schiller's ballads for Blackies' 'Little German Classics' series, which she professed to enjoy. She played the piano in the evenings, and read English novels. There were friends from the university who came to dinner – Weekley was close to Professor Kipping, an organic chemist, and his wife – but there was little gaiety.

When her younger sister Johanna came to visit (married now to a staff officer, Max von Schreibershofen, and elegantly dressed), Frieda felt herself pitied, though she knew Johanna's husband was a compulsive gambler – he was soon forced to resign his commission. Johanna's amorous conquests and glittering social whirl seemed enviable compared to the Mapperley routine of shopping in the morning, visits in the afternoon, and set times for every household task. Frieda did not require much to make her happy, but she found Mapperley dull and lonely.

It is not surprising that she turned to extramarital affairs to relieve her boredom. Unlike Lawrence's other women, who had wanted to make their own way in the world, and had a low opinion of sexuality, Frieda had no intellectual ambitions. She simply wanted, as Emma Bovary had, to live more fully.

Will Dowson, a well-to-do lace manufacturer, was her first lover. He was said to have owned the first motor car in the neighbourhood, and would drive Frieda into Sherwood Forest for their assignations. His wife was a suffragette, and it is easy enough to see what he found in Frieda; but she was uninvolved emotionally, and was always eager to return from her afternoons with him to be with her children, whom she loved with much greater passion. Weekley suspected nothing of this affair, though Lawrence hinted darkly in the posthumously published *Mr Noon* that he would have been willing to connive at his wife's liaison.

On a visit to Munich in 1907 Frieda entered into a much more dangerous affair. Her sister Else was staying with a childhood friend who was married to Dr Otto Gross, a psychiatrist, who delighted in being part of an unconventional circle of expressionist painters, poets and homosexuals, which occasionally included the presence of a genius such as the sexually outspoken playwright Franz Wedekind.

Dr Otto Gross was thought by that circle to be a genius himself; he was thirty, a tall, slim, fair-haired man who fascinated women even though, with his hooked nose and weak chin, he was far from conventionally handsome. Gross was a disciple of Sigmund Freud, of whom Frieda had never heard, and he explained some of Freud's theories and his own extension of them to her. He believed that erotic fulfilment was at the very centre of human experience, and that to be able to give and receive sexual pleasure was a mark of worth as a human being. Frieda, intoxicated by a vision of freedom, took Otto for a lover. For the first time she felt admired as she needed to be, and there was extra satisfaction in discovering that she was preferred to her sister Else, who had already had an affair with Gross, and had had a child by him. When Frieda returned to Nottingham, even her children recognised that she had changed profoundly: one of them said to her, 'You are not our old mother. You have got our old mother's skin on, but you are not our mother that went away.'[2]

Frieda continued to write to Otto on her return, and was unable to bring herself to burn the letters he wrote back. In those letters he praised the strength of her sexuality as a divine gift, and made her see herself as both unusual and important, when she had felt herself dwindling into middle age in a lifeless suburban world; from Otto she drew the conviction that if only people were allowed to indulge their sexual appetites freely the world would become a paradise. But there were things she did not know about Otto Gross. He was a cocaine addict, and treated his complaisant wife Freidel, whom he was soon to abandon, tyrannically. Perhaps Frieda did sense he was wrecking his own life, however, for although they met passionately once more, and he persistently urged her to leave her husband, she never agreed to do so.

When Lawrence entered Frieda's life in 1912, five years had passed since the episode with Otto Gross. She was bored – 'sleepwalking', she called it. Her husband treated her well enough, and she loved her children, but she had nothing to satisfy the hunger for life Lawrence instantly recognised.

Her husband had shown her some of Lawrence's writing, most likely pages from 'Paul Morel' – her son Montague remembers seeing her reading it in bed – and according to her daughter Barbara, Weekley had mentioned that he had 'a genius in his evening class', so Frieda was well prepared to find Lawrence impressive. Her first image of him was of a long, thin figure, with straight legs and light, sure movements. She must also have seen his physical frailty.

Lawrence, fired by his recent disappointing conversations with Jessie about 'Paul Morel', talked with his usual animation about women and how he was tired of them. Frieda was surprised to hear such an intense harangue before lunch: he seemed altogether fiercer than any Englishman she had met. We know they spoke of Oedipus, but whether of psychoanalysis or Sophocles is not clear. Although Lawrence had only been invited to lunch, he stayed until evening, and walked home through the fields in the darkness.

What Frieda responded to at once in Lawrence was his air of spiritual authority. He did not treat her with respect, but was critical of her from the first. At their second meeting he pointed out, 'You are quite unaware of your husband, you take no notice of him.'[3] Later, as she watched him making paper boats for her children, she saw how completely oblivious of her presence he became, and was at once overcome by tenderness. This recalls Jessie Chambers' response to seeing Lawrence in a similar attitude as he attempted to fix his brother's umbrella. Not exactly an erotic tug, it is closer to a maternal impulse; but no less powerful for that. Frieda recognised in Lawrence someone who would need her, in a way neither Weekley nor Gross ever needed her, with the whole of his being. He was at once vulnerable and demanding.

Lawrence saw the beauty of Frieda's mischievous face, listened to her low, foreign voice, and saw her sexual confidence. Nothing could have been more different from the timid reluctance of the girls he had known, or even the ready sensuality of Alice Dax.

It was Frieda who made the first sexual overtures. One Sunday when her husband was away, she suggested that Lawrence stay the night with her. He was unsurprised. Their conversation had already made it clear to him that she did not find sex frightening, or even such a serious matter as the other women he had known. Nevertheless, he refused to do as she asked, saying, 'I will not stay in your husband's house while he is away, but you must tell him the truth and we will go away together, because I love you.'[4]

It was a risky move. Lawrence knew he had met the one woman he wanted; he would have felt dishonest and contemptible if he had accepted her offer of a clandestine affair. He was also aware that he was asking a woman he had known only six weeks to choose between himself and her whole comfortable life. Frieda knew, as Lawrence did not, that her husband would be devastated. Moreover, although she had left her children for short holidays before, she could hardly bear to think of being separated from them.

At first Frieda tried to persuade him to accept a compromise. She suggested that he accompany her to Germany, which she had already arranged to visit to attend her father's celebration of the fiftieth anniversary of his entering the army. In return, she promised to tell Weekley how unhappy she was in her marriage.

Lawrence was thrown into a fever of suspense, as he could not be sure of Frieda's intentions. Would she really commit herself? In a letter to Edward Garnett, who was looking after his literary affairs, he comforted himself: 'We could have at least one week together.'[5] Before they set off for Germany, he was able to take Frieda to visit Garnett at The Cearne in Kent. Lawrence had written: 'Mrs Weekley is perfectly unconventional, but really good, in the best sense. I'll bet you have never met anyone like her, by a long chalk.'[6]

As late as 30 April, three days before their intended departure, Lawrence was still not certain Frieda would go away with him. His letters show him in an agony of suspense. He implored her to tell him all her movements precisely, particularly the times of the trains. 'For goodness sake tell me something and something definite. I would do anything on earth for you, and can do nothing . . . I am afraid of something low, like an eel which bites out of the mud and hangs on with its teeth.'[7]

Frieda kept part of her word, and told her husband some of the truth about her unhappiness; but she put off the interview until the last minute before her departure, and even then, although she admitted that she had been unfaithful with Will Dowson and Otto Gross, she did not tell Weekley she was leaving for Germany with Lawrence. Still less did she announce a permanent separation.

Frieda left her son behind in Nottingham, and took the two girls to their grandparents' house in Well Walk, Hampstead. She was stunned with the misery of parting from her children. Lawrence had written, 'I shall get to Kings Cross tomorrow at 1.25. Will that do? You see I couldn't come today because I was waiting for the laundry and for some stuff from the tailors.' Frieda needed to be brave as she

78

read on: 'I hope you've got some money for yourself. I can only muster eleven pounds.'[8]

They crossed the Channel on 3 May 1912, sitting on old ropes and watching England disappear until there was nothing but their own, almost childlike, sense of being alone together on a grey sea.

Telegrams and letters from Weekley pursued Frieda to Germany. Her parents realised something was wrong, but she took some pains to conceal from them the fact that she was travelling with a man.

When they reached Metz, Lawrence booked into a small hotel. Frieda took a room there too, as the family house was filled with relatives and friends who had come for the celebration; but it was far from the honeyed time together that Lawrence had imagined. He could see that Frieda was restless and undecided, and seemed reluctant to introduce him to her sisters Else and Johanna. She was indeed wondering what her more successful sisters would make of him.

Else was the first to meet him, at Metz railway station. She thought he looked gentlemanly and was not shy. A few days later, while Frieda and Johanna were at a fair together in Metz, they bumped into Lawrence wandering around on his own in a cloth cap and raincoat, and the confrontation Frieda had feared took place. Johanna was a worldly woman, used to a Berlin society of upper-class officers. She saw Lawrence's Englishness, his gawkiness, and his poverty, but she also saw that he was personally confident. She told Frieda she thought he could be trusted.

Alone in his hotel room, abroad for the first time in his life and acutely aware of Frieda's indecision, Lawrence was wretched. He either wandered round the town (which he disliked) on his own, or sat in his hotel room writing gloomy letters to Frieda. 'Now I can't stand it any longer, I can't. For two hours I haven't moved a muscle – just sat and thought.'[9] He could not bear the 'subterfuge, lying, dirt, fear' and, worst of all, the suspense. The situation was 'round my chest like a cord'.[10]

A grotesque incident, however, brought Lawrence's presence into the open as far as the rest of the family were concerned. He and Frieda were discovered by an officious policeman talking in English near the fortifications of Metz. The suspicion of espionage, which could have led to arrest, had to be rebutted, and for this Frieda turned to her father, Baron von Richthofen.

So it was that Lawrence was brought to have tea with the Baron, a miner's son confronting an aristocrat. It was an awkward occasion. In 1920 Lawrence described a similar episode in *Mr Noon*, in which Gilbert Noon, facing a perplexed father, makes mistakes in the gender of French words, and falls into obstinate silence. That afternoon in Metz, the Baron was more dismayed by the situation than he allowed himself to appear; later he wrote to his daughter sadly that she had chosen to travel about the world like a barmaid.

Lawrence was bustled off to Trier, about two hours by train from Metz, to be out of danger of arrest, and settled down to wait for Frieda to visit him. Surprisingly, some of his sprightliness returned. He began to work on his novel again, and set off to visit his Krenkow relatives eighty miles away in Waldbroun in the Rhineland, responding to the new landscape with pleasure. At the Krenkows' he continued to work, and flirted with his young married cousin, Hannah. He admitted to Edward Garnett that everything was still vague and undecided, but to Frieda he was able to write 'I love you' without his usual English reticence. He also managed to write an article describing his impressions of Germany for Walter de la Mare on the *Westminster Gazette*, even as he waited for Frieda to sort her situation out.

Lawrence had little understanding of Ernest Weekley's unhappiness, which he hugely underestimated. He thought Weekley was content to accept Frieda's affairs with other men, whereas in fact he had been driven nearly mad by her disclosures about Dowson and Gross. Weekley did not yet know about Lawrence, but he was certainly suspicious, as his telegram in early May asking Frieda if she were with a man makes clear.

Lawrence's wish to bring the situation to the conclusion he desired made him ruthless. He wrote to Weekley himself, stating that he and Frieda loved one another (the letter was produced as evidence in the divorce proceedings eighteen months later). Lawrence was not prepared for Weekley's response. He demanded nothing less than Frieda's total admission of guilt, so that he could arrange a divorce which would not cost him his post at the university, and made it clear that he was going to be altogether uncompromising about allowing her access to the children. 'We are not,' he said contemptuously, 'like rabbits.'[11]

The stark choice thus presented to Frieda threw her into panic. She attempted to calm her nerves by flirting with an old friend, Udo von Henning, an army officer. Lawrence, when he heard about this, was determined not to be bullied. 'If you want Henning, or anybody, have him,'[12] he wrote to Frieda, contemptuously comparing her sexual use of the man to a dose of morphine. This apparent licence for infidelity may have been a shrewd bluff. It was hardly consistent with Lawrence's own temperament. He had lived in a world of puritanical sexual mores until his meeting with Frieda; he had slept only with Alice Dax, whom he did not love, and Jessie Chambers, with whom he found sexual relations difficult. After meeting Frieda, he was to sleep with no other woman. With great astuteness, and without any belief in unrestrained sexual freedom, he refused to play the role of the jealous and fearful lover, and mocked Frieda instead about Henning. 'I think you're rather horrid to Henning. You make him more . . . babyfied . . . Where is Henning to get his next feed?'[13]

What kept Frieda in such an agony of indecision was her fear of losing access to her children altogether. Nevertheless, on 24 May she set off to Munich to rejoin Lawrence, and they travelled south together. A friend lent them a three-roomed flat in Beuerberg with a balcony which overlooked the river Isar. Frieda's sister Else had lent them some money. They only had about fifteen shillings a week, but on this they were able to afford good black bread and fresh eggs, and they found delicious berries to eat. It was a time of great beauty; both had the gift of finding happiness in the world about them, and now they found it together.

Yet they argued about everything. When Frieda lost a heel from one of her shoes, she threw both away and walked barefoot; Lawrence was indignant at the waste. He was also irritated by her untidiness, and tried hard to make her more orderly, and put woollen, silk and cotton clothes in separate drawers as his mother would have done.

Lawrence and Frieda disposed the roles usually accorded to literary genius and spouse in an unusual way; he did most of the work, bringing her breakfast in bed with a bunch of flowers every morning, and she lay about being pampered. He had already observed her incompetence when she struggled with the gas taps at Mapperley, and now he scolded her for her helplessness; even a common woman, he said, could make a better cup of coffee. But when she was distressed by her own mistakes, for instance when she burnt the pigeons they had bought for supper, he treated her with gentle indulgence.

There was one misery, however, that could not be exorcised; Frieda grieved for the children she had been forced to abandon. When Lawrence's attempts at consolation failed, her grief made him blind with rage and, for all the love he had felt for his own mother, he came to curse the mother in Frieda. In 'She Looks Back', one of the *Look! We Have Come Through!* poems written at Beuerberg, he reproaches her bitterly for being like Lot's wife:

> *Nevertheless, the curse against you is still in my heart*
> *Like a deep, deep burn.*
> *The curse against all mothers.*[14]

Chapter 7

THE WANDERERS

L
awrence and Frieda's first night of love in England had not
been a success. The poems in *Look! We Have Come Through!*
make that clear, and the 'Argument' at the start of that volume
declares how intensely personal a case history it is. 'First Morning',
written in Beuerberg, opens:

> *The night was a failure*
> *but why not –?*[1]

In the poem, Lawrence puts this failure down to his inability to 'free
myself from the past, those others', but does not explain why the
thought of other women should haunt him in Frieda's bed, or why it
should produce 'confusion'. He might be thinking that the spirit of
his mother was sabotaging his sexuality with Frieda, as it did with
Jessie, though that does not explain the plural 'others'. *Mr Noon* makes
it clear that, whatever Lawrence and Frieda's difficulties were, they
continued through many of their early attempts at lovemaking, and
in the light of Lawrence's later obsessive anger at women's insistence
on their own sexual satisfaction, it seems likely that Frieda found him
a poor lover from early on.

It is hardly surprising. Not only did he not have the least idea of
how to arouse a woman by his caresses, his later writing suggests
that he came to think that no woman should need him to do so. That
Lawrence and Frieda were passionately in love is not in dispute, but
all the evidence suggests that it was not an attachment based on the
'lineaments of gratified desire'.

The praise Johanna, the character based on Frieda, gives to Gilbert

Noon's sexual prowess in *Mr Noon* is a little unconvincing: 'Do you know I was rather frightened that you weren't a good lover? But it isn't every man who can love a woman three times in a quarter of an hour so *well*, is it?'[2] However, Lawrence wrote these lines nearly ten years later, and by then needed to stress an aspect of the bond between Frieda and himself which was fast disappearing. Even as they stand, the lines bear witness to Lawrence's adolescent potency rather than his ability to give pleasure.

It may be that Lawrence found Frieda's frank sensuality overpowering: Frieda, unlike all the other women he had known, was neither virginal nor intellectual. 'One sits so tight on the crater of one's emotions . . . I am just learning – thanks to Frieda – to let go a bit.'[3]

Lawrence may have been frequently overwhelmed by desire for Frieda, yet the satisfying of that desire presented him with problems; something, at any rate, was awry. In the early months of the relationship, there was a quarrel over a poem Lawrence had written for his dead mother which had been reverently copied into one of Lawrence's notebooks by Louie Burrows. It is not a particularly good poem, but it was hardly an aesthetic response that led Frieda to write so vehemently alongside some lines in which Lawrence speaks of his mother as his love, 'I hate it.' At the end of the page, she added a comment that suggests a far more intimate source for her fury:

I have tried, I have fought, I have nearly killed myself in the battle to get you into connection with myself and other people, sadly I proved to myself that I can love, but never you. Now I will leave you alone for some days and I will see if being alone will help you to see me as I am. I will heal again by myself, you cannot help me, you are a sad thing. I know your secret and your despair. I have seen you ashamed – I have made you better, that is my reward.[4]

We can only conjecture about the secret and the shame, but that they were sexual seems likely. It is also likely that, with her genius for sexuality, as Gross had described it years earlier, Frieda had done much to cure whatever was wrong. Lawrence and Frieda's sexual failure was, in the upshot, not particularly important. On their first morning they were happy together, in spite of the disappointment of the previous night. The same is true of the lovers in *Mr Noon*; in spite of sexual failure they are 'happy just being together'. If Frieda already guessed she would not enjoy with Lawrence the sexual delights she had experienced with Gross, in the last analysis she chose against their significance.

There are intimations in the poems, however, of darker conflicts to come. Frieda wakes in the night disturbed by the choice she has made, intuitively fearing something destructive in Lawrence. He uses words in the poem that are actually hers:

> *. . . No, I'm a thing of life. I give*
> *You armfuls of sunshine, and you won't let me live.*[5]

Her uncertainty is resolved in going back to sleep in Lawrence's arms: a soothing which is notably far from the erotic.

Whatever else, Lawrence was overwhelmingly in love with Frieda, and the desire he felt for her was very different from the nervy, electrical desire he had felt for Helen Corke: 'I think, when one loves, one's very sex passion becomes calm, a steady sort of force instead of a storm. Passion, that nearly drives one mad, is far away from real love.'[6]

Their lovemaking was unhampered by birth control: for all Frieda's understandable alarm at the thought of having children, Lawrence did not believe in preventing conception 'when people love each other' – an interesting comment on his feelings about Jessie, with whom he had always used condoms, and even Helen, for whom he had prepared such precautions, as well as an acknowledgement of Frieda's much greater recklessness.

The joy he takes in Frieda's physical beauty and her calm pleasure fill 'Gloire de Dijon':

> *She drips herself with water, and her shoulders*
> *Glisten as silver.*[7]

The consummation of Lawrence's love is described in 'Song of the Man Who is Loved':

> *So I hope I shall spend eternity*
> *With my face down buried between her breasts;*

> *And my heart full of security,*
> *And my still hands full of her breasts.*[8]

That image of satisfaction resembles a nursing child falling asleep, and it seems likely that the passionate connection between Lawrence and Frieda was closer to a biological tie than that of erotic love. This is not incompatible with the 'wonderful naked intimacy' that Lawrence described in a letter to Sallie Hopkin, his Eastwood friend, in which he also wrote that he ought not to have blamed women as he had in the past, but himself 'for taking my love to the wrong women'.[9] Frieda, writing much later in *Not I, But the Wind*, thought the real tie between herself and Lawrence was 'the wonder of living' which they drew from their daily lives.

Altogether, the new relationship made Lawrence feel sure of himself in a new way, but at the same time he was already alarmingly aware of his emotional dependency on Frieda. And he did not entirely enjoy the knowledge that she was necessary to him. Frieda's account in her memoirs of these early days of their relationship gives little indication of the doubts she felt at the time. As late as July, she had been tempted to accede to Weekley's proposal to set her up with her children in a flat in London. This would not have involved her in divorce proceedings, and would have left her free, provided she did not live openly with Lawrence. It was the kind of arrangement her sisters would have found perfectly acceptable, if not ideal, and they may well have tried to talk her into it.

The narrator of *Look! We Have Come Through!* is devastated by any such possibility:

> *Perhaps she will go back to England*
> *Perhaps she will go back*
> *Perhaps we are parted for ever.*[10]

Yet Lawrence had too much pride to plead with Frieda to stay for his sake. 'She almost hates me because I won't say "I love you – stay with me whatever happens". I *do* love her. If she left me, I do not think I should be alive six months hence.'[11]

After a week in Beuerberg they moved up the river Isar to Icking, and there Frieda's mother made a violent incursion into Lawrence's life; she was to be important to him as a correspondent and occasion-ally as a subject of his fiction. On this occasion she came to scold him for taking her daughter off to live in poverty. Lawrence, who saw that these anxieties were legitimate, accepted her tirade, rather to Frieda's irritation. On her return to Munich, the Baroness confessed to her daughter Else that she had thought Lawrence both lovable and reliable.

Lawrence's second novel, *The Trespasser*, had come out in England in May 1912, the month in which he left the country. Edward Garnett (who continued to act as Lawrence's mentor and unpaid editor and literary agent for many years) sent him the reviews, which were kind rather than enthusiastic. The *English Review* found the book 'somewhat disappointing', and the *Saturday Review* reflected: 'Had it been the work of almost any other man, it would have satisfied.'

While Lawrence and Frieda were staying at Icking, Garnett's twenty-year-old son David, holidaying in Munich, called to see them. David, slightly patronisingly, thought Lawrence cheeky and amus-ing, but he described Frieda as a lioness. For his part, Lawrence envied the boy's swimming in the Isar: 'He simply smashes his way through the water.'[12] Frieda, too, seemed impressed by David's athleticism.

We know a good deal of what Frieda and Lawrence talked about at this time from *Not I, But the Wind*. He told her about the people he had known in his childhood, the poverty of his family, how he had felt when a friend at school rejected him because he was a collier's son. She told him how the nuns at her convent school had tried to tame her wild spirits, and how her father had picked asparagus. She also told him about her earlier affairs, and made no secret of the powerful influence Otto Gross had had upon her life and thinking. Lawrence argued against promiscuous sexual love because, he claimed, he couldn't see how anyone could be physically in love with more than one person at a time. His behaviour in the preceding year might suggest otherwise, but perhaps he was not then in love.

Their different attitudes to promiscuity were founded in their differ-ent backgrounds. Lawrence had been much impressed by the 'utterly non-moral' attitude of the Baroness when he met her at the Richthofen home, and was fascinated to learn that Frieda's elder sister Else had 'gone with two other men (in succession) ... Lord, what a family.

I've never seen anything like it.'[13] Nor had he: people did not live like that in Eastwood or Croydon.

Frieda's sisters and their friends had all reached understandings with their husbands; sexual liberation and open marriages were the assumed norm among them. But it was not an exciting affair that Lawrence wanted; there is no more talk of play, as there had been with Agnes Holt and Jessie. He wanted commitment above all, as he had written earlier from the Krenkows when Frieda had accused him of being indecisive: 'I know in my heart "here's my marriage". It feels rather terrible – because it is a great thing in my life – it is my *life* – I am a bit awe-inspired, I want to get used to it.'[14] Lawrence could never separate sexual passion from the idea of lifelong monogamy. He believed in marriage, even if it had hardly brought his parents happiness.

Soon after Frieda's mother's visit, Lawrence and Frieda left the security of their borrowed flat and walked south, with knapsacks on their backs, into Italy on 5 August. David Garnett and his friend Harold Hobson, a consulting engineer, joined them in Mayrhofen in the foothills of the Alps. Lawrence entertained the party with his excellent mimicry of Yeats, whom he had met through Ezra Pound in 1909. The countryside was marvellously beautiful, and there was an abundance of food – delicious coffee and many kinds of bread. Lawrence felt some qualms about their new friends, Garnett and Hobson: 'Those spoiled well-to-do children of the Fabian middle class with their enviable happy picnicky childhoods,'[15] as he put it in *Mr Noon*. Their easy childhood gave them more in common, both with each other and with Frieda, than he could ever have.

It was on this trip through the Tyrol that Lawrence first discovered how little he could trust Frieda sexually. As he watched a lusty young peasant dancing with Frieda he could see exactly what he was hoping for, and also that Frieda might well have acceded. She came to Lawrence's bed that night, but on 12 August, less than four months after taking up with Lawrence, she seduced David Garnett's handsome young friend Harold Hobson.

We owe this story to David Garnett. If we are to believe the account in *Mr Noon*, Frieda confessed the episode to Lawrence, who forgave her. So much in that novel reads like a factual account that it is strong supporting evidence for the incident. Two men accompany Gilbert

Noon and Johanna on their trip through the Tyrol, and Gilbert observes their relationship without suspicion. Crossing the mountains, Johanna confesses that she has had sex with one of the men. The incident is beautifully told: Gilbert is so surprised by Johanna's confession that he feels no pain, and after a few moments observes only that people do things without knowing the reason, and that it doesn't matter because he loves her.

In the novel, Johanna is made a little testy by this magnanimity, just as Frieda may have been annoyed that she could not provoke Lawrence to a straightforward expression of jealousy. According to David Garnett, Hobson was not the only lover Frieda took on that trip. He claims that once, after a quarrel, she swam across the river to where a woodcutter was working, made love to him, and swam back, just to show Lawrence she was free to do what she liked.

The truth of this second incident is hotly denied by Frieda's daughter Barbara Weekley Barr. She was not present, however, and her mother's general propensity for erotic adventure is unquestioned. Aldous Huxley, who was not in the Tyrol either, and who only grew close to Lawrence much later, added several Prussian cavalry officers and some Italian peasants to the possible list of Frieda's lovers.

None of the quarrels that were so marked a part of Lawrence and Frieda's relationship seem to have centred on Lawrence's sexual jealousy. The verbal aggression tinged with spite which (if we can trust *Mr Noon*) Lawrence was already showing in the Tyrol, was usually directed at a foolish remark of Frieda's, sometimes at the very 'gushing' quality of speech he had once so admired. Gilbert Noon makes fun of Johanna's address to fireflies in the rye fields in that spirit. The violence of the argument which then erupted was in such marked contrast to the importance of the occasion that one may suspect another, possibly sexual, source for the passion. Whatever it may have been, it is certain that it was there in the Tyrol that Lawrence recognised with a horrible shock that, whatever Frieda did, his very being was now dependent upon her, and that if they were to part 'the soul must bleed to death'.

Chapter 8

GARGNANO

L awrence had been told about Lake Garda by Ezra Pound; on 18 September 1912 he rented, for three guineas a month, the first floor of the large Villa Igea, in the village of Gargnano, overlooking the lake. Fifty pounds arrived from Duckworth for *The Trespasser* just when they needed it to pay the landlord. There were vineyards and olive trees and lemon gardens, and Lawrence was delighted at the way the residents of Gargnano stood and gossiped in the town square.

Frieda usually lay in bed smoking and reading novels until lunchtime. Lawrence never complained at her neglect of domestic chores; he liked doing them, as he had once liked helping his mother. He got up every morning at eight and brought Frieda her breakfast in bed, then worked until lunchtime. He knew that Frieda had left behind a comfortable life in which she could be as idle as she wished, and he enjoyed looking after himself. He could cook, cut wood, scrub floors and even milk a cow, while Frieda was impractical and slovenly. She made some attempt to master the huge charcoal stove and gleaming copper pans, but the stove was too much for her. And it was in Gargnano that she tried to wash the sheets and found their size and wetness impossible to cope with. In her memoir, Frieda reports Lawrence's amusement at her misery when he rescued her: 'The One and Only (which name stood for the one and only phoenix when I was uppish) is drowning, oh dear!'[1]

They lived well on little money; so well that Frieda could not understand why everyone did not do the same. Lawrence himself had the genius for living he found in Frieda; he taught everyone near him to be grateful 'simply for life itself'[2] as she put it.

They both learnt Italian. Frieda read novels, including *Anna Karenina*, which she then sent to her husband in the hope of softening his heart. Carelessly, she had left a letter in the book from Will Dowson, her former lover, who had written to say she would have been better advised to run off with him. When Weekley found the letter he maliciously sent it back to Lawrence.

Lawrence and Frieda identified with Anna and Vronsky because Karenin, like Weekley, had used a husband's legal power to keep a child from his mother as a weapon against his adulterous wife; also because they were living in comparable isolation. It says something for their relationship that they were able to sustain it as Anna and Vronsky could not. Unlike Vronsky, of course, Lawrence had not been taken away from the main purpose of his life; in fact he now had the chance to dedicate himself altogether to his writing. Frieda suffered most. There was very little in her life other than Lawrence, and she missed her children so badly that one cold day she went down to the lake fully clothed and let the water lap over her in her misery.

In the seven months they lived in Gargnano, Lawrence finished the last draft of *Sons and Lovers*, and began 'The Sisters', which was to become *The Rainbow* and *Women in Love*. Edward Garnett had made extensive notes on *Sons and Lovers*; now Lawrence worked over the whole novel again, reliving his experience in the process. It was the first book Lawrence had written with Frieda at his side, and in her memoir she claims to have written parts of it. Her contribution was far more than responding to enquiries such as 'What do you think my mother felt like then?'[3] as fully as she could. She wrote 'little female bits', [4] gave advice about Mrs Morel and Miriam, and helped to draw the portrait of Clara Dawes. She was very pleased with her contributions, asserting to Edward Garnett that before her help 'I think L. quite missed the point in "Paul Morel",'[5] and in the same letter spoke of the love Paul felt for his mother as 'sort of Oedipus'. She certainly introduced Lawrence to the ideas of Freud she had heard from Gross.

It is unlikely that Lawrence knew much about Freud before this reworking of *Sons and Lovers*, as there was no translation of Freud available in 1912, and it was not until 1914 that he was to meet knowledgeable Freudians. In Gargnano he learnt to see Paul Morel's problems in Freudian terms; Frieda had only the sketchiest idea of psychoanalysis, but she was altogether convinced by what she thought she understood, and so she played a crucial part in changing the final shape of the novel. In the process, some additional animus against Jessie crept in: Frieda always argued that Mrs Morel deserved her victory over Miriam, since Miriam did not feel enough 'warmth' for Paul. But Lawrence was writing out of his own soul: he found Freud's ideas too clinical. The essential emotional shape was his, and the book is evidence for Freud's theory rather than for Lawrence's use of it.

To be at Lawrence's side, as the handmaiden of his genius, may have been exhilarating, but it demanded a spiritual toughness few women could have matched. When Lawrence wrote of his mother's death, for instance, he became ill with grief, and Frieda sometimes felt defeated by his misery. Luckily, she had a very different temperament from Jessie Chambers. When she found Lawrence's grief more than she could bear, she wrote a skit on his intensity called 'Paul Morel: or His Mother's Darling'. Neither Jessie nor Helen Corke could write as freshly as Frieda. Her personal vivacity comes out clearly in her letters, which are unstuffy, colloquial and sometimes as naturally charming as those of Lawrence. Some are acutely perceptive. To Edward Garnett, she appended a note on 14 November 1912 after reading his play *Jeanne d'Arc*:

> *Of course she is really a fearfully jolly, healthy girl with a bit of peasant cunning, and then her weird Mysticism throws a veil over her and I like it . . . I like the way you treated her. L. always wants to treat women like the chicken we had the other day, take its guts out and pluck its feathers sitting over a pail . . . Poor Jeanne in her simple broken vitality! Don't you men all love her better because she was sacrificed! Why are all heroines really Gretchen? You don't like the triumphant female, it's too much for you!*[6]

Gargnano was no idyll, for all the happiness Frieda and Lawrence found there. Weekley talked of divorce, but set no proceedings in motion and alternated between pleas and threats. Frieda's sister Else continued to press Lawrence to give up his claim on Frieda's love. He wrote in reply:

*If Frieda and the children could live happily together, I should say 'Go'
– because the happiness of two out of three is sufficient. But if she would
only be sacrificing her life, I would not let her go if I could keep her . . .
that would sap their strength because they would have to support her life
as they grew up. They would not be free to live of themselves – they
would first have to* live for *her, to pay back.*[7]

For all the intelligence of this, Lawrence was still far from calm, and
explaining to his Croydon friend Arthur McLeod why he had written
no stories over the months, he wrote, 'The business with Frieda
squashes little things out of me.' Weekley sent Frieda a photograph
of her children and assured her that she would never see them again
unless she returned to him. 'I have done with you. I want to forget
you and you must be dead to the children.'[8] The law, as Frieda knew,
was on his side. In December Weekley threatened to come to Italy
and kill both of them. This visit never took place, though Lawrence
imagined Weekley's arrival in his play *Fight for Barbara*, which he
began to write in October 1912.

At first Lawrence tried to console Frieda for the loss of her children,
but soon her despair began to anger him. He took her grief as evidence
that he was not sufficient for her, as she was for him, and the thought
made him cruel. The problem was exacerbated by Weekley's
behaviour. Lawrence sent the children some money for Christmas,
but Weekley returned it. Frieda's tears at this so maddened Lawrence
that he actually invited what he most feared, demanding that she
return to her husband if she was miserable, and insisting that he would
not try to stop her if she wanted to go back to England. He refused
to acknowledge she had legitimate grounds for pain, and his sneers
began to take on some of the sadism that was to characterise his later
rages. Frieda said in a letter to Edward Garnett: 'Over the children I
thought he was beastly; he hated me for being miserable, not a
moment of misery did he put up with.'[9] Lawrence was to become
pathologically jealous of Frieda's children; he might well have felt the
same about children of his own if they had been able to have any.

Nevertheless, on Christmas Day 1912 Lawrence wrote to Sallie
Hopkin that even if the skies fell on them it wouldn't destroy what
was between Frieda and himself. His good mood was in part induced
by a visit from Harold Hobson, which broke their isolation. In the

general good humour Lawrence found it perfectly possible to put Frieda's earlier infidelity with Hobson out of his mind. But Lawrence was still subject to fits of rage. He sometimes gave Frieda a 'tonguelashing', rather as his mother had attacked his father. Those changes of mood were very frightening, and even Frieda could not handle them. Like Jessie, Frieda recognised Lawrence's fear of powerful women: 'In his heart I think he always dreaded women, felt that they were in the end more powerful than men.'[10] She saw his vulnerability, even though she felt 'like a cat without her kittens'. She knew 'he needed me more than they [her children] did'.[11]

On 5 April 1913 Lawrence, writing to his sister Ada about a possible return to England, mentioned that Frieda had used something Ada had once said as evidence for 'what a difficult and unpleasant person I am to live with'.[12] A note in Frieda's hand shows no repentance for doing so and adds with spirit, 'Yes, so shall I . . . your letter just came when L. had made me so miserable that I began to think I was the scum of the earth, unfit for human being – *his* misery was all my doing, so your letter came as a help to me from the Almighty.'

Lawrence had not altogether cut himself off from the life he had led before he left England. He had received a letter from Louie Burrows while in Italy, and replied gently enough by telling her that he was going to marry the woman he was living with, and that the best thing she could do was to put him out of her mind and, if necessary, hate him.

He had also written to Jessie several times. Before he left for Germany he had written to her that he was going on with 'Paul Morel' and that she would have to forgive him. A few weeks later he wrote excitedly to tell her about Frieda, claiming to have confided this secret only to his sister, though in fact many of his new friends were already aware of it. Jessie was shocked by Frieda's marital situation, and although in her memoir written after Lawrence's death she spoke of the release the news gave her, it was nevertheless a blow 'comparable to a kind of death'.[13] The future that lay ahead of her looked barren, and in whatever she tried to read she saw only the wreckage of her life.

For a time, Helen Corke and Jessie Chambers had been close. Helen had been to stay at the Chambers' farm, and they exchanged intimate letters. Through 1911 Helen served as a link with Lawrence, but while she recognised that the arrival of Frieda in his life was like 'the sun of a new day',[14] Jessie could not feel so generously. During the summer of 1912, Helen saw a change in Jessie's personality, 'as if the lamp in her spirit burned low',[15] and when the two of them went for a holiday to the Rhineland together, Jessie could take no pleasure in the visit. The only experience that seemed to reach into her depressed spirit was reading Dostoevsky's *Crime and Punishment*. For her part, Helen felt as if she were abroad alone.

The following year, Lawrence had his publisher send Jessie a copy of his *Love Poems and Others*, published in February 1913. She remembered most of them from his old college notebook, and wrote to thank him, offering a few comments as she had always done. His reply came together with proof sheets of *Sons and Lovers*. He took no account of her comments, which had once been so important to him, asserting instead that 'the little book was all right'[16] and inviting her to stay with Frieda and him in Italy.

Jessie hardly dared look at the proofs; as she says in her memoir, 'I was by no means sure of my capacity to recover a second time.' Her sister May, to whom she showed Lawrence's letter, suggested she return it to him unanswered; this she did, along with the packet of proofs, a gesture she clearly felt to be both daring and cruel. She remembered Lawrence once saying to her, 'Any woman will give a man a ton of generosity, but is there a woman who will give him an ounce of justice?'[17] Posting back the letter, and the proofs which contained Lawrence's version of the life they had once shared, she reflected, 'Here is your ounce of justice.'

Jessie miscalculated the pain she had the power to inflict. Lawrence was not certain the gesture had been intended as a deliberate snub, but felt it would have been a good thing if it had. For himself, he put any sense of guilt aside. As he had complacently explained to Willie Hopkin when writing *The White Peacock*, 'If I need any woman for my fictional purpose, I shall use her. Why should I let any woman come between me and the flowering of my genius?'[18]

Lawrence and Frieda decided to return to England in the summer of 1913 so that she could be near her children. Lawrence himself did not want to return; he loved Italy, but was afraid to let Frieda go alone, fearing that seeing her children again might make her choose against staying with him. And perhaps, having accepted her sexual infidelity with such equanimity, he was reluctant to share her love with the children. But they were returning to a situation in which the balance of power in their relationship was about to shift. And they were about to make new friendships which would prove important to them for the rest of their lives.

Chapter 9

THE WIDENING CIRCLE

The effect of Frieda's desertion on the Weekley family had
been devastating. Weekley, to make a complete break with
the past, dismissed the nanny Frieda had brought from Germany and sold both his own house in Nottingham and his parents'
house in Hampstead. He and the children were now living in Chiswick
with his parents, an unmarried aunt and a bachelor uncle. Weekley
commuted to Nottingham each week. He refused to mention Frieda,
and the other adults did all they could to make the children think of
their mother as evil. The two elder children, Monty and Elsa (aged
twelve and ten when Frieda left them) were inclined in any case to
take their father's side; but Barbara (then aged eight) was a rebellious
spirit who found herself identified with her mother when she did
wrong, and grew up with a more complex pattern of allegiance. Much
later, when she was staying with Lawrence and Frieda in Italy, Barbara
gave an account of what life had been like in the Weekley household.
Lawrence used it in his story 'The Virgin and the Gipsy' in 1926,
where anger against a runaway wife smothers all vital experience in
a household.

In the middle of June 1913 Lawrence and Frieda returned to England and stayed at The Cearne in Kent with Edward Garnett. All
Frieda's thoughts were centred on seeing her children again. She knew
they were living in Chiswick, but did not know the exact address: she
wandered along the streets, hoping to find them. At length, recognising some curtains she had bought in Nottingham, she rushed into the
house and ran upstairs to find the children. It was a disastrous attempt.
Her sudden appearance frightened the children, who had been told

many times to think of their mother as a disgusting creature, and she was humiliatingly chivvied out.

When she had recovered from that failure, Frieda realised that a more complicated campaign would have to be mounted. With David Garnett and the writer Katherine Mansfield, whom she had recently met, she walked around in front of St Paul's School in south-west London, hoping to catch a glimpse of Monty.

She saw him, spoke to him, and took him off to a sweet shop – an incident he luckily did not mention at home. A little later Frieda met her daughters by chance in the street. They danced with delight to see her, and asked her when she was coming back. She hugged them and explained they would have to wait. For a time she felt optimistic, but unfortunately the girls were less discreet than their brother, and when Frieda tried to meet them again they had obviously been instructed to have nothing to do with her. In her memoir Frieda describes the little white faces looking at her in silence as if she were 'an evil ghost'.[1]

Lawrence still had connections in Eastwood, and he was far from indifferent to how he was regarded there. He wrote detailed letters describing his plans to Enid Hilton and Sallie Hopkin, whom he asked to conceal his impending visit from Alice Dax. He had written to his sister Ada from Italy of his likely return to England, observing that she had kept a discreet silence in her letters about *Sons and Lovers*, which had been published in May. He may have suspected the reason for this. His sisters had to outface people in the streets of Eastwood who had read the book, and his elder brother George told Harry Moore in 1952 that when he read the book he had wanted to thrash Lawrence for the picture it gave of his mother and father.[2] George might have been imprudent and reckless when he was young, but in the intervening years he had become a lay preacher, and he was by now exceedingly pious. He had deeply disapproved of his brother going away with a married woman. With some misgivings, Lawrence particularly sent his love to his father in the same letter to Ada, and wondered what he might have been told about his portrait as Walter Morel.

Reviews of *Sons and Lovers* had been very favourable. The *London Saturday Review* found 'none to excel it' among the important novels of the year; the *Athenaeum* had some reservations about the autobiographical element, but added 'we are held captive from the first page to the last'; while the *Saturday Westminster Gazette* thought the novel 'charged with the beauty of atmosphere and observation'. Although Duckworth's edition had lost money, Lawrence returned to find himself accepted as a serious author. This introduced him to a new circle of possible acquaintance.

When Lawrence and Frieda first met John Middleton Murry and his wife Katherine Mansfield in the summer of 1913, they were living in three rooms in Chancery Lane. The four of them took to one another instantly. They had a number of things in common; Katherine was waiting for a divorce from her first husband, George Bowden, as Frieda was waiting for a divorce from Weekley. Both women were older than their men, and from substantially more privileged backgrounds. And both Katherine and Frieda, as the more sexually sophisticated, had taken the initiative. Katherine had first offered Murry a room in her flat, then asked him to make her his mistress; to persuade him, she had to overcome terrors created in his mind by an early encounter with a prostitute in Paris, an experience he had found loathsome, and which had given him gonorrhoea.

Katherine Mansfield was born in 1888 in Wellington, New Zealand, and lived there for the first fifteen years of her life until her father, Chairman of the Bank of New Zealand, decided his children needed an English education. John Middleton Murry was a year younger than her, the son of a poor clerk at the War Office, who had won scholarships to Christ's Hospital and Brasenose College, Oxford. Katherine had a fine creative talent. She had already written a well-received book of short stories, *In a German Pension,* published in 1911. Murry too had literary ambitions, and had been influenced by a vacation spent in Paris to begin a little magazine called *Rhythm*, which he and Katherine now edited together. *Rhythm* was cheaply produced, but intended to be much wider in scope than an undergraduate magazine. Contributors ranged from Francis Carco, a twenty-five-year-old French poet Murry had befriended in Paris, to Walter de la Mare. In January 1913 Katherine had written to Lawrence in Italy asking him to contribute and, though he knew it would not pay, Lawrence agreed. It was business with *Rhythm* (which he thought a 'daft paper',[3] since the contributors were of such uneven merit) which brought Lawrence to Chancery Lane. There are many tributes to Katherine's bold elegance and doll-like prettiness; her sleek dark hair brushed close to her head, and her pale face, as Dorothy Brett described it, 'like a quiet mask, full of hidden laughter'.⁴ Frieda admired Katherine's elegance, particularly praising her long legs. Both Lawrence and Frieda were also attracted to Murry's dreamy good looks. He was twenty-four – four years younger than Lawrence – and was strikingly handsome, with a 'lovely frightening mouth',⁵ as Katherine called it.

On that first trip back to England, Frieda thought their acquaintance with Katherine and Murry was 'the only spontaneous and gay friendship we had'.⁶ She loved the way they made faces, and stuck out their tongues at each other like children. Later, Katherine herself recognised the childlike quality of their love; their joint impracticality was dangerous; neither had the commonsense of Lawrence about looking after themselves. For the moment, though, they were busy and happy.

Murry gives a vivid picture of the four of them sitting in an omnibus as they went off to lunch somewhere in Soho: 'Lawrence was slim and even boyish; he wore a large straw hat that suited him well. Mrs Lawrence, a big Panama hat over her flaxen hair. Straw hats, sunshine and gaiety.'⁷

Frieda treated Katherine like a younger sister. Katherine was indignant at the way Weekley was bullying Frieda, and was eager to help by taking messages to the children. She was also ready to confide secrets of her own. Nevertheless, they were very different creatures. Katherine was inordinately ambitious. The bisexual strand in her had no counterpart in Frieda, who preferred men to women, and had no close, adoring women friends as Katherine had. Frieda had never shown the slightest interest in developing her own literary talents, and was completely uncompetitive as a creative artist. Katherine was not merely determined to make her own way as a writer, she could not be content without recognition: that is why she was so reluctant to admit that her first published story, 'The-Child-Who-Was-Tired', was an adaptation of a story by Chekhov she had come across in a German translation. (Katherine's failure to acknowledge this debt made it easier for Floryan Sobieniowski, a Pole who had been her lover in Germany before she met Murry, to blackmail her in 1920.) Both women had abandoned the conventions of the day without much anxiety but in a very different spirit. Katherine was dark and intense, with a teasing manner; she always cared about what people thought of her and was not above trimming a little to make a good impression. Frieda was forthright to the point of recklessness; everything in her life had confirmed her sense of her own worth as a woman. Katherine was driven by inner forces Frieda was untroubled by. Murry too was eager for literary success; it was in order to be part of the literary world as much as to live with Katherine that he had thrown away his chance of a good Classics degree at Oxford. He was also something of a snob, and had cut off his links with his poor London family.

The foursome had a weekend in Broadstairs, Kent, at the end of July, where they went swimming and feasted (for all their shortage of money) on steak and tomatoes. Lawrence gave Katherine and Murry a copy of *Sons and Lovers*, which confirmed Murry's conviction of his stature as a novelist.

No wonder Frieda thought their relationship with the Murrys was the only happy one they had formed. The placid cheerfulness of that expedition is in stark contrast to the weeks Lawrence and Frieda had spent with Edward Garnett and his wife Constance at The Cearne.

The Garnett family had been close to Lawrence for some time, close enough for Constance to wish Antonia Almgren, the niece of an old friend, on them in Gargnano. Constance had been much taken by Frieda's characteristic summing-up of the troubled girl, who at that time was being pursued by a mad husband: 'I like Tony for many things; she is chasing greatness as if it were a rabbit and she wants to put salt on its tail.'[8]

The Lawrences turned up at The Cearne unexpectedly, and had necessitated a good many household rearrangements, but Constance found Lawrence instantly charming. She saw, as her son David had observed, that Lawrence 'couldn't buy a stamp without starting some intimate contact'.[9] Lawrence, in turn, was happy to pass a morning netting raspberries, and was flatteringly full of praise for Constance's fluent translations of Dostoevsky, whom at this stage he still considered an admirable writer.

Frieda, who had reached a crisis in her attempts to see her children, felt her concerns pushed to one side by a group of friends who were more interested in Lawrence than herself; but she knew how to make sure Lawrence continued to be aware of her. They were soon fighting hammer and tongs, and their rows distressed Constance, whose sympathies went out to Lawrence. She could see Frieda was suffering over her children, but thought her tactless, and believed it was her insensitivity that made Lawrence literally scream in anguish. David was unashamedly partisan for Frieda, and thought the rows were engendered by Lawrence's jealousy of her children and his own spitefulness.

Constance was so put out by these quarrels that she took up the matter with Lawrence. She could not imagine any relationship surviving such conflict, but, as she told Edward: 'He says I don't understand that his love is of the permanent sort and it is all that Frieda only *half* loves him.'[10]

After Constance's rebuke, Lawrence began to behave with more restraint, presumably in deference to his hostess. As the month-long visit came to an end, Constance observed to Edward that while Lawrence was quite sweet, having helped her in the house and in the vegetable garden, Frieda was rather trying.

Lawrence assumed that Katherine and Murry had more money than he did, and was astonished to hear from the poet Edward Marsh, who had asked him to contribute a poem to his anthology *Georgian Poetry*, that lack of funds might account for their not coming down to visit them when they moved to Kingsgate, a village on the Kent coast. When Lawrence and Frieda returned to Italy in October 1913, the hope was that Katherine and Murry would soon join them, but this was not to be. Murry's magazine *Rhythm* appeared to be going under; he was more than usually anxious about money, and not for the last time he was miserably uncertain about his ability to make Katherine happy. Lawrence wrote advising him to pack in his hack reviewing and live in Italy with them on Katherine's small annuity. His insights were based on his shrewd observation of the couple's interaction in London:

> *Be more natural, and positive, and stick to your own guts. You spread them out on a tray for her to throw to the cats. If you want things to come right – if you are ill, and exhausted, then take her money to the last penny, and let her do her own housework. Then she'll know you love her. You can't blame her if she's not satisfied with you . . .*[11]

In stressing Katherine's impatience with Murry's passivity, however, Lawrence missed her need for someone to 'nurse me, love me, hold me, comfort me',[12] as she was soon to be lamenting in her journal. Perhaps Lawrence assumed the creative fire lay with the male half of the couple. At any rate, the diatribe did not help Murry. He could see well enough that Katherine was unsatisfied, and was too dependent on her to think about whether she was satisfying him or not. Lawrence, well aware of his own need for Frieda, was proudly resolved never to be beaten into any such submission. He knew Frieda was indifferent to financial stress and believed that Katherine too did not really need Murry to work to buy her luxuries, since 'a woman who really loves a man would sleep on a board'.[13]

Back in Italy, Lawrence and Frieda set up house in Fiascherino, on the Gulf of Spezia. Lawrence did much less work there than he had in Gargnano. There were money worries and irritations, and problems over Frieda's divorce continued. They also had several visitors. Among these was Ivy Low.

Ivy Low had published two mildly successful novels – *Growing Pains* and *The Questing Beast* – when she visited Lawrence in Italy. She was twenty-five and full of enthusiasm for *Sons and Lovers*, which she thought 'the most marvellous novel I had ever read'.[14] She had written a rapturous letter to Lawrence, care of his publishers, and Lawrence had replied from Italy using crested notepaper, with a note saying that she was not to let the crest upset her because 'my wife's father was a baron',[15] and that he was simply using up the paper. It would be easy but inappropriate to condemn the palpable pleasure Lawrence took in Frieda's title: he was a creature of his times and, though he was later to assert a defiant pride in his working-class origins, he still bore the influence of his mother's attitudes, and Frieda did nothing to discourage his snobbery. On this occasion he was both trying to impress Ivy and to put her at her ease.

Ivy was confident enough in appearance when she arrived. She was an ebullient girl, whose family was part of the English Jewish intelligentsia. She wore an embroidered blouse – her clothes were borrowed from a friend, the writer Catherine Carswell – and this went down well, she observed, noticing at the same time that Frieda was not very elegantly dressed.

Ivy's account of her visit suggests she was given a warm welcome.

Lawrence seemed insecure, and asked her what she thought of him. Comforting him in what she called the 'Oxfordy' accent she had learnt from her mother, Ivy said she saw a working-class man full of life, who gave her a great deal of flattering attention. Whether Lawrence was as keen to ask Ivy's opinion of him as she claimed seems doubtful, since on no other occasion does he behave in this way, but with her enthusiasm they got on well enough at first.

After four or five days, however, the situation changed. Lawrence revised his opinion of Ivy and began, as she put it, 'to find out my defects one by one, and quite a few that nobody else had ever discovered'. He criticised her for not offering to help him prepare the meals. This seemed unfair when, as Ivy could not but notice, Frieda 'did not have to do anything – it was all right for her just to *be*'.[16]

Frieda's biographer Robert Lucas suggests that Frieda was jealous of the amount of time Lawrence spent walking and talking with his new friend. Ivy, in her account, openly declares how much she would have liked to usurp Frieda's place in Lawrence's bed. None of this quite explains the vicious harangues Lawrence began to direct at every area of her insecurity. Ivy had confessed that she was anxious about her friendship with Viola Meynell (daughter of the poet Alice Meynell), who sometimes did not introduce her to her more distinguished friends, and Lawrence tormented her about this mercilessly. He also made fun of her drawling accent with his usual superb mimicry.

Ivy Low left Fiascherino after six weeks, returning home to England with her confidence shaken, sure that she would never write again; nor did she write another novel for fifteen years. She appears as a rather flustered figure in later incidents: once, when Lawrence and the Murrys were meeting near Hampstead tube station, Katherine disappeared to avoid having to speak to her. It was perhaps her lack of social grace which prevented Ivy from entering the close band of Lawrence's admirers, though the two remained friendly, and it was through Ivy that Lawrence met Viola Meynell, who was to lend him and Frieda a cottage in Greatham, Sussex, in 1915. When Lawrence heard that Ivy had married Maxim Litvinoff (then working for a publisher in London, but subsequently to become Soviet Foreign Minister) he wrote and asked if she would like a kitchen table and chairs he had left with the artist Mark Gertler. Lawrence was later befriended by Ivy's uncle Dr David Eder and his sister-in-law Barbara Low, who were both well known psychoanalysts.

Constance Garnett and her friend Vera Volkhovsky, the daughter of a Russian exile, also visited Fiascherino early in 1914. Lawrence rowed them across the bay of Spezia on their first morning, and took them for many walks. He and Frieda had dinner with them at the Albergo delle Palme, 'talking and arguing'. Lawrence, who was working on a new novel, 'The Sisters', had received a note from Edward suggesting it badly needed rewriting, but he seemed unperturbed by this. Constance, however, was worried about him living so far from the sources of his material: 'The life he's leading now doesn't seem likely to provide fresh stuff for him.'[17] There she was wrong, but she saw other things acutely enough: 'Frieda and he seem to have been having a set-to yesterday and the day before – and both looked as if they had been crying – but today they are both happier again.'[18]

Constance was outspoken to Lawrence about his behaviour, and gained, rather against her will, the confidence of Frieda, who went to her to 'pour out my Lawrence woes'.[19] A few months later, after her return to England, Constance was writing to Edward: 'Don't ask the Lawrences down as you may be tempted to when you see them – I don't feel I could stand his fervid intensity over his personal emotions and Frieda's trivial second-hand generalisations just now (though you know I am fond of them both really).'[20] As her son David unkindly remarked, Lawrence 'used up his human relationships rather fast'.[21]

In May 1914, Lawrence and Frieda heard that Frieda's divorce from Weekley had gone through (with Frieda, as the guilty party, forbidden to contact her children), and they returned to England to marry. There they found the Murrys were altogether less cheerful; *Rhythm* was still losing money, and the allowance Katherine received from her father had been used up to pay the magazine's debts; Murry was overwhelmed by the number of articles he was having to write for the *Westminster Review*, and both of them had been ill. They were delighted, however, to see Lawrence and Frieda again, and they attended their wedding at Kensington Register Office on 13 July 1914. On the way to the ceremony, while Lawrence was buying a ring, Frieda took off her old wedding ring and gave it to Katherine. This charming gesture signalled more than affection. The Lawrences' relation with the Murrys was one in which all of them were appreciated as equals. However,

Lawrence and Frieda were about to enter a world in which Frieda was no longer perceived to be as interesting as Lawrence.

At about this time, Lawrence began to draw to himself several women who admired his writing and perceived him as something between a moral teacher and a therapist; in turn, he addressed them like a prophet, often with insight, always with authority. If he enjoyed the fact that some of these women were titled or wealthy, he did not betray it, and if he found them sexually attractive, he took no advantage of their attachment to him. He was interested in women; he understood their problems, and felt he knew how to help them understand themselves. They gave him an attentive respect he could not command from Frieda, who continued to absorb all his sexual energy. One way or another all the women were emotionally needy: three of them – Catherine Carswell, Mary Cannan and Ottoline Morrell – had husbands who were mentally unstable. It was their spirits he was interested in, and these lonely, aristocratic and often talented women responded to his insights with ardour. Like his family and friends from Eastwood and Croydon, they all appeared in his books.

Chapter 10

PASSIONATE FRIENDS

It was while on holiday at Kingsgate, Kent, in 1913, after his stay with the Garnetts, that Lawrence first met Lady Cynthia Asquith, who was staying nearby in Broadstairs. He was impressed by her beauty, and pleased to be graciously received by her when he and Frieda were known to be living in sin. He had been introduced to Lady Cynthia by Edward Marsh, the Georgian poet who had included Lawrence's 'Snap-Dragon' in his anthology of Georgian poetry.

Lady Cynthia was the daughter of the Earl of Wemyss. She had been born in a great country house in Wiltshire in 1887, presented at Court, and painted by Sargent and Augustus John. She was a radiant beauty of twenty-six; but unlike her sisters she had married a man with relatively little money, Herbert Asquith, a barrister, and the second son of the Prime Minister; so for all her grandeur she was usually short of cash.

Lawrence had recently been much praised for *Sons and Lovers*, and though Lady Cynthia claims in her memoirs that she knew nothing of him other than the fact that he wrote poetry and was the son of a coalminer, his reputation must have preceded him. Lady Cynthia loved writers, and was excited by anything to do with the profession of letters. In her book *Haply I May Remember* (1950) she writes well of the intoxication of seeing her own work in print.

In the weeks Lawrence and Frieda spent at Kingsgate, he and Cynthia often took walks together, on which he opened her eyes to the natural world around her. Randolph Churchill described her as 'the greatest flirt that ever lived';[1] she was a little vain, and very much needed the reassurance of feeling young men were in love with her. Lawrence was well aware of Cynthia's vanity; in a portrait of her as

Lady Daphne in the story 'The Ladybird', written in 1921, he wrote: 'she loved her loveliness almost with obsession'. He made no secret of his admiration for her frailty and her lovely blue-green eyes, but quite soon after their first meeting he could write to her with remarkable assurance of her 'whining and grizzling'.[2]

In mid-February 1915, Lady Cynthia visited the Lawrences while they were staying in Viola Meynell's cottage in Greatham, Sussex. She much enjoyed her visit, though Lawrence might not have liked the description she wrote to a friend of 'a whimsical poet in corduroys [who] cooked the kippers etc with which he fed me and his delightful, ebullient German wife'.[3] Murry, who was also visiting at the time, found Cynthia 'much better than the women the L's usually pick up, though there was a great deal too much "Lady Cynthia" about it all'.[4]

Though no one could miss the delight Lawrence took in being accepted by the aristocracy, he valued a more important quality in Cynthia than either her rank or her beauty, writing: 'She is something of a stoic with a nature as hard and sad as rock . . . There is something sea-like about her, cold and with a sort of passionate salt, that burns and corrodes.'[5]

He thought of Cynthia rather as he had of Helen Corke, or Helena in *The Trespasser*, whom he described as a 'dreaming woman, with whom passion exhausts itself at the mouth. Her desire was accomplished in a real kiss.'[6] Characters Lawrence based on Cynthia usually have husbands who do not offer much physical love, and at the time when Lawrence knew her best, Cynthia showed a stronger interest in admiration than in sexual fulfilment. Indeed, she had never had a lover whom Lawrence would have called 'real', and she believed in remaining technically faithful to her husband 'Beb'.

Cynthia had married for love, but after the initial excitement of being married had worn off, she quickly became bored. 'Beb' was part of her own circle, but was not a strong character; both of them needed a great deal of flattery to bolster their self-esteem. Cynthia felt she ought to be allowed the luxury of admirers, and was happy to be adored by much older men, like Lord Basil Blackwood. When in August 1916 she learnt he was in love with her, she behaved in a way Lawrence customarily loathed; she allowed him to kiss her, but refused to become his mistress. In her diaries Lady Cynthia mentions how much more she enjoyed the winning of affection than the act of love. As things turned out, Basil Blackwood was killed in 1917, before Cynthia could discover whether he would have made her sexually happy in a way Beb did not.

Lawrence was a little in love with Cynthia Asquith himself, and often dreamed of her, but he pressed no sexual demands on her; he treated all his female admirers very chastely. The writer Richard Aldington, who knew Lawrence, commented on the attraction he had for women: 'What interested them was his "genius", the fine qualities which went to his making as a great artist. They were interested in him, attracted by him, not because he was "a lurid sexual specialist" but because he wasn't.'[7] In her memoir, Lady Cynthia states that not only did she not discuss sex with Lawrence, she could not remember him ever using the word.

Lady Cynthia had many close non-sexual relationships with male writers. What she most liked to do was talk about herself, and no one was more intuitively able to do so than Lawrence. As their friendship deepened, Lawrence came to be her adviser on all her domestic distress.

After Lawrence's death, Lady Cynthia declared that no one could be in his presence for more than two minutes without being struck by his difference from other people; like Aldous Huxley (whose introductory essay to Lawrence's letters she had by then read, and who uses the same phrase) she found him 'different not only in degree, but in kind'. He wasted no time on small talk. Walking with him, she was excited by his vivid perceptions of birds, flowers, or moonlight, and found that to be with him brought her to life.

Lady Cynthia was physically frail; she had been diagnosed as tubercular, and when she first met Lawrence she had only just returned from a sanatorium on the River Dee in Scotland. He showed great solicitude for her, and they became so close that Lady Cynthia's family suspected her of having an affair with him. Nevertheless, she aroused no jealousy in Frieda. With unerring instinct, Frieda saw that in this friendship there was nothing to fear. Lady Cynthia in turn readily acknowledged Frieda's generosity of nature: from first to last they never perceived each other as rivals, and Frieda confided some of her own problems to Cynthia.

Like most of the women who became his followers, Lady Cynthia accepted Lawrence's strictures. She was drawn to his perceptiveness, and said she had never known 'such an X-ray psychologist'.[8] The elder of her two sons, John, was autistic and given to outbursts of rage. In the summer of 1915, when he was four, he started to cause her serious worry. Soon her anxiety turned to terror, as she realised the boy might actually be mad. (The later course of John's life was altogether tragic. He died in an institution near Dumfries at twenty-six.) Lawrence and Frieda were staying with Cynthia and observed John's wild moods; two days later Lawrence set down the way he thought Cynthia should deal with the angry child, with acute sensitivity: 'Don't try to make him love you, or obey you – don't do it . . . That you fight is only a sign that you are wanting in yourself . . . Your own soul is deficient so it fights for the love of the child.'[9] Later, when Cynthia's younger son Michael felt that his mother only began to love him when he promised to be successful, Lawrence tried to help her deal with that problem too. But he gave her great pain by claiming that John's illness derived from the Asquiths' marriage, and that her need for Michael, along with the demands she made on him, arose from her lack of fulfilment. 'The Rocking-Horse Winner', written very much later, in 1926, was inspired by the unhappiness of the Asquith family.

In June 1915, as Frieda and Lady Cynthia strolled together on a beach in Kent, Frieda complained that people, 'particularly women – particularly one woman', treated her as a mere appendage, and would insist on 'explaining' her own husband to her, telling her he was a 'being dropped straight from the sky'.[10] It may well be that the 'one woman' Frieda was referring to was the literary hostess Lady Ottoline Morrell. If so, her words support Lady Ottoline's belief that the cause of the tension between them was Frieda's jealousy.

Lady Ottoline was an altogether more powerful figure than Lady Cynthia. She was the daughter of Lieutenant-General Arthur Bentinck, Colonel of the Seventh Dragoon Guards, half-sister of the Duke of Portland, and wife of Philip Morrell, a Liberal Member of Parliament. Her family owned a considerable number of the Nottinghamshire coalfields where Lawrence's father had worked. A handsome woman, with a long pale face and strong masculine features, she was in her early forties when she and Lawrence first became friends in the spring of 1914. She had written him an admiring letter about his work, and invited him to her house in Bedford Square, and subsequently to her country home near Garsington in Oxfordshire, a splendid Elizabethan manor house surrounded by an estate of five hundred acres. Lytton Strachey, who was a regular guest at Garsington, described the extraordinary luxury of the house, with its marvellous silk curtains and Persian carpeting, as 'gilded and preposterous',[11] but this did not prevent him enjoying, indeed soliciting, Ottoline's hospitality. As his biographer Michael Holroyd puts it: 'he seems to have felt that by ridiculing Ottoline as a perpetual hostess, he would avert ridicule from himself as an inexplicably persistent guest'. [12] Ottoline loved to invite artists, writers and distinguished politicians to Garsington. Those who visited her were allowed to work quietly during the day, and expected to take part in brilliant conversations in the evenings. In a letter to Cynthia Asquith in November 1915 Lawrence wrote: 'It is England – my God, it breaks my soul – this England, these shafted windows, the elm trees, the blue distance – the past, the great past.'[13]

Lady Ottoline was a woman of perceptiveness and magnificent generosity, yet she was often caricatured, even by those she had helped. In part it was her appearance; her features were too strong for charm, even while she suggested sensuality. The portrait by Augustus John shows her mouth a little open, hinting at something between uneasiness and ferocity. She liked grand hats and striking clothes in rich materials, which attracted attention to the angularity of her body. Her voice and laugh were manly, according to Aldous Huxley's portrait of her as Priscilla Wimbush in *Crome Yellow*, written in 1921, and she had dyed red hair which she wore in an elaborate coiffeur. Lady Ottoline was as original a personality as any of her notable guests, and was far more interested in anyone with a claim to genius than in members of her own class.

Even as a duke's half-sister, she altogether outranked an impoverished baroness, and Frieda must have felt as much. They never liked each other. On 15 June 1914, Lady Ottoline's journal notes with pleasure that Lawrence and Frieda had come to stay at Garsington, but makes the first of many caustic observations about Frieda's behaviour. A room was being repainted, and Lawrence, entering into the spirit of things, began to help, while Frieda sat and mocked the enterprise. There was a measure of sulkiness in Frieda's manner, which Ottoline describes as that of a tigress which might spring and attack either Lawrence or another guest at any moment. Frieda's own memoir confirms that this was in part due to envy: Ottoline suggests it was not jealousy over Lawrence's affections, so much as his social success and Frieda's sense of being treated as an 'appendage'. In the world of Garsington, Frieda could not be considered as interesting a person as her husband. It is a theme which was to recur as the relationship between Lawrence and Frieda developed; all that was clear from the first encounter with Lady Ottoline was that she looked formidable enough to displace Frieda as Lawrence's knowing guide to the world.

Garsington, for all its grandeur, is modest in size, and the Lawrences' bedroom was not far down the corridor from Ottoline's. On that first visit the Lawrences could be overheard quarrelling the whole of one night, and Lawrence came down the next morning looking whipped and forlorn. Like many of Lawrence's friends, Ottoline felt that Frieda was exceedingly bad for him; but she also saw that he was 'by tradition and instinct faithful to a wife and far too timid and sensitive to face life alone'.[14]

Lawrence visited Garsington several times in 1915, often without Frieda, while he was working on the novel which was to become *The Rainbow*; he took an interest in Ottoline's plans for the garden, and was delighted when she went with him to Oxford to look at the illuminated missals and books in the Bodleian; they got on well together in Frieda's absence. Like most people who explored the world with Lawrence, Ottoline took great pleasure in the childlike excitement he found in it.

Lawrence began to extol Ottoline's virtues so frequently that even her gifts of a coloured counterpane for the marital bed and an opal for Lawrence failed to please Frieda. He genuinely admired Ottoline's grandeur of spirit, and liked the fact that she was 'a great lady'. He enjoyed talking to her about the Nottinghamshire countryside they had both known as they walked about the gardens at Garsington or the fields nearby. As if this was not enough, Frieda soon began to hear gossip that Ottoline thought Lawrence would be happier if he left her, which increased her antagonism.

Ottoline's biographer Miranda Seymour suggests a reason for the lack of compassion Ottoline felt for Frieda's situation – as a divorced wife refused access to her children. When Ottoline made the acquaintance of the Lawrences, her love affair with Bertrand Russell was at its height. Russell was pleading with her to leave her husband and throw in her lot with him, but she lacked the courage to do so. Frieda, she knew, had given up a decent husband and children she adored because the man she loved was unwilling to settle for an extramarital affair; Ottoline felt the comparison bitterly.

Lawrence was eager for Ottoline and Frieda to be friends, and Ottoline wanted to help him, whatever she thought of Frieda. She made a generous offer of a gardener's cottage near Garsington which the Lawrences could have when they left Greatham in July 1915. Lawrence apparently wrote back with suggestions for rather expensive improvements. When Ottoline, without resentment, offered another building, Frieda replied with an even more extensive list of repairs, and the offer had to be withdrawn.

Ottoline's insights into Frieda are biased, but should not be ignored; she admired her robust health and her vitality, but thought she behaved like a spoilt child in need of constant flattery. When Lawrence and Frieda visited Garsington at the same time as the musician Philip Heseltine and Dikran Kouzoumdjian (who became the novelist Michael Arlen), Ottoline observed the eagerness with which Frieda responded to their attentiveness, as if that proved how intense was her need for praise.

It was soon after this visit that Frieda wrote to Ottoline complaining about her relationship with Lawrence. To Lawrence, Ottoline represented a world of intelligent and cultured privilege, and Frieda felt her friendship with Lawrence in some way reduced her own importance for him; at any rate, of all the women to whom Lawrence became close in this period, Ottoline was the one for whom Frieda felt most jealousy. She feared exactly the spiritual bond which Ottoline found so exciting. 'I would not mind if you and he had an ordinary love-affair – what I hate is this "soul mush".'[15]

Ottoline had a profound desire for religious belief, and Lawrence's sense of wonder at life in all its forms was rooted in a similar impulse, though he had not shared his mother's Congregational faith since adolescence, and no longer believed in a personal God. His letters to Ottoline are couched in the language of a preacher, and would have seemed grossly impudent to anyone less impressed by his genius. Ottoline, however, responded with warm friendship, and always spoke of Lawrence with loyalty, notably when *The Rainbow* was published in September 1915, and he was badly in need of praise. It is worth noting that it is to Garsington that Lawrence was to post the manuscript of *The Rainbow* for safekeeping after it had been banned.

In June 1914, Lawrence formed another important attachment: to the writer Catherine Carswell.

Catherine Carswell was a friend of Ivy Low; it was to her that Ivy had proudly read out Lawrence's reply to her first letter. She had admired the work Lawrence had published in the *English Review*, and met him for the first time when he and Frieda called on her in Hampstead on their return from Gargnano. She saw in him at that meeting a working man who would have risen to a position of authority in any career he had undertaken; and she admired Frieda both for her careless generosity and the courage with which she accepted a life without security. Catherine walked with Lawrence past Hampstead parish churchyard, where a child of hers was buried, and found him so sensitive to her feelings that she was soon talking to him as if she had known him all her life.

Catherine Carswell was born into a Presbyterian businessman's family in Glasgow in 1879; that is, she was exactly the same age as Frieda. She attended Glasgow University and then the Frankfurt Conservatory, where she studied the piano. In 1904 she married Herbert Jackson, an artist who had fought in the Boer War; after their marriage Jackson seems to have lost hold of reality. He threatened Catherine with a pistol when she told him she was pregnant, as he believed himself incapable of sexual intercourse. He was subsequently declared insane and after a sensational trial Catherine was granted a decree of annulment. She worked to provide for herself and her daughter, who was born in 1905, as a literary critic on the *Glasgow Herald*, in which she favourably reviewed *The White Peacock*. She became the mistress of Maurice Greiffenhagen, a married professor at the Glasgow School of Art who was seventeen years her senior. The year after she met Lawrence, she married Donald Carswell, a barrister. Short of money as he was at the time, Lawrence sent her a pretty plate as a wedding present. Donald Carswell was to prove too shy to succeed in his profession, and he later became depressed, alcoholic and a compulsive talker.

If Lawrence was sexually attracted to Catherine, he only showed it in his uneasiness about such incidents as when, on a visit in 1916, he reproved her for walking about his house wearing an ankle-length petticoat topped by a long-sleeved woollen vest. There are fewer portraits of Catherine in Lawrence's writing than of others of his female acquaintances, but she said of Isabelle Pervin in the story 'The Blind Man' that its truth 'smote' her. Lawrence used the vicarage where the Carswells were living in 1918 as a background to that story, which turns on the black depression of Isabelle's husband: 'She felt she would scream with the strain, and would give anything, anything to escape.' When a friend comes to visit them, the husband feels left out, and his fumbling attempt at making intimate, touching contact with his wife's visitor is felt as a horrible intrusion. Catherine wrote in her memoir *The Savage Pilgrimage* of Lawrence's relationship to her husband: 'Though there was an enduring respect between him and the man I had married, there was no particular gush of sympathy.'[16] Nevertheless, Lawrence turned hopefully to Donald Carswell for legal advice at the time of the prosecution of *The Rainbow*.

Lawrence treated Catherine with great kindness. After she had met him a few times, she asked him to read the manuscript of her first novel, and though he criticised her 'indirect and roundabout' style, he also encouraged her to believe she could be a writer 'if she worked at it'. She had a sober, commonsense intelligence Lawrence appreciated all his life, and he wrote to her: 'I think you are the only woman I ever met who is so intrinsically detached, so essentially separate and isolated as to be a real writer or artist or recorder ... And to want children and common human fulfilments is rather a falsity for you, I think. You were never made to "meet and mingle", but to remain intact, essentially, whatever your experiences may be.' He even offered to help her with her writing. He was no flatterer of her poems, however, and directly advised her to change both their form and diction and always to 'break the rhyme rather than the stony directness of speech'.[17]

For her part, Catherine never doubted Lawrence's genius, and of the many memoirs of him written after his death, hers was the most unqualified in its admiration. Even she, however, recorded the 'spin-sterish tartness' in some of his edgier comments about their friends. Catherine made few emotional demands on Lawrence, and Frieda was never jealous of her. Indeed, the two women liked one another, despite Catherine's description in her memoir of her first impression of Frieda as a 'typical German frau of the blonde, gushing type'.[18]

Mary Cannan, the talented actress wife of the popular novelist Gilbert Cannan, also became Lawrence's friend in 1914. The daughter of a publican, she had been married for thirteen years to the playwright J. M. Barrie. They had divorced in 1909, but Barrie was still fond of her, and continued to give her a generous annual allowance. She was in her mid-forties, still fine-featured and beautifully made-up when Lawrence and Frieda came to live near the Cannans in Buckingham-shire in 1914. Mary's second marriage was not an easy one. Gilbert Cannan had been cited as a co-respondent by Barrie, and afterwards felt bound to marry her, even though Mary was seventeen years older than he was. David Garnett wittily described Cannan's marriage as 'a dish heaped with a profusion of inedible fruits'. Catherine Carswell, on a visit to the Lawrences in Buckinghamshire in 1915 saw a great unhappiness in Gilbert which Mary's chirpiness could not dispel. The Cannans got on so badly with each other that they were always eager for company, and Frieda and Lawrence were among the many friends invited to visit the converted windmill in which they were living. Gilbert, after one mental breakdown, took a mistress and got Mary's maid pregnant. By 1917 the Cannans' marriage was dissolved.

Lawrence enjoyed Mary's elegance, her ability to 'dart into the rag-shops like a sparrow into a scullery and emerge with a waistcoat'.[19] She flew in and out of the Lawrences' lives rather like such a bird, as their travels crossed hers. Lawrence also liked her gossip, knowing all the while she was kind underneath her love of scandal.

In the early summer of 1914 Lawrence acquired a wealthy American patroness when Amy Lowell invited the Lawrences to dine with her at the Berkeley Hotel in Piccadilly; Richard Aldington and his wife, the poet Hilda Doolittle ('H. D.'), were among the guests, and Edward Marsh (then private secretary to Winston Churchill) brought rumours of imminent war. The conversation, however, was more concerned with the latest conflicts in the world of poetry.

Amy Lowell, herself a poet, and an enthusiastic supporter of the Imagists, had quarrelled with Ezra Pound, who thought she was trying to take the movement over. She now wanted to recruit Lawrence as a contributor to her own anthology of Imagist verse, and placed him at her side as guest of honour, expressing her admiration for his work. Lawrence wasn't an Imagist, but didn't mind his work appearing under that banner, and he enjoyed the warmth of Amy's praise. Amy Lowell may have been obese and bossy, but she had a genuine and discriminating love of poetry, and was a loyal champion of Lawrence and H. D., among others. Not only did she publish his poetry in her anthologies, she sent him money when he was sick or hard-up, and even tried to collect royalties that were due to him from Mitchell Kennerley, the American publisher of *The Trespasser*. Lawrence in turn was solicitous about her health, wrote sympathetically when she was grieving for her brother, and was moved by her generosity even when it was elicited by a begging letter from Frieda. When on 4 November 1916 he received a cheque for £60 he wrote, 'This I shall always treasure up, the kindness, even if I can pay you back the money.'[20] He was not, however, obsequious, and could deliver a sudden rebuke: 'Why don't you always be yourself. If it doesn't come out of your heart, it is no good, however many colours it may have . . . I suppose you think me damned impertinent. But I hate to see you posturing, when there is thereby a real person betrayed in you.'[21] Amy Lowell was good-natured enough to accept this, and she and Lawrence stayed in touch until her death in 1925.

It was in 1915 that Lawrence first met the Honourable Dorothy Brett, who was to be unselfishly devoted to him to the end of his life. Her father, the second Viscount Esher, was a Liberal Member of Parliament who had once been influential at Court; he had married as a cover for his homosexuality, and had gone out of his way to make his daughters feel stupid. Dorothy's early deafness was mocked by her brothers during her childhood, and she had to use an ear trumpet all her life. She also had very prominent teeth, which gave her a rabbit-like appearance, and Frieda mocked both that and her receding chin.

Brett, as she was always called, was a student at the Slade School of Art when she met Lawrence, through the painter Mark Gertler. They did not immediately form a bond of friendship. On their first meeting she remembered him speaking very maliciously about a mutual acquaintance; soon afterwards they were both present at a party which Murry and Mansfield also attended, Murry having to be propped up, amiably drunk, against a wall. Brett did not enter into any kind of intimacy with Lawrence until 1923. She was too shy, and perhaps also too plain for Lawrence to be interested in finding out much about her. Lawrence described Hilda Blessington, a character based on her in *The Boy in the Bush*, written in 1923, as 'one of the odd borderline people who don't and *can't* really belong'. Possibly for that reason, she liked to attach herself to talented people who needed care and attention, and she lavished both on Katherine Mansfield as she battled with tuberculosis. Her attachment to Lawrence from 1923 onwards was both open and intense.

Chapter 11

THE WAR

Two years had passed since pneumonia made it necessary for Lawrence to abandon teaching, but his lungs were still vulnerable to colds, and he and Frieda intended to return to Italy for his health. The declaration of war with Germany on 4 August 1914 changed these plans completely. They needed to find somewhere inexpensive to live in England, and began by renting the Triangle, a cottage in Bellingdon Lane, near Chesham in Buckinghamshire, for six shillings a month. They stayed there until January 1915. Lawrence was unwell, and the cottage was damp and cold. Even in 1913 Edward Marsh had thought Lawrence looked 'terribly ill', and David Garnett claimed to have seen spots of blood on his handkerchief. From now on the contrast between his frailty and Frieda's buxom good health was to strike everyone they met.

The outbreak of war caused a crisis of loyalty for Frieda; she had two von Richthofen cousins in the German air force (they were to become its greatest heroes), and she was not the kind of person to toe an acceptable line socially. Lawrence himself had been drawn to Frieda's family, though he had described the dark side of German militarism clearly enough in 1913 in the story 'The Prussian Officer', which drew on his observation of soldiers herded together in Metz, and tells the story of an orderly bullied savagely by a brutal officer whose homosexual feelings are aroused.

Lawrence could see no reason for the war, and disliked the British jingoism that assumed the Germans had no sense of fair play. In any case, he could hardly see the point of such notions in the barbaric war that was beginning. And he resented not being able to return to Italy, where he felt he would have been healthier. It is hardly surprising that by 25 August he was saying: 'I can't say we're happy because we're not.'[1]

There is an impression of Lawrence and Frieda (as Daniel and Hildegarde Rayner) at the Triangle in Compton Mackenzie's novel *The Four Winds of Love*. Mackenzie had been introduced to the Lawrences by the Cannans, who lived close by. Daniel Rayner has a squeaky voice with a broad Midlands accent, and Mackenzie describes their cottage with some disdain. Rayner is discovered on his knees scrubbing the floor, and his wife Hildegarde has to roll off the bed to come down to talk to visitors while her husband makes tea. Hildegarde is large, genial and handsome; and quite extraordinarily tactless in her approbation of the German army, who were at that time being widely accused of committing atrocities in Belgium. Lawrence and Frieda were to suffer severely and unfairly as suspected German spies throughout the war, but in part they brought it on themselves by their unguarded behaviour.

There was a worsening of the quarrels between them at this time. Murry visited them in Chesham, and said that the mere mention of Frieda's children was enough to make her burst into tears. All access to them was still denied her, and by now she was desperate to see them. In December 1914, after a visit to Lawrence's family, Frieda went to see Weekley to ask about possible meetings. The visit did not bring much hope. Weekley began to insult her, saying that the commonest prostitute was better than she was. Frieda responded in an uncharacteristically crestfallen and humble manner to whatever he said; even so, he told her crushingly before she left that his solicitors had instructions to have her arrested if she attempted to interfere with the children.

Lawrence and Frieda were also short of money. Amy Lowell, who came to visit in a maroon automobile driven by a maroon-clad chauffeur, saw as much at once. She did not like to offer Lawrence money, and instead delighted him with the suggestion that she provide him with a typewriter. When it arrived he wrote to thank her, describing himself as 'bubbling with joy'.[2] Soon after this, the Royal Literary Fund made him a grant of £50. Without it, it is hard to see how they could have survived.

Both Lawrence and Frieda were delighted when the Murrys came to look for a cottage to rent close by. Katherine stayed with Frieda while Murry searched for something suitable. He found Rose Tree Cottage in Lee, about three miles away, and Lawrence helped get it ready for occupation with his usual enthusiasm, expressing some scorn for Murry's lack of briskness with a paintbrush. In both couples it was the creative writers who did most of the chores. Lawrence had always done the housework; Katherine did as much for Murry, and Frieda was struck by her capacity for hard work, which was in marked contrast to her own indolent ways.

While she was at the Triangle Katherine confided many of her earlier experiences (some of which she had never told Murry about) to Frieda – including a lesbian encounter with Edith Bendall, a beautiful woman nine years older than her, with whom she enjoyed a brief erotic passion in New Zealand in 1907. In due course the story was transmitted to Lawrence, and found its way into the chapter called 'Shame' in *The Rainbow*, in which Ursula goes swimming naked with Winifred Inger.

Lawrence continued to correspond with his close women friends, admonishing, lecturing and flattering by turn; creating a whole network of support which Frieda had to survive without, and which made her angry and jealous. Congratulating Catherine on her marriage to Donald Carswell, he assures her that she has 'a complete right to be happy. I only want to know people who have the courage to live,'[3] while he wrote grandly to Lady Ottoline that 'life is an affair of aristocrats'.[4]

Not everyone took kindly to his comments. Lawrence met E. M. Forster when dining at Ottoline's house in Bedford Square in January 1915, and Forster was initially much impressed by him. He visited the Lawrences at the Meynells' cottage in Greatham, Sussex, to which they moved that month, but was offended to be taken to task about his repressed sexuality, which Lawrence thought should be directed towards a woman. Forster was both a homosexual and a deeply private man, and he made no attempt to disguise the repugnance he felt for Lawrence's intrusive advice. Lawrence appears to have been surprised that his analysis was rejected, and in a letter to Bertrand Russell he wrote, 'Why can't he act? Why can't he take a woman and fight clear to his basic, primal being?'[5] Frieda's appended notes to Lawrence's letters of this period very much reflect the best of her, but Forster objected, saying that he did not like to 'have dealings with a firm'. A note from Frieda attached to Lawrence's invitation to Forster comments: 'This is a very angelic letter but I know the flapping of wings won't quite make you overlook the little twisted horns and the hoof.' A week later, she began a joint letter to Forster by praising *Howards End*, but added:

> *We had violent discussions over your letters, Lawrence and I – (three cheers for the 'firm') . . . Hope and that sort of thing is not your strong point – you are so frightened of being let down, as if one couldn't get up again! As to the firm you did hit a little sore point with me – Poor author's wife, who does her little best and everybody wishes her to Jericho.*[6]

Lawrence loyally took Frieda's part.

Most visitors to the Triangle came for intimate conversation with Lawrence, and had less interest in Frieda, and her resentment of this was often outspoken. Bertrand Russell, however, on a visit to the Lawrences at Greatham in June 1915, wrote to Ottoline Morrell about Frieda:

> *I mind her much more when you are about. Lawrence wrote you a long letter yesterday, but she possessed herself of it and tore it up. Then he wrote another which I hope will reach you. He was very angry. She appeared on the little wall by the flowerbed, jeering. He said, 'Come off that, lass, or I'll hit thee in the mouth. You've gone too far this time.'*[7]

After Russell's visit, Frieda wrote to him:

> *You were a little cross with me – It seemed to you that I did not respect enough your work, which I could never understand; that particular man-made thing you call it intellect is a mystery, rather a thrilling one to me . . . It's rather jolly it's your form of 'Wille zur Macht' [will to power], I should always be frightened of your intellect I feel it against women, at present anyhow.*[8]

Bertrand Russell had been introduced to Lawrence by Ottoline in February 1915. He was spellbound by the energy and force with which Lawrence propounded the superiority of instinct and intuition to rational thought, and, perhaps just because of his own commitment to the academic intellect, he was soon writing to Ottoline that he loved Lawrence more and more, and was almost coming to believe in his ideas. At this time Lawrence was drawn to a welfare state in which men would receive wages whether they were sick or well, and to this Russell was sympathetic. Both men were opposed to the war, and for a time it seemed as if they could become close friends; they even arranged to give a lecture course together.

One weekend in March 1915, when Lawrence was invited to Trinity College, Cambridge, the atmosphere changed. Lawrence, who had coped easily enough with aristocratic houses in London, felt oppressed by the snobbishness of a Cambridge college, and was repelled by the open homosexuality of several of Russell's friends, notably John Maynard Keynes. After he returned to Greatham, he wrote to Russell that Cambridge made him feel very 'blank and down . . . I cannot bear its smell of rottenness, marsh stagnancy.'

When in July Russell sent him the lecture notes that were the basis of his first popular book, *Principles of Social Reconstruction*, Lawrence crossed out and corrected his work with an arrogance that incensed Russell: it was his letter of 14 September, however, criticising Russell's essay 'The Dangers to Civilisation', which ended the friendship. Lawrence wrote: 'You are simply *full* of repressed desires, which have become savage and anti-social. And they come out in this sheep's clothing of peace propaganda . . . Your will is false and cruel. You are too full of devilish repressions to be anything but lustful and cruel . . . It is a perverted, mental blood-lust.'

The violence of this attack so overwhelmed Russell that, as he later wrote, 'For twenty-four hours I thought that I was not fit to live, and contemplated committing suicide'.[9] When he recovered his balance, Russell broke off the friendship. Ottoline Morrell, who received a similarly abusive letter from Lawrence condemning her treatment of her protégée Maria Nys – a young Belgian girl who had an adolescent attachment to Ottoline – was more forgiving.

In his 'Portraits from Memory', Russell claimed that Lawrence had anticipated 'the whole philosophy of fascism before the politicians thought of it'; he went much beyond a condemnation of Lawrence's belief in blood-consciousness as 'frankly rubbish', and asserted: 'I did not then know that it led straight to Auschwitz.'[10] This is clearly over the top. Nevertheless, Russell was right to suggest that Lawrence's ideas were related to those of the Fascist movement.

As early as January 1913, Lawrence had formulated a faith in the body and impulse, as opposed to mind and reason, to justify his elopement with Frieda: 'My great religion is a belief in the blood, the flesh, as being wiser than the intellect. We can go wrong in our minds. But what our blood feels and believes and says is always true.'[11] His dislike for the mechanised killing of the war, as opposed to killing in anger, for which he could have human sympathy, confirmed his belief in the health of instinctual responses rather than those of mind and reason, and his dislike of democracy grew as a whole generation of young men were sent to the slaughter. If democracy permitted such carnage, so much the worse for democracy, as he insisted to Russell in July 1915: 'You must drop all your democracy. You must not believe in the people ... The whole must culminate in an absolute Dictator ... Can't you see the whole state is collapsing?'[12] These strands in his thinking were similar to those which drew other English writers to dictators of both left and right.

In addition, however, Lawrence was anti-Semitic. No doubt the origin of this was provincial ignorance, but Frieda, whose father was similarly prejudiced, offered no counterweight, even though her sister Else had married a Jew. Lawrence's identification of Jews that he meets is at first merely habit; when he is angry on some other matter, Jewishness becomes immediately relevant. Of the publisher William Heinemann, who had been unimpressed by *The Trespasser* and was now considering his poems, Lawrence wrote to Walter de la Mare on 8 July 1912: 'I hope the rotten little Jew won't have them.'[13] His casual anti-Semitism comes out in a letter he wrote from Kingsgate in 1913, explaining why he disliked the place: 'What have I to do with fat, fatherly Jews and their motor cars and their bathing tents.' A day later, as if pleased with the idea, he was writing to Edward Garnett, 'I feel horribly out of place among these Jews' villas and the babies and papas'.[14]

Nor did he revise his views when he formed close friendships with Jews such as Mark Gertler. Gertler, a brilliant painter from an East End Jewish family, was a friend of Brett from Slade days, and had much in common with Lawrence. His early drawings and his observation of immigrant family life were as shrewd as *Sons and Lovers*. Like Lawrence, he was deeply attached to his mother. Like Lawrence too,

udio portrait of the Lawrence family, taken in about 1897.
ck: Emily, George, Ernest. *Front*: Ada, Lydia, David Herbert, Arthur.

LEFT Ernest, probably in the Lawrence house in Walker Street.

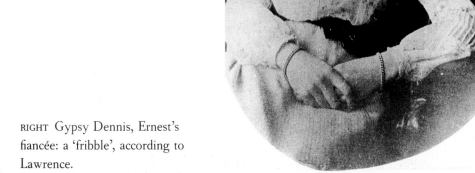

RIGHT Gypsy Dennis, Ernest's fiancée: a 'fribble', according to Lawrence.

RIGHT Ada Lawrence as a young woman.

BELOW The Chambers family in 1906. *Back*: May, Alan, Jessie, Hubert, Bernard. *Front*: Mollie, Edmund (the father of the family), the youngest son David, and Sarah Ann, Edmund's wife.

LEFT Jessie Chambers.

ABOVE Lawrence in 1908, at the time of his graduation from Nottingham
University College.

ABOVE LEFT Alice Dax and her daughter in 1916, about five years after her affair with Lawrence.

ABOVE Helen Corke.

LEFT Lydia Lawrence in her wheelchair at Lynn Croft during the last months of her life in 1910.

uisa Burrows in 1910,
e year in which she and
wrence became
gaged.

The young Frieda von Richthofen.

ᴏᴠᴇ Katherine Mansfield
1913.

ɪɢʜᴛ John Middleton
Murry.

LEFT Lady Cynthia Asquith, the beautiful daughter of the Earl of Wemyss. She was a close friend of Lawrence and Frieda for many years.

RIGHT Lady Ottoline Morrell was a friend and admirer of Lawrence until she was caricatured by him as Hermione in *Women in Love*. This portrait is by Augustus John, who was for a time her lover.

…toline Morrell photographed by Cecil Beaton.

LEFT Catherine Carswell at about the time she met Lawrence in 1914. An attractive, determined woman, she was one of his most loyal admirers.

BELOW Lawrence's wedding day, 13 July 1914. Left to right: Lawrence, Katherine Mansfield, Frieda, John Middleton Murry.

RIGHT Amy Lowell, an American poet from a wealthy and influential family who became Lawrence's patron and friend.

LEFT Mary Cannan. A stylish actress, first married to J.M. Barrie, then to the novelist Gilbert Cannan, she was described by David Garnett as 'charming, chirpy, and a little overwrought'.

LEFT Aldous Huxley, Dorothy Brett and Mark Gertler, photographed by Ottoline Morrell at Garsington in 1917

BELOW Mabel Dodge, the daughter of a wealthy American banker, invited Lawrence and Frieda to be her guests at Taos, New Mexico.

wrence and Frieda at their house near Lake Chapala in Mexico, 1923.

LEFT Lawrence and Frieda leaving America in 1925, after he had suffered his first serio haemorrhage in Oaxaca.

BELOW Angelo Ravagli with family.

his talent and personable good looks meant he was able to find patrons among the aristocratic circle at Garsington.

Lawrence was acutely aware of Gertler's Jewishness, and ascribed the despair he saw in Gertler's painting *The Merry-Go-Round* to it. He wrote to Gertler on 9 October 1916 after praising it as the best modern picture he had seen: 'It is a terrifying coloured flame of decomposition, your flame . . . It would take a Jew to paint this picture. It would take your national history to get you here, without disintegrating you first . . . At last your race is at an end – these pictures are its death cry.'[15]

Lawrence meant these words admiringly, and a postscript to the letter adds, 'I'd buy it if I had any money.' Nevertheless, he always saw Gertler as belonging to a different race. When Gilbert Cannan published *Mendel* in 1916, a novel based on Gertler's love for Dora Carrington, Lawrence was indignant at the vulgar travesty of his friend's life. His reaction, however, was to blame Gertler rather than Cannan. To Catherine Carswell he wrote, 'Gertler, Jew-like, has told every detail of his life to Gilbert.'[16]

Gertler was always kind to Lawrence, even offering to lend him money when he had little himself. Lawrence, in gently refusing a loan on 5 December 1916, wrote: 'It is a principle with me to borrow from the rich as long as I can, not from the poor.'[17] Gertler's generosity to Lawrence did not prevent him from using Gertler as a model for the corrupt sculptor Loerke in *Women in Love*.

Another close friend was Samuel Solomonovich Koteliansky, a Russian Jew from the Ukraine, who came to London on a scholarship from the University of Kiev in 1910. He worked as a secretary and translator in a law office in High Holborn, and made literal versions of Tolstoy, Dostoevsky and Chekhov for Mansfield, Murry and the Woolfs. Leonard Woolf describes 'Kot's passionate approval of what he thought good . . . his inability to tell a lie . . . If you knew Kot well, you knew what a major Hebrew prophet must have been like 3,000 years ago.'[18]

Lawrence greatly admired Kot, and wrote more letters to him than to any other friend, occasionally reflecting in them on the nature of Jewishness. In 1917 he wrote: 'Why humanity has hated Jews, I have come to the conclusion is that the Jews have always taken religion – since the great days that is – and used it for their own personal and private gratification, as if it were a thing administered to their own importance and well-being and conceit. This is the slave-trick of the Jews – they used the great religious consciousness as a trick of personal conceit.'[19]

Nevertheless, Kot admired Lawrence all his life. Despite Lawrence's sense of Jews as racially different, and the echo of Nietzsche in that phrase 'slave-trick', Frieda was surely right to rebuke Russell for calling Lawrence a Nazi when she read the first of his attacks on Lawrence in *Harpers* in 1953: 'You might as well call St Augustine a Nazi.' Lawrence did not live long enough to see Hitler come to power, and may well have been repelled by Nazi thuggery, even had he been attracted to a rhetoric that signally resembled his own.

For the moment, the central story for Lawrence was his relation to Frieda. This he began to explore in his new novel.

The novel we now know as *The Rainbow* was written between August 1914 and May 1915, after a third draft of 'The Sisters' (called 'The Wedding Ring') had been rejected by Methuen as too frank to be publishable. The life between Lawrence and Frieda flowed into the new novel, and Lawrence was proud of the autobiographical source of the work. He had been quite properly teased by Frieda for his depiction of Clara Dawes, who leaves her husband only to return to him, in *Sons and Lovers*, and he determined to put that right by showing women like Frieda as confidently in control of their own lives. He felt ambiguously about that confidence, however, and confessed another intention: to show Frieda 'in her Godalmightiness in all its glory'.

Lawrence needed to believe in the health of the marriage he and Frieda had made. They were capable of the most intense happiness together (as a record of such happiness *The Rainbow* is almost unequalled), so he was prepared to accept the raging quarrels that so dismayed his friends, and even to insist they had moral value. But these quarrels were no longer only about Frieda's lament for her lost children. There was another, more intensely felt dynamic, and the novel explores its source.

Set between Nottinghamshire and Derbyshire and spanning three generations, from the Industrial Revolution to the First World War, *The Rainbow* has a traditional novelistic shape. There is no one character that Lawrence identifies with as he had with Paul Morel in *Sons and Lovers* (though Tom Brangwen, at the heart of the first part of the novel, is described as 'mardy' like Lawrence, and suffers from the same awed and anxious feelings about women); what matters is that every male in the book is given a pattern of feelings which resembles Lawrence's relation to Frieda. On Tom's first sight of the Polish Mrs Lensky (whom Lawrence names Lydia, after his mother), he immediately recognises the woman he wants. 'That's her,'[20] he exclaims. Like Frieda, Mrs Lensky is well-born and self-possessed, has already been married, and is six years older than Tom. These attributes free Tom from his usual sexual anxiety, and make him feel confident enough to ask Mrs Lensky to marry him.

Mrs Lensky has a mysterious separateness which contributes to her sexual charm; she often seems to ignore Tom (as Miriam never could ignore Paul Morel), and there is a mixture of fear and worship in his desire. He is no longer afraid his passion will soil her (as he had felt with local girls), but as the relationship deepens he comes to be maddened by that separateness, which rouses him to raging fury.

There is nothing imaginary about the separateness that threatens him once Lydia becomes pregnant. Then he speaks of feeling 'deposed',[21] as if the only place he had were being taken away by a child. Indeed, Lydia's daughter by her first husband does try to oust Tom from her bed. Tom's jealousy (rather like Lawrence's quivering hatred whenever Frieda expressed her longing for her children) is presented as an overwhelming need for attention. At one point he reflects: 'He would smash her into attention.'[22] Nevertheless, the description of Tom's relationship to his stepchild has rarely been matched; the tenderness with which Tom carries the sobbing child into a lantern-lit, warm-smelling cowshed while Anna is giving birth is imagined memorably:

He opened the doors, upper and lower, and they entered into the high, dry barn that smelled warm, even if it were not warm. He hung the lantern on the nail and shut the door. They were in another world now. The light shed softly on the timbered barn, on the white-washed walls, and the great heap of hay; instruments cast their shadows largely, a ladder rose to the dark arch of a loft. Outside there was the driving rain, inside the softly-illuminated stillness and calmness of the barn.

Holding the child on one arm, he set about preparing the food for the

cows, filling a pan with chopped hay and brewers' grain and a little meal.
The child, all wonder, watched what he did. A new being was created in
her for the new conditions. Sometimes, a little spasm, eddying from the
bygone storm of sobbing, shook her small body. Her eyes were wide and
wondering, pathetic . . .

There was a noise of chains running as the cows lifted or dropped their
heads sharply; then a contented soothing sound, a long snuffing as the
beasts ate in silence.

The journey had to be performed several times. There was the rhythmic
sound of the shovel in the barn, then the man returned walking stiffly
between the two weights, the face of the child peering out from the shawl.
Then the next time, as he stooped, she freed her arm and put it round
his neck, clinging soft and warm, making all easier.

The beasts fed, he dropped the pan and sat down on a box, to arrange
the child.

'Will the cows go to sleep now?' she said, catching her breath as she
spoke.[23]

As the marriage develops Tom has to learn to make do with less sex
than he wants, and it may be that Lawrence was already having to
do the same; perhaps, like Lydia Lensky, Frieda only wanted her
husband in her own way and to her own measure. For her part, Lydia
complains that Tom needs her excessively, and does not do enough
to make her love him. It is hard to see how Lawrence could have
done more for Frieda: he earned all the money, attracted all the
friends, and did all the housework; Lydia's accusation, in my view,
nevertheless arose from Lawrence's own experience, and relates to
the amount of pleasure he gave Frieda in bed. With another author
this would be an unwarrantable conjecture, but Lawrence's later writing, with its condemnation of foreplay and disgust at women who seek
too greedily for their own sexual satisfaction, makes the speculation
legitimate. In any case, his quarrels with Frieda were by now openly
about their sexual relationship. During the autumn of 1914, Murry
and Lawrence had many long and intimate conversations about sex;
partly because the Lawrences' public quarrels invited it. On one
occasion Murry heard Frieda accuse Lawrence of taking her 'as a dog
does a bitch',[24] and there were angry words which suggested Frieda
no longer wanted Lawrence sexually in any way.

Lydia is always sympathetically portrayed, and even Tom is some-times aware that she feels lonely, isolated and unsure, for all her apparent self-confidence. She complains that he makes her feel as if she is 'nothing', and he echoes that unhappiness, though his sense that his life amounts to no more than the long marital embrace affirms something more enduring: Lawrence's life-long fidelity to Frieda, in spite of the many women who admired him. At one point Lydia asks Tom if he wants another woman, just as Frieda might have asked Lawrence. No more than Tom Brangwen could Lawrence have turned elsewhere. As Tom affirms on his daughter's wedding day, he cannot conceive of a man saving his own soul alone; he can only imagine entering heaven as a married soul.

With Lydia's daughter Anna and Tom's nephew Will, Lawrence looks at a relationship in which the man is dependent to the point of sickness, and the woman glories in her separateness as 'Anna Victrix'. Again, it is hard to miss the resemblance to Frieda in her 'Godalmight-iness'. Anna, with her contempt for ordinary people, and her polecat obstinacy as a child, chooses her cousin Will for her lover as Frieda had chosen Lawrence. Like Frieda, Anna persists in her choice against parental disapproval and the obvious poverty of Will's expectations.

Anna and Will have a honeymoon period of sexual happiness which is so intense that they forget the world outside their bedroom, and even forget they are hungry. Will is ashamed not to be up and busy, however, while Anna can stay in bed shamelessly (recalling Lawrence and Frieda's days in Gargnano). Nevertheless, the power of Anna over Will is seen as destructive, just as Lawrence was to fear that Frieda's power over him was destructive. The gain was to be com-pletely absolved from any sense of sin; but the loss was nothing less than the whole outside world.

In the novel, it is Anna who tires of such withdrawal, and gives a tea party to let the outside world in. Thrown out of their private world, and spoken to as a child, Will feels one of those black rages which Lawrence so often felt towards Frieda. In the grip of that hatred, everything Anna does is detestable, and it is only when he sees Anna weeping alone that Will suddenly recognises she is unhappy. He touches her wet face with his mouth and trembles with love; it is almost as if the rage between them made their lovemaking more tender. The loving reconciliations between Lawrence and Frieda, which so many of their friends witnessed, had a similar component.

Nevertheless, Will finds Anna's independent being unbearable. When he comes home full of love and finds her sitting at a sewing machine, his face goes stiff with rage at the evidence that she has not been anxiously waiting for him; he feels that if she can manage without him, he is not sufficiently necessary to her. The marvellous scene in which Anna dances by herself, a strange and elated creature, her belly big with child, is an image of that independent being. All their battles spring from Will's desire to have every minute of her day in his power, while Anna feels she has to fight him to continue to have any life of her own. We can hear Frieda's voice when Anna complains, 'You don't let me sleep, you don't let me *live*.' For all their battles, Will cannot imagine leaving Anna. He can only envisage going to another woman, which he fears would change nothing; he would simply become dependent on her in the same way. So Lawrence suspected there was no sense in leaving Frieda. He knew he depended on her, as Will depended on Anna, 'like a child depended on its mother'. When his daughter Ursula is born, Will turns to her for love, as men who have lost domestic power may turn to their female children.

It is in this part of the book that Lawrence begins to develop an analysis of sadism as an element in male sexuality. Will develops a strangely sadistic attitude to his own child, daring her to soar higher and higher on a swing (as Lawrence once tried to compel Jessie Chambers) until she feels sick. And sadism infuses Will's experience with a girl he picks up after a long bout of hostility with Anna. That oddly erotic episode seems to foreshadow some of those given to Gerald Crich in *Women in Love*. Will carries his enjoyment of power, which leads from caress to near rape, back to his wife, who at once responds sexually. Lawrence attributes their new sensuality to Anna's sense that there is something new in Will which she cannot reduce; but he also characterises their lovemaking, with a certain frisson, as immoral, since each one was seeking only their own gratification. It is a prefiguring of the theme of 'bad sex', which is attributed to Gerald and Gudrun in *Women in Love,* and some evidence that in these matters also Lawrence was extrapolating as much from his own experience as conjecturing about the sexual world of Murry and Mansfield, from whom those later characters are in part drawn.

In the third section of the book, which centres on Will and Anna's daughter Ursula, lust is shown at its most destructive. Ursula, like Louie Burrows (whose personality she partly shares, and whose cottage is the setting for Will and Anna's life), sees her own emancipation as a matter of being 'able to pay her own scot'; Jessie, Helen Corke and probably Lawrence's own mother would have thought the same. But Lawrence has begun to hate such importance being given to a person's job, so that 'marriage and home becomes a little side show'. Ursula's teaching doesn't bring her freedom, but shuts her in a kind of prison. It has to be said that in this respect Ursula (a very different creature from Ursula in *Women in Love*) barely resembles Frieda, who never had much desire for a job of any kind. The episode in which Ursula falls passionately in love with her teacher Winifred Inger was modelled on the experience which Katherine Mansfield confided to Frieda at Chesham: it is some evidence that modernity, women and Mansfield were already moving together in Lawrence's mind.

Lawrence was unembarrassed by personal revelations, but with Murry he always made sure they spoke of what was wrong with Murry's relationship with Katherine, rather than of his own difficulties with Frieda. Lawrence liked to lay the blame on Murry's timorous inability to assert himself. For his part, Murry was hostile to Frieda. He found her stupid, and had difficulty in not being rude to her. Other friends who visited Lawrence at Chesham also took against her. It was at this time that the Lawrences began to see a good deal of Koteliansky. He and Frieda disliked one another immediately, though Kot idolised Lawrence.

Kot became impatient whenever Frieda complained about her lost children; once he told her that since she had thrown in her lot with Lawrence, she should put up with the separation. Frieda stood up and left without a word, making her way through the rain to Rose Tree Cottage and Katherine. Shortly afterwards, Katherine appeared at the door, in wellingtons and with her skirts tucked up, evidently enjoying the drama. She brought a message from Frieda announcing that she would never return. To this, Lawrence shouted, 'Damn the woman, I never want to see her again!'[25]

This quarrel was resolved, but Kot made his opinion of Frieda plain enough for Lawrence to write and rebuke him. Lawrence did not say it, but Kot had failed to notice Frieda's growing awareness of her own displacement; she had indeed thrown in her lot with Lawrence, while he himself seemed to have only too many new admirers.

After that first intriguing vision of Katherine Mansfield in wellingtons Kot was bewitched, and over the next few weeks he made his adoration plain. He had a natural generosity of spirit which contrasted with Murry, and Katherine soon began to use him as someone to whom she could complain, though she still claimed to love Murry.

For a time, however, all these quarrels could be forgotten in the preparations for Christmas, which both the Murrys and the Lawrences meant to make as cheerful as possible. With Mary and Gilbert Cannan, they planned festivities together. Lawrence made punch, and guests came from London. Among them was Mark Gertler, looking as pretty as a Fra Lippo Lippi cherub. On Christmas Day, everyone drank a great deal. And Gertler kissed Katherine Mansfield.

The episode took place during a game of charades, which had been suggested by Kot. Katherine, Gertler and Murry were to act out a scene in which Katherine was supposed to flirt with Gertler and then return to Murry, but in the event she refused to go back to him. Murry did not make a great issue of this, but Lawrence was exasperated by his meekness, which was exactly what he felt led Katherine to torment him.

Katherine had already decided that her affair with Murry should come to an end, though she had no designs on Gertler; all through January she was writing feverish letters to the French poet and painter Francis Carco, who had once published in *Rhythm*; she finally set out to join him in Paris in February 1915. One of her first actions on reaching France was to write to Frieda. The confidential sisterly relationship between them still continued.

The previous month, the Lawrences had moved to the pleasant cottage in Greatham, Sussex, which had been lent them by Violet Meynell. Murry, lonely and low after Katherine's departure, came to visit and caught a serious chill after a soaking walk across the local marshlands. For several days Lawrence nursed him tenderly, an incident which found its way into *Aaron's Rod*, written in 1921. For all his emotional frailty, Murry was becoming Lawrence's most intimate friend. As a consequence, though he did not risk intervening in the

Lawrences' squabbling, his dislike for Frieda increased. By May 1915 he was writing to Katherine that he was planning to take Lawrence away for a summer holiday to see if he could 'urge him to the point of leaving her'. With some innocence, and complete trust, he spoke of Lawrence being happy with him because 'he would know I am loving him'.[26] Katherine sent a caustic rejoinder.

The love Murry had in mind was far from physical, and Lawrence himself was going through a period of extreme anxiety about the homosexuality of some of his acquaintances in the Bloomsbury Group. He had even recently asked David Garnett to choose between his homosexual friends and him. Garnett chose his friends. Yet the sense that he and Murry shared a loving relationship helped Lawrence to bear his difficulties with Frieda. At the same time it increased Frieda's resentment of Murry. Over the next few months Katherine returned from France several times. Her love affair with Carco had never been a great passion: the picture she gives of him in her stories 'An Indiscreet Journey' and 'Je ne parle pas Français' suggests someone even more passive than Murry. She was soon living with Murry again, having persuaded him to abandon his flat in Elgin Crescent, Notting Hill, for a house in St John's Wood. And she was ill once more.

The Lawrences moved from Greatham to the Vale of Health in Hampstead in August 1915, and found themselves living next door to the poet Anna Wickham, whom David Garnett described as 'a beautiful and powerful woman'. It was a time of optimism; Lawrence and Anna spent a good deal of time walking on the heath. And he and the Murrys launched their short-lived magazine *Signature*. They rented an office for a shilling a week in Red Lion Square, and held literary meetings on Thursday nights. The magazine only appeared three times. Katherine Mansfield wrote some fiction for it under the pseudonym Mathilda Berry, and Lawrence wrote an essay, 'The Crown', which was spread over the three issues and explored the perpetual conflict of the senses and the spirit.

Lawrence was hoping for a pot of gold from the imminent publication of *The Rainbow*, and at the end of September he brought the Murrys a pre-publication copy of the novel, lovingly inscribed to both of them. Then, on 5 October, the Meynells' friend Robert Lynd's review appeared in the *Daily News*, calling the book a 'monstrous wilderness of phallicism', and drawing attention to the lesbian episode.

Lawrence was devastated. There were soon attacks by Clement Shorter in the *Sphere* and James Douglas in the *Star*. To Lawrence's horror, a thousand copies of *The Rainbow* were seized from the printers by Scotland Yard, and the book was charged with obscenity. A hearing was fixed for 13 November, at Bow Street Police Court.

Frederick Delius, who had been told of Lawrence's difficulties by his fellow composer Philip Heseltine (Peter Warlock), had offered Lawrence a small house in the orange groves of Florida, and he began to think of leaving England for America; the thought would recur several times during the war years. First, however, Lawrence felt he should fight the order for the suppression of *The Rainbow*. He hoped that the Society of Authors would take up his cause (they refused), and he also counted on the help of several titled friends, Members of Parliament and famous writers among his acquaintance. Not all of them were as enthusiastic about the book as he could have wished. Ezra Pound was surprisingly squeamish about the explicit sexuality. Lady Cynthia Asquith, who had read and commented on sections of the book earlier, had ventured very little in the way of evaluation, but in a letter written to her close friend Desmond MacCarthy on 3 June 1919, she said: 'A strange bewildering, surely morbid book. It is full of his obsessions about sex conflict (all the lovers hate one another) and the "amorphousness" of actual life.'[27]

Five days before the hearing, Lawrence was staying at Garsington. He did not talk about the trial but seemed to find solace in long walks across the fields on his own, or in helping Ottoline Morrell to set iris bulbs around one of the small garden pools. Ottoline, with characteristic kindness, had contributed £30 for the intended trip to Florida. Lawrence and Frieda had their passports ready, but although he hoped to be leaving England within a month, he was not to be allowed to do so.

The authorities who found Lawrence's novel pornographic specifically mentioned Ursula's lesbian bathing with Winifred Inger and her lovemaking with Anton Skrebensky, which reduced him to a passive role. They seem to have been less worried by the perversity of the lovemaking between Anna and Will, even though certain passages suggest sodomy. The book's publisher, Methuen, who had asked Lawrence to deal with other objections earlier in the history of the manuscript (according to J. B. Pinker, who had succeeded Edward Garnett as Lawrence's agent in 1914, he left unchanged only one passage of which they complained), put up little resistance when the courts invoked the 1857 Obscene Publications Act. They voluntarily surrendered all the remaining copies of *The Rainbow*, which were destroyed, and took no steps to have either Lawrence or themselves represented, being mainly concerned to escape with the lightest possible penalty. Lawrence was outraged both at Methuen's betrayal and at the unfairness of the proceedings; the prosecution drew largely on unfavourable comments in the press and did not call the author to give evidence. He cursed them all, 'body and soul, root, branch and leaf, to eternal damnation'.[28] No fine was imposed on Algernon Methuen, who was made a baronet the following year.

The Morrells did try to help Lawrence in his legal battle, but to no avail; perhaps the reason Philip's interventions attracted little support was that he was known to be a pacifist. As Lady Ottoline said, 'Philip did all he could in the House of Commons to get the ban removed, but without success.' In fact Philip's questions in the House may even have confirmed the suspicions of those who believed that pacifism and sexual immorality were somehow connected.

Catherine Carswell reviewed *The Rainbow* very favourably for the *Glasgow Herald*, although she found it puzzling and even disappointing after *Sons and Lovers*. The review cost her her job. Murry, on the other hand, the friend to whom Lawrence had most fully explained his intentions in writing the novel, did not like the book and did nothing for it. Indeed, many of the writers who might otherwise have been willing to help felt the same.

The waspish malice that had always been in Lawrence came more frequently to the surface at this time. He was affectionate and grateful to Ottoline in her presence, but spiteful behind her back. Dorothy Brett describes a tea in December of that year which was spent in 'tearing poor O. to pieces'.[29] A little nervous that Ottoline might get to hear of this, Lawrence subsequently wrote advising her not to believe everything Brett might say. While Lawrence stayed in London to see what could be done for *The Rainbow*, Catherine Carswell felt she had to preserve a little distance between them: 'the need to save myself, even to save myself up'.[30] It is rather as if, even for a friend as loyal as Catherine, Lawrence's neediness at this juncture was too draining to be tolerable.

Lawrence and Frieda together were even more demanding. Catherine had a dread of emotional mess: 'His marriage to Frieda was a step which inevitably created a morass about the paths of friendship. I saw one person after another flounder in that morass. For me, I preferred to signal across it.'[31]

Chapter 12

CORNWALL

In the event, it was not to Florida but to the north coast of Cornwall that the Lawrences retreated. The writer J. D. Beresford had offered them a cottage near Padstow for the first two months of 1916, and once there Lawrence found it was possible to rent accommodation exceptionally cheaply.

When they arrived in Padstow in the last week of December 1915, Lawrence was ill, defeated and without income. He was already in some financial difficulty: that spring he had been pressed for the costs of the Weekley divorce, which the courts had awarded against him, and with the suppression of *The Rainbow* he was denied any profit from his labours of the last two years. Worse, he was, as Richard Aldington put it, 'publicly stigmatised as obscene, and his name was made so notorious that publishers and periodicals for a long time avoided using his work'.[1] The tuberculosis he was always to deny was beginning to make itself felt. He badly needed emotional support from Frieda; at the simplest level he needed her to demonstrate that she respected him. Frieda, who had been loyal through humiliating poverty, and had put up with his desperate rages, could not manage it now. She developed a mocking manner in dealing with the return of his rejected manuscripts, and even used this to score marital points about his habits of speech and thought.

Before the Lawrences left for Cornwall, Frieda saw her children on several occasions – once in an interview timed to last half an hour at a lawyer's office. The children were very nervous, and Frieda was both excited and tearful. Her daughter Barbara Barr says that everyone was relieved when the lawyer's clerk brought the interview to an end. On another occasion, Frieda took them to *The Marriage of Figaro*, and afterwards gave them ten shillings each (the money was formally returned by Weekley). Lawrence noted, perhaps a little optimistically, that she had almost ceased to fret about the children, and they were certainly no longer the commonest cause of their quarrels, which now centred on Lawrence's demand to be acknowledged as the more important figure.

Lawrence had always claimed that he wanted equality between the sexes, but now he began to speak vehemently of his need for a woman who would recognise his will as absolute. He had previously demanded precedence as a genius, but that was not so easy to do when no one seemed to want his work. So he began both to claim precedence as a man, and to look for other bonds. His marriage no longer gave him sufficient emotional support, and there was no sign of children. The medical reason for that cannot be established now, though Frieda's daughter Barbara hazarded a guess that Lawrence was sterile as a result of an attack of mumps in childhood. It may be so. It is also possible that Frieda took precautions which she concealed from Lawrence, who disapproved of interference in the matter of conception. At any rate, in the absence of a family he began to think of an ideal community of like-minded souls in which he could take refuge from an increasingly hostile world. He called it 'Rananim', a word derived from the Hebrew phrase 'Ranenu, Rananim', 'Rejoice in the Lord, O Ye Righteous', which Koteliansky delighted to chant.

Sometimes visitors produced their own eddies and currents in the Lawrences' arguments. One such was Philip Heseltine, to whom Ottoline Morrell had unwisely confided her dislike of Frieda. Lawrence did his best to make as little as possible of Heseltine's gossip about this, but Frieda wrote Ottoline a furious letter and, although Ottoline wrote back in soothing terms, war between them was now open. Ottoline never came down to Cornwall, though she was one of the friends around whom Lawrence hoped to build Rananim.

It was while Lawrence was reeling from the suppression of *The Rainbow* that Katherine Mansfield heard that her much-loved brother Leslie had been killed in France. In November she and Murry went off to Bandol in the south of France to help her recover from the blow; but the weather was very cold, and Murry contracted food poisoning and soon retreated to London, where he thrived best. Katherine, alone, ill and desperate for letters, wrote to Lawrence, who castigated Murry for leaving her, and suggested her illness was due to his continuous whining and indecisiveness. At the same time Lawrence began to hope that the four of them might set up a community together. When Murry set off to rejoin Katherine in Bandol, Lawrence wrote to them as if they were happy and naughty children – 'Cari Mei Ragazzi' he called them – delighted they should be together again. There is a charm and tenderness towards Katherine in all his letters at this time. Frieda, too, wrote to her: 'I am so anxious now to *live* with no more soul harassing, we are *friends* and we won't bother any more about the *deep* things, they are all right, just let's live like lilies of the field.'[2]

In February 1916 the Lawrences moved to Higher Tregerthen, about five miles north of St Ives, where they had found a one-up, one-down stone house for only £5 a year. It adjoined another, more substantial structure, at £16 a year, which had big windows, a large study and dining room at ground level, and three bedrooms. Lawrence identified it eagerly as ideal for the Murrys, and wrote enthusiastically inviting Katherine and Murry to join them. There was no running water and no indoor sanitation in either cottage, which worried neither Lawrence nor Frieda, but Lawrence knew Katherine was more concerned with such matters, and arranged to have an outside privy moved so as not to appall her too much. He also described the granite village under the high, shaggy moor-hills covered with gorse as 'the best place I have been in, I think'.[3] Frieda later described it as a 'granite hole',[4] but agreed that they had made it pleasant to live in.

The Murrys were not the only friends Lawrence tried to persuade to join them, but they were far the most important emotionally. Lawrence wrote to Murry: 'I feel you are my only real friends in the world.' All he wanted was that the four of them should love and be happy. 'Let us be happy together,'[5] he pleaded. Tempting as this communal life may have sounded, it is still surprising, after Lawrence's indignant interference over the Gertler episode and Katherine's reaction to Lawrence and Frieda's quarrels in Buckinghamshire, that Katherine was eager to try it again.

The north coast of Cornwall is bleak and windswept; the sea is treacherous, and that spring of 1916 there was snow and fog. Lured by Lawrence's offer of love and friendship, the Murrys arrived on 1 April, on a cart piled high with chattels, but even while they waited in a small hotel for their cottage to be made ready, Katherine admitted to Murry that she feared she would never like the place.

On 11 May, three weeks after they moved in, Katherine was already writing to Kot: 'It may all be over next month; in fact it will be,'[6] and hinting that she was irritable with Murry as well as the Lawrences. She was working hard, doing all the domestic chores, and Murry saw nothing wrong with that. Meanwhile, he was giving his most intimate companionship to Lawrence. But what really made life in Higher Tregerthen a nightmare was the worsening relationship between Lawrence and Frieda.

The Lawrences' arguments were constant and often physically threatening. Katherine writes of saucepans and flat-irons being thrown. Once, when Frieda gave an opinion of Shelley with bland assurance, Lawrence accused her of showing off. This enraged Frieda, who on this occasion, according to Katherine, was the first to lose her temper. In his account, Murry stresses Lawrence's conviction that Frieda was simply taking up a contrary position in order to annoy him: 'What do *you* care? If you *dare* to say another word about Shelley, I'll . . .'[7] At dinner time a few hours later, Lawrence began to chase Frieda round the kitchen table, punching her and pulling her hair. Katherine gives an amusing picture of their relative physical strengths: even as he pursued Frieda, Lawrence looked green and puny, while Frieda was a 'big, soft woman'[8] who easily absorbed the blows he dealt her.

When Lawrence and Frieda made up, as they always did, Katherine was astounded by the evidence of Lawrence's humiliating dependence on his wife: the morning after this quarrel, he not only trimmed a hat for Frieda, but ran about preparing her a breakfast in bed. And this was at a time when Lawrence was quite seriously ill. Consumption had been suspected in November 1915, but when Lawrence's fevers and debility so alarmed his friends that Dr Maitland Radford (the brother of the poet Dollie Radford, who had been a friend of Lawrence's since the Greatham period) went down to examine him in Cornwall, Lawrence insisted that he had found only nerves, stress and a 'referred inflammation in all the internal linings'.[9] It seems likely that although a formal diagnosis of tuberculosis was not made until June 1916, when he was rejected for military service, Lawrence was already suffering from the disease.

Lawrence was powerless to reverse a situation in which Frieda seemed so overwhelmingly the stronger, and one must suppose that a sense of this entered their sexual relationship. The composer Cecil Gray, who was living nearby, conjectured that Lawrence was already impotent. There is no evidence to support this, but there is certainly an odd counterpoint between Lawrence's passionate assertions about male supremacy and the situation between him and Frieda at this time. This did not stop him from criticising the Murrys for what he felt was wrong in their relationship, which he insisted was shallower than his and Frieda's because it was less turbulent. Murry always thought the reason Lawrence had such an intensely quarrelsome marriage with Frieda went back to his relations to his mother; there may be something in that hypothesis. Lawrence had set up a situation which repeated the violent quarrels between his father and mother. It was his loss of power that Lawrence himself felt was the key: his father's anger was caused in part by a similar loss. In a later letter, Lawrence explained the source of his fury very plainly to Katherine: 'I do think a woman must yield some sort of precedence to a man, and he must take this precedence. I do think men must go ahead absolutely in front of their women, without turning round to ask for permission or approval from them.'[10] The trouble was that Lawrence's lack of literary success meant he now needed Frieda's approval desperately, and she refused to provide it. His attempts to impose a harmonious relationship on her led him into a kind of frenzy: 'He raves, roars, beats the table, abuses everybody,'[11] as Katherine put it, observing that after such attacks he was ill, haggard and broken.

Katherine blamed Frieda for what was happening: 'Of course, Frieda is at the bottom of it . . . he has chosen Frieda and when he is with real people he knows how fatal that choice is.'[12] Close as she had once felt to Frieda, she now expressed little compassion for her, and suspected her of relishing the fights. Even Frieda's new surge of domestic activity irritated Katherine. (Frieda had learnt to wash clothes, and did so in huge tubs of water, with a great deal of noise and energy.) Katherine was sorry for Lawrence. He was so like herself. With her usual wit, she saw him, her dear friend, 'like a little gold ring in that immense German Christmas pudding which is Frieda'.[13]

Katherine had other complaints against Lawrence: he and Murry set off with rucksacks on their backs and left her alone; she found his obsession with sexual symbolism tedious, and teased him by suggesting that he should call his cottage 'The Phallus'.

Murry always claimed to be astonished when Frieda told him that the characters of Gerald Crich and Gudrun Brangwen in *Women in Love* were based on himself and Katherine, and it has to be said that the intense struggle of wills between Gudrun and Gerald is much more like the extreme violence of Lawrence's own marriage. Still, Murry could not but recognise something of his relation to Lawrence in Rupert Birkin's wish for blood brotherhood with Crich, and he must have identified Lawrence's theory, evolved in Cornwall, that what his marriage needed to balance it was a loving, brotherly relationship with Murry.

Murry was frightened at the prospect, imagining some black magic rite performed on the Cornish moors, although he did not entertain (or so he claims) any suspicion that Lawrence was making a homosexual advance. Murry's biographer, Frank Lea, tells us that Murry had had an extreme aversion to homosexual acts since he had been the object of an assault when he was a schoolboy. Perhaps Lea is right about Murry's innocence: Lawrence too was, with one side of himself, shocked by homosexuality, which he had found so disgusting on his visit to Bertrand Russell in Cambridge in 1915 that he was led to dub John Maynard Keynes and his friends evil. His revulsion had impressed Russell, who wrote to Ottoline Morrell: 'Lawrence has the same feeling against sodomy as I have; you had nearly made me believe there is no harm in it, but I have reverted.'[14]

What Lawrence had in mind was not sexual, but spiritual; the blood brotherhood was to include Katherine, though she was thought to be uneasy about it. Murry saw Lawrence was ill; the tuberculosis he never admitted already had him in its grip. But whatever Lawrence wanted as a counterweight to his battling relationship with Frieda, Murry could not give it. He was too afraid of losing Katherine to respond unguardedly. For her part, Katherine sat up in her room, smoking cigarettes and brooding.

Murry thought, sensibly enough, that Lawrence's insistence on an intimate relationship with a man must stem from some insufficiency in his relationship to Frieda. Lawrence was disappointed in himself, in the rejection of his work, and may have also disliked what was happening in the marital bed. Yet he needed to believe that the relationship between Frieda and himself was still real and life-giving: it was to make that clear that he stressed the contrast between his own and the Murrys' relationship, and insisted that his wild alternations between hate and love were the bedrock reality on which life ought to be built. That is also why he comes across as less a suitor than a bully when he sneers at the love between the Murrys as false, and his observations jar, even though the precariousness he had recognised in their relationship was genuine.

It is not surprising that the Cornwall experiment at communal living was an explosive failure. All four were fond of one another, but the tensions were too great. As Lawrence said, they 'all had to pretend a little, and we couldn't keep it up'. After only two months, Murry and Katherine announced that they were moving away to the south of Cornwall, and Lawrence accepted their decision, though it affected him badly. He began to have fits of delirium at night: Murry claims that was the context in which Lawrence was heard to shout that he was 'an obscene bug sucking his life away',[15] though both the 'obscenity' and the 'sucking' could have had a different explanation in a delirious dream.

Katherine knew she needed to escape from Murry as well as the Lawrences. She began to write to Ottoline Morrell in an attempt to establish a more intimate relationship with her, as an insurance against falling out of Murry's network of literary friendship. Even after their move, Katherine was writing to beg an invitation for herself to Garsington without Murry.

The Murrys moved out in June 1916, and Lawrence, with characteristic generosity, helped them to load up their cart. Murry set off feeling he had said goodbye to Lawrence forever. This was far from the case, though the relationship between all four never recovered. Nor did Lawrence propose a blood brotherhood between them again. As he wrote to Amy Lowell while he was typing out the manuscript of *Women in Love*, 'I take so unkindly to any sort of machinery. But now I and the typewriter have sworn a Blutbrudershaft.'[16]

Lawrence shrewdly observed to Kot that Katherine and Murry had 'worn out anything there was between them', and guessed that what Katherine needed was 'to be quiet, to learn to live alone, and without external stimulant'.[17] For a time that was what happened. Even though in the tug-of-war with Lawrence over Murry's affections Katherine might seem to be the victor and therefore the enemy, Lawrence had come to like her better than Murry. He thought about her with real friendship and, for most of *Women in Love*, which he was then writing, the portrait of Gudrun is charming and affectionate, and has much of Katherine's wit and gaiety.

Murry must have been thinking of breaking free from Katherine himself. He was becoming a successful author, with two books published that year, and though the novel, *Still Life*, was a poor thing, the study *Dostoevsky* was important. On his return to London he had also found a clerical niche at the War Office, which not only saved him from military service but gave him a decent salary.

That summer, Murry visited Garsington several times, and he had begun to think a great deal about Ottoline. On 31 August he wrote to her: 'I have a queer suspicion I may be in love with you.'[18] Indeed, he continued to write letters and go for moonlit walks with her even as he and Katherine grew close again. For a time he liked to think Ottoline was in love with him. There is no sign in Ottoline's account of those days that she was much involved emotionally, though she was aware of Murry's good looks.

Chapter 13

INFIDELITIES

Affter the Murrys' departure for Mylor, on the south coast of Cornwall, the Lawrences were very low. Lawrence's health was poor, and they were particularly strapped for money. Indeed, Lawrence wrote to his agent J. B. Pinker that he had only £6 in the world. Lawrence and Frieda could make do on very little, but at this time they could not have managed without help from their more fortunate literary friends, including Amy Lowell and Ottoline Morrell, to whom Lawrence wrote blaming the bleak countryside for the Murrys' departure and reflecting that he had found Murry 'rather horrid when he was here'.[1]

Until the Military Service Act of 1916 the British army had been made up of volunteers; now the death toll of the war made conscription essential, and it was not long before an official letter arrived summoning Lawrence to present himself to the the army authorities. On 28 June 1916 he travelled to Penzance, then to Bodmin, sixty miles away, where he had to submit to a medical examination lasting two days and a night. He had not brought night clothes, and disliked having to wash at a communal zinc trough. The humiliation of that experience went into the chapter of *Kangaroo* entitled 'The Nightmare': 'When it came to Somers' turn to be examined, and he took off his clothes and sat in his shirt in the cold lobby, the fat fellow pointed to his thin delicate legs with a jeer.'[2]

Lawrence was found to be tubercular, and although he had hated the prospect of fighting in the war, he found his rejection for military service ignominious, and had to struggle to throw off the resulting sense of physical inadequacy. 'Let them label me unfit,' he said to himself. 'I know my body is fragile in its own way, but also it is very strong, and it's the only body that would carry my particular self.'[3]

Catherine Carswell stayed with the Lawrences in Cornwall for Christmas 1916. They walked, talked about Dostoevsky and Murry's book, washed dishes together and looked after the cottages. She also witnessed the terrifying end of a row. Lawrence was singing to himself while washing the dishes, and Frieda came up behind him and broke a dinner plate over his head. 'It hurt him very much and might of course have injured him seriously,'[4] says Carswell, who could not explain what had driven Frieda to do it. Lawrence was too astonished to hit back. Catherine was rather given to saying how grateful she would be to have a man like Lawrence to fight with, but she did not imagine that Frieda's aggression was unprovoked, and reports Frieda's saying that she would have to leave Lawrence with some sympathy.

In *The Savage Pilgrimage*, her account of Lawrence's life, after giving a fair appraisal of Frieda's special qualities, Carswell says:

> *Sometimes it seemed to us that he had chosen rather a force of nature – a female force – than an individual woman. Frieda was to Lawrence by turns a buffeting and a laughing breeze, a healing rain or a maddening tempest of stupidity, a cheering sun or a stroke of indiscriminate lightning ... At times she hated Lawrence and he her. There were things she jeered at in him and things in her that maddened him – things that neither would consent to subdue. But, partly for that reason, how he admired her!*[5]

Catherine Carswell's is a dissenting voice among those friends who saw a sexual source for Lawrence and Frieda's quarrels. She believed that, 'if Lawrence had not been potent in body as well as in spirit, he could never have had Frieda to wife or, having her, he would not have kept her'.[6]

Meanwhile, Lawrence continued to write *Women in Love*, in which two couples with contrasted kinds of sexuality work out their lives against the background of a great house much like Ottoline Morrell's. It is perhaps significant that, although Murry lived next to Lawrence and spoke to him every day for two months, he neither saw nor heard anything of the novel on which Lawrence was working.

Lawrence and Frieda were now often estranged as well as quarrelsome, and Lawrence tried to develop new emotional ties.

When the American journalist Esther Andrews came into Lawrence's life at the end of 1916 she was attached to Robert Mountsier,
who was to become Lawrence's American agent in 1920. Lawrence
was keen to gain an audience in America, which he hoped would
be less priggish than England, and he liked the couple's gentleness.
Mountsier and Esther visited Lawrence in Tregerthen in November
and December 1916; they were unmarried, and attracted some suspicion in Cornwall for this: Lawrence's Christmas Eve celebrations
were interrupted by police arriving to inspect Mountsier's papers.
Mountsier became the model for Monsell in *Kangaroo*, who was questioned by the police in Cornwall, and later arrested and strip-searched
in London.

Esther was unhappy with Mountsier, and when he went back to
London she stayed on with the Lawrences from Christmas to mid-
January 1917. She returned for another visit in the spring of that year,
during which Frieda fell ill with colitis. Lawrence and Esther spent a
great deal of time together. He liked her very much, calling her 'Hadaf-
fah' (a version of the Hebrew 'Hadassah', an alternative name of the
biblical Esther) and writing about her affectionately in several letters.
To judge from her photographs, she was a beautiful woman with a
sexually provocative allure, quite different from any other woman
Lawrence had known. There is no reason, however, to suppose that
Lawrence's relationship with her was sexual, any more than it had
been with his other admirers.

At Christmas, Catherine Carswell saw that Esther was glamorous
but very unhappy, and 'could not resist ... trying to match her
strength against Frieda's, disastrously to herself'.[7] It is probable that
Esther would have liked to sleep with Lawrence, and that Frieda
realised this, and was never sure if she had or not. In Frieda's memoir
she blames her loneliness in the summer of 1917 on Lawrence's attachment to Esther. According to Lawrence's American patron, Mabel
Luhan (whose jealousy of Frieda makes her an unreliable witness),
Frieda told her that Lawrence had betrayed her with two people in
Cornwall, one an American girl, and the experience was a miserable
failure. Frieda may well have told her this. She probably also mentioned Lawrence's relationship with William Henry Hocking.

Hocking was a handsome fellow who worked on a nearby farm. He and Lawrence were much of an age, but Lawrence's obviously superior education meant that Hocking treated him with a most satisfying respect. He had left school at thirteen, though he had an interest in books and languages.

Lawrence made friends with the entire family, rather as he had with the Chambers. He enjoyed teaching William's younger brother Stanley to speak French, and there were picnics out on the moors with his sisters Mabel and Mary. Frieda sometimes took tea with them, but she never found it easy to relate to simple people as Lawrence did. He enjoyed working in the fields, in spite of his ill health, and showed the Hockings how to tie sheaves in the Midland manner he had learnt at Haggs Farm. Lawrence had never been more in need of simple affection, which is what the Hocking family offered.

He also found something 'independent and manly' in William Henry; a dark, Celtic quality, which put him outside the Christian traditions to which Lawrence was becoming increasingly hostile as the European war progressed. In turn, he widened William Henry's expectations of what the world could offer, and wrote several letters to friends on his account, for instance to Barbara Low in August 1916:

> *He is desirous of the intellectual life, yet he isn't in the least fit for anything but his farming . . . He looks to me as if I could suddenly give him wings – and it is a trouble and a nuisance . . . So if he does come to London for a bit after harvest is over, perhaps Eder [the psychoanalyst] might talk to him . . . But it isn't analysing he wants – it is some real relation with the intellectual life.*[8]

In the prologue to *Women in Love* (suppressed by Lawrence himself, who feared it would be considered obscene after *The Rainbow*), Lawrence attributes to Rupert Birkin an overwhelming physical desire for a Cornish man of William Henry's physical type: 'Then again Birkin would feel the desire spring up in him, the desire to know this man, to have him, as it were to eat him, take the very substance of him . . . as if the satisfaction of his desire lay in the body of the young strong man opposite.' And he explicitly states of Birkin: 'Although he was always drawn to women, feeling more at home with a woman than a man, yet it was for men that he felt the hot, flushing, roused attraction which a man is supposed to feel for the other sex.'[9]

None of this necessarily means that Lawrence acted on any such desires himself, or that William Henry (who married two years later) would have welcomed any attempt to do so. But William Henry felt Lawrence had some homosexual inclinations: 'He used to come down to the farm and talk about it a lot.'[10] Talking may have been all there was to it, but the possibility of an intense homosexual episode cannot be ruled out.

Lawrence denied it to Catherine Carswell, and he was certainly made extremely uneasy by homosexuals. He remarked in a letter to Kot that he dreamt of beetles when he thought of them, but then he had dreamt of beetles when Murry was in Cornwall, and he had described his early feelings of homosexual arousal in *The White Peacock*. There had always been something in Lawrence which identified strongly with women – Jessie Chambers' brothers spoke of him as 'a woman in a man's skin', and this identification sometimes had an erotic charge, as the unedited text of *Sons and Lovers* makes clear: there, Paul Morel is drawn to a pair of stockings lying over a chair in Clara's bedroom, and gets up stealthily to put them on himself. The novelist Angela Carter pointed out in an essay on *Women in Love* that Lawrence showed an unusual interest in women's stockings (taking pleasure in cross-dressing, of course, does not necessarily indicate homosexual practice).

Helen Corke, too, observed the sexual ambivalence of Lawrence's nature, and he echoed this himself in a letter to Henry Savage, a journalist who had praised *The White Peacock* in the *English Review* in December 1913. Writing to Savage about Richard Barnham Middleton, a young writer who had committed suicide in 1911, Lawrence conjectured:

> *Perhaps if he could have found a woman to love, and who loved him, that would have done it, and he would have been pure . . . he would have loved a man, more than a woman: even physically; like the ancients did . . . I believe it is because most women don't leave scope to the man's imagination – but I don't know. I should like to know why nearly every man that approaches greatness tends to homosexuality, whether he admits it or not: so that he loves the* body *of a man better than the body of a woman – as I believe the Greeks did, sculptors and all, by far.*[11]

The only evidence of actual homosexual behaviour, however, is second- or third-hand. Hilda Doolittle recalled that in 1917 Frieda complained that Lawrence only liked men sexually, and in a letter to her former husband Richard Aldington in 1949, she spoke of Lawrence's 'passionate attachment' in Cornwall. Most tellingly, in a letter to Murry in which she spoke of rescuing Lawrence from his homosexual impulses, Frieda said: 'I think the homosexuality in him was a short phase out of misery – I fought him and won – and that he wanted a deeper thing from you.'[12] The 'misery' to which Frieda alludes had many sources. It is not clear whether Lawrence's 'passionate attachment' would have arisen if he had not fallen into despair about Frieda, or whether a growing awareness of his own sexual preferences was the cause of the trouble between them. In either case, Hocking was a sign that their long battle had moved into a new phase.

Frieda spent a good deal of time with their near neighbour Cecil Gray while Lawrence was visiting the Hockings. Gray, who was to be satirised in Aldous Huxley's *Antic Hay* as Mr Mercaptan, a 'sleek, comfortable young man', had an allowance of two hundred pounds a year from his parents. Lawrence never particularly liked Gray, who purported to know a great deal about his sexual problems, and it may well be that in asserting that Lawrence was, if not absolutely impotent, not very far from it, Gray was repeating Frieda's words (though it was not a complaint she made to other friends). Certainly she saw a lot of Gray at a time when she was lonely and unhappy, and sought some form of consolation from him. Knowing Frieda's disposition to see herself as first and foremost a sexual creature, it seems likely that they were lovers.

The main evidence for a sexual relationship between them comes from Hilda Doolittle. In her novel *Bid Me To Live* (1960) she portrays a group of characters who resemble Lawrence, Frieda, herself and Gray, and suggests that Frieda encouraged Lawrence to sleep with H. D. so as to have more time for her own affair with Cecil Gray. There are some oddities here: Frieda had only too much time on her hands while Lawrence was with William Henry Hocking, and Lawrence needed no urging to take an interest in H. D. He had written her some very ardent letters, but when on one occasion they did find themselves alone together he backed off hastily, to her disappointment. He may have been tempted by Esther Andrews' prettiness, but the last thing he needed was a woman of H. D.'s genius. In the end, whatever the relations between Frieda and Gray in Cornwall, it was H. D. who went off with Gray and had a child by him.

Gray was envious of the women who clustered round Lawrence. As Lawrence took little sexual advantage of the situation, Gray dubbed him a Cornish St Anthony, and wrote to Lawrence suggesting that he was allowing himself to become the object of a kind of esoteric female cult. Perhaps Frieda sensed the same wish. Lawrence wrote to Gray demanding that he give up 'your hatred of me, like Frieda's hatred of me'.[13] This bracketing together is suggestive, and Lawrence commands them both to acknowledge the difference between their idea of sexual relations and that which existed between him and his female followers: 'You want an emotional sensuous underworld, like Frieda and the Hebrideans: my "women" want an ecstatic, subtly intellectual underworld, like the Greeks – Orphicism.'[14]

It is against this background that Lawrence finished *Women in Love*. There is much marvellous writing in the book – descriptions of woods near a waterside in darkness, sounds and smells and seasons – all charged with Lawrence's peculiar gift for registering a physical world infused with a happiness that recalls Tolstoy:

> *The boat rustled lightly along the water. They passed bathers whose striped tents stood between the willows of the meadow's edge, and drew along the open shore, past the meadow that sloped golden in the light of the already late afternoon. Other boats were stealing under the wooded shore opposite, they could hear people's laughter and voices. But Gudrun rowed on towards the clump of trees that balanced perfect in the distance, in the golden light.*[15]

The novel continues the story of the Brangwen family from *The Rainbow*, this time focusing on the sisters Ursula and Gudrun, who work as teachers in a small town dominated by a colliery owned by the Crich family. Ursula falls in love with Rupert Birkin, an inspector of schools, while Gudrun has an affair with Gerald Crich, the son of the colliery owner. Birkin and Crich have a close, even loving relationship; indeed, an earlier draft of the book begins not with the Brangwen sisters discussing matrimony but with Gerald and Birkin on holiday together, silently aware of all they feel for one another. Neither man is happy with his life: Birkin is having an unsatisfactory love affair with the 'nerveworn' Lady Hermione Roddice, whom he cannot desire, and Gerald, who as a child accidentally killed his brother, has found meaning only in trying to make the Crich mines more productive.

Part of Lawrence's intention in *Women in Love* was to portray the ruin of the England he had loved by industrialisation, but his main theme was the difficulty in finding salvation through sexual love; he shows a modern, creatively active woman, Gudrun, seeking a sado-masochistic form of eroticism which in the end destroys the man who loves her, Gerald. If this is intended as a prognosis of the Murrys' marriage, it is a markedly inaccurate one. Catherine Carswell once asked Lawrence why he used friends who were 'so far removed from the general run' as the central characters of *Women in Love*, and he replied that it was in the exceptional people that one could tell where the rest of humanity was tending.

The sisters are drawn with great affection, particularly the elegant Gudrun with her brightly-coloured stockings. Ursula has a jolliness which instantly recalls Frieda; she enjoys everything. When Hermione points out that to marry Birkin one would have to suffer for him, Ursula replies, 'I think it is degrading not to be happy.'[16] It is easy to see why Frieda acknowledged and liked her representation in this book. We can also hear her voice in Ursula's outbursts of anger: 'You go to your women ... you've always had a string of them trailing after you – and you always will. Go to your spiritual brides – but don't come to me as well because I'm not having any, thank you.'[17]

Birkin's ideas are usually Lawrence's, and his struggle to have Ursula accept his sexual terms is essentially an account of Lawrence's struggle with Frieda. Birkin is close to hating any form of sexuality:

He knew his life rested with her. But he would rather not live than accept the love she proffered. The old way of love seemed a dreadful bondage, a sort of conscription ... True, he hated promiscuity even worse than marriage ... On the whole, he hated sex, it was such a limitation. It was sex that turned a man into a broken half of a couple, the woman into the other half ... He wanted sex to revert to the level of other appetites, to be regarded as a functional process, not a fulfilment.[18]

In a delirious rage when he is ill Birkin is filled with hatred of female power. 'It filled him with almost insane fury, this calm assumption of the Magna Mater, that all was hers because she had borne it.'[19] All through the book the women apprehended through Birkin's sensibility are alarming, even murderous in intent: Hermione hits Birkin over the head with a lump of lapiz, and even old Mrs Crich is described as a harpy. The strongest loving attraction Birkin feels is towards Gerald.

The scenes between a man and a woman most highly charged with eroticism are those between Gerald and Gudrun, and these are infused with a 'hellish' recognition of a delight taken in the infliction of pain. Gerald forces his horse to stand close to the railway line, and Gudrun faints when she sees him bring down his spurs on the animal's bleeding sides. In a later episode, she thrills illicitly when he catches a terrified rabbit. It may be these hints of sado-masochistic sexuality that led Murry to call the novel 'bestial'.

It is hardly the aspect of sexuality Lawrence appears to single out for condemnation, as he charts the destruction of Gerald at the hands of Gudrun. If we ask why Birkin feels Gudrun is so dangerous to Gerald, and if we accept that there is a counterpart of that fear in Lawrence's response to Katherine's relation to Murry, the answer lies somewhere in that very independent gaiety which makes the portrait of Gudrun such a charming one. The source of Gudrun's independence is her sense of herself as an artist – unlike Ursula, whose only interest is love (in this resembling Frieda). Gudrun's talent is as important to her as any love affair (Birkin insists her gifts are small, but Lawrence said the same of Katherine). When Gudrun appraises Gerald as a sculptor would, Birkin feels peculiarly apprehensive. As she innocently touches him on the chin, 'to Birkin it was as if she killed Gerald with that touch'. Lawrence seems alarmed at the thought of the female half of a pair being the creative artist. Birkin is, of course, also sexually jealous. The only physical expression of his love for Gerald is the naked wrestling scene which leaves the two men in one another's arms, exhausted as if they had made love. It is the closest they can become, since blood brotherhood appealed to Gerald as little as it had to Murry.

At the close of the novel, the two couples take a holiday in the Swiss Alps, a cold landscape Birkin can only bear because he has

Ursula's warm body close to him. There he and Ursula make licentious love: Birkin enjoys with Ursula the sodomy he is unable to practise with Gerald. 'They might do as they liked – this she realised as she went to sleep. How could anything that gave one satisfaction be excluded? What was degrading? Who cared?'[20]

When Gudrun is attracted to the ambiguously sexed sculptor Loerke, and tells Gerald that their love affair is a failure, Gerald almost kills her, but at length he turns his misery against himself and walks off into the snow, leaving Birkin disconsolate but vindicated. As a pattern of relationships, *Women in Love* is one of the subtlest pieces of writing Lawrence ever achieved, with each character of the quartet having a weight of their own, but it is odd that the book should ever have seemed to carry prescriptive moral advice – as it came to in the fifties – when it charts so clearly Lawrence's own sexual unease.

Two other episodes made 1917 particularly painful: in June Lawrence was summoned for a second military medical examination, at which his tuberculosis was confirmed and he was classified C3, unfit for service. And he and Frieda were expelled from Cornwall.

Lawrence had been under police surveillance the whole time he had been in Cornwall. The war was going badly in the autumn of 1917, and he was suspected for a number of reasons. He had been constantly outspoken in his criticism of the war. He had a German wife, and the Cornish folk were disconcerted by Frieda's behaviour. She once ran about gaily with a white scarf flowing in the wind, which might well have looked as if she was signalling to submarines. And Lawrence had not joined the army, even though he looked fit enough as he worked on the Hockings' farm. He never spoke of his tuberculosis.

Once two policemen jumped out from behind a bush on the moors and accused Frieda of photographing coastal installations. Lawrence and Frieda were visiting Cecil Gray one night in October 1917 when two policemen burst into the house because a light was showing. Gray had to pay a very heavy fine. When the Lawrences returned home they found that their cottage had been ransacked for 'suspicious material'; Lawrence's botany notebooks were carefully scrutinised, and the following day a policeman, accompanied by dogs, came to read out a court order instructing the Lawrences to leave Cornwall within three days.

William Henry Hocking never told Lawrence that he knew he was being watched by the Cornish police. He drove the Lawrences to the station, but he behaved cautiously, and some of his family even refused to say goodbye.

Frieda said something changed for ever as a result of that forced removal from Cornwall. Lawrence's hatred of the war, and of England itself, rose to a fever pitch, and he began to wish desperately to leave the country altogether, but this was far from easy. He had tried to get his passport renewed on 5 January 1917, and had been refused in the interests of national security; his escape continued to be blocked by suspicious authorities.

Katherine Mansfield had continued to be loyal to Lawrence as an artist, for all their difficulties in Cornwall: sitting with Kot and Gertler in the Café Royal in Regent Street in September 1916 she had over-heard two men making fun of Lawrence's recently-published early poems, *Amores*. She went over to their table, politely asked to see the book, and then strode out of the restaurant with it. This magnificent gesture was used by Lawrence in the 'Gudrun at the Pompadour' chapter in *Women in Love*, which he added to the manuscript in October 1916, and Katherine never reproached him for the portrait of her as Gudrun.

Lawrence called to see Katherine in London on his return from Cornwall; he was alone, as Frieda had gone down with 'flu. Katherine found him his 'old, rich, merry self'. Lawrence, seeing how ill she was despite the months she had spent in Bandol, felt rather disgusted to see Murry looking so fit. That Christmas they exchanged gifts, and Katherine was present enough in his thoughts for him to dream of her cured of consumption and to write as much to her, adding, with poignant affection, 'I wish it was spring for all of us.'[21]

By February 1918 Lawrence was telling Mark Gertler: 'I feel nothing but a quite bloody, merciless and almost anarchistic revolution will be any good for this country, a fearful chaos of smashing up.'[22]

Lawrence wrote to Catherine Carswell: 'I heard from Ottoline Morrell this morning, saying she hears she is the villainess of the new book.'[23] Claire Tomalin, in her biography of Katherine Mansfield, hazards a guess that Murry was responsible for Ottoline's suspicions, as it was at this period that he was enjoying his intimate conversations with her on his visits to Garsington.

Lawrence was understandably reluctant to allow Ottoline a sight of the manuscript of *Women in Love*. When she did read it, she was shocked and hurt to find Hermione, whom she easily identified as herself, described as wearing 'dirty dresses like an old hag',[24] and resented the suggestion that she was Lawrence's discarded mistress. Incensed by the minutely accurate description of Hermione's house, which was clearly based on Garsington, Ottoline wrote to Lawrence asking for an explanation. Lawrence's rather lame response was to claim that she had mistaken his intentions and that Hermione was a very fine woman.

It was not only by her house that Hermione could be identified as Ottoline Morrell. Ottoline's sing-song drawl and characteristic syntax are minutely recorded and ascribed to Hermione. And it was hardly over-sensitive of Ottoline to dislike descriptions of her face as 'macabre'. Hermione is portrayed as manipulative throughout the book, and utters a stream of earnest platitudes which often do little more than echo Birkin's thoughts. Even her intelligence and her passionate interest in books are ridiculed. Ottoline particularly disliked the way Lawrence represented the struggle between Hermione and Ursula for Birkin's regard, which mirrored the antagonism between Frieda and herself, and the suggestion of a perverted sexual attraction between the women. It was Frieda's voice she could hear in Ursula's tirade against Hermione: 'Is that spiritual, her bullying, her conceit, her sordid materialism? She's a fishwife, a fishwife, she is such a materialist ... She wants power, immediate power, she wants the illusion that she is a great woman, that is all.'

The offensive portrait of Hermione tortured Ottoline with the secret anxiety that Lawrence had divined a monstrosity in her of which she herself was unaware. She tried to believe that the most malicious parts of the book were Frieda's work, but although Frieda did hand-correct part of the manuscript, there is no evidence of the intimate collaboration she had offered Lawrence in *Sons and Lovers*. Ottoline had often attracted satire, and she would eventually forgive Aldous Huxley for his caricature of her as Priscilla Wimbush in *Crome Yellow*, but she found it difficult to overcome the pain *Women in Love* caused her. As she also indignantly pointed out, there had never been a sexual relationship between her and Lawrence, and we must look elsewhere for the emotional source of Lawrence's animus against Hermione.

Lawrence's surprise at Ottoline's anger was in part genuine. He had always used the people around him as characters in his books, and he seems to have expected them to accept his portraits as they accepted his verbal strictures. He had often upbraided Ottoline for her wilfulness, and urged her to see herself as a priestess rather than a salon lady or a bluestocking. Even while he was writing her into *Women in Love*, Lawrence was inviting Ottoline to Tregerthen, and as he set down his hurtful descriptions of her he was accepting her help in the form of clothes, blankets, food and books.

Apologists for Lawrence generally take the line that what offended Ottoline was the savage accuracy of the portrait; yet in fact it is disappointingly superficial. Ottoline had indeed taken lovers (including Augustus John and Bertrand Russell), as a result of a marriage that was often painfully humiliating. On her wedding anniversary in 1937 she wrote unhappily in her journal that her husband Philip had never found her sexually attractive, and had only been urged to marry her by his snobbish family. Although to all appearances the dutiful husband, he had a series of affairs with typists and maids, and on one occasion had confessed to making two women pregnant. He also had a series of mental breakdowns. These cannot be laid at Ottoline's door: since adolescence Philip had been disturbed by his parents' preference for another son, who committed suicide. His sense of inadequacy was not altogether unfounded: he could have had few illusions about his worth as a politician.

Although she was to have a passionately physical love affair with a stonemason only a few years later, Ottoline at this stage of her life was less interested in sex than in intelligent companionship, and she valued above all things the influence she could have on her friends' lives; it was the source of the friendship she and Lawrence had once enjoyed. Her religious feelings, though unconventional, were genuine. Lawrence had once been under the spell of Ottoline's dominant personality and aristocratic origins: she might even have seemed a candidate to fulfil Lydia Lawrence's dream for her son of marriage to a great lady. Lawrence had enjoyed her admiration and generosity, and had taken on the role of her mentor and prophet. Ottoline was right to see that the source of Lawrence's hostility was probably autobiographical, and the suppressed prologue to *Women in Love* offers some clues to this. The 'soul mush' which had so incensed Frieda in Lawrence's relationship with Ottoline resembled the passionate companionship he had shared with Jessie Chambers, and the account of Birkin's sexual failure with Hermione necessarily draws on his encounters with Jessie, since Lawrence's range of experience was so limited.

As he looked at the pattern of Ottoline's marriage, Lawrence saw a powerful, independent woman and a subordinate man. The power of patronage and money gave Ottoline a female confidence which Lawrence was now coming to hate and fear, though he had once admired it. Frieda was delighted with her own portrait as Ursula in *Women in Love*, perhaps especially since it is Hermione who is murderously able to rob men of virility by killing sexual desire, even if this also had its basis in Lawrence's marriage to Frieda.

A similar displacement of anxiety can be found in Lawrence's analysis of the quality of Katherine's relationship with Murry, which by 1918 became a matter of obsessive concern for him: he projected onto this too aspects of his own struggle with Frieda, tried to explain Katherine to herself as a *Magna Mater* figure, and felt Murry's psychological dependency on her was repellent. He must have been aware of the parallel with his own marriage, and in December 1918 he wrote to Katherine: 'In a way Frieda is the devouring mother. It is awfully hard, once the sex relation has gone this way, to recover. If we don't recover, we die.'[25] In the same letter he talks about the necessity for women to yield precedence to men. It was precisely to exorcise his fear of Frieda's strength that he separated out all the good elements that he wanted in Frieda and gave them to Ursula, and dispersed all her wicked powers to the other women in the novel.

Women in Love was to end any intimacy between Lawrence and Ottoline until 1928. Philip Morrell went to Lawrence's literary agent, pointed out that the book was obviously libellous, and threatened to bring an action against any publisher who brought it out. Lawrence received the news calmly enough: after the banning of *The Rainbow*, publishers weren't trying very hard to buy *Women in Love* anyway. Indeed, Lawrence was unable to publish the novel until November 1920 when the small, new publishing house of Thomas Seltzer brought it out in New York; it was May 1921 before Secker risked publication in England. The only book Lawrence had had published in 1917 was the collection of poems *Look! We Have Come Through!*, for which the critics had little good to say. *The Times* declared: 'The Muse can only turn away her face in pained distaste.'

Lawrence was desperately short of money, and filled out forms applying for a grant from the Royal Literary Fund. Kot, knowing his plight, offered to lend him his last £10. Catherine Carswell thought Lawrence should go back to teaching, but it was clear that few schools would open their doors to a writer who had been prosecuted for obscenity.

During the second half of the war, Lady Cynthia Asquith saw much less of Lawrence, although in the autumn of 1917 she took him to the opera in London (he made use of this in *Aaron's Rod*, where the privilege of being given a box at the opera enabled those who shared it to flirt and gossip). Lawrence's mild boredom with Cynthia did not mean he was diffident about asking her to approach anyone in her social group who might help him to find a secretarial job at the Ministry of Education, which his teaching qualifications seemed to fit him for. In October 1918 his own efforts procured a job writing articles on education for *The Times Literary Supplement* which would have brought in £3 a week, but he found the chore impossible to fulfil. Lady Cynthia treated Lawrence to lunch at a good restaurant in November of that year, and she noted that he drank a good deal of red wine, became truculent and urged her to go back to her house in the country, where she could make use of her time by doing her own housework. Although she found his railing against their acquaintances amusing enough, she did not like being called a 'duffer' herself, nor did she enjoy Lawrence's criticism of her whirl of social activity. By the end of November she was recording in her diary, 'I felt very tired and disinclined for Lawrence – but I couldn't put him off.'[26] They continued to exchange letters through 1919, though the volume of correspondence much decreased and, although they met once or twice during the twenties, Lady Cynthia could no longer be numbered among Lawrence's very close friends.

After leaving Cornwall, the Lawrences had stayed for a time in a room lent by the Aldingtons in Mecklenburgh Square, and it was there that Lawrence made the acquaintance of Dorothy Yorke, an exotic beauty who was in love with Richard Aldington. In December Lawrence and Frieda moved on to a cottage in Berkshire belonging to their friends the Radfords. Lawrence loved the soothing, wooded landscape of Berkshire, but by April they were forced to uproot once more, when Dollie Radford needed the cottage herself. Lawrence's sister Ada then found them a cottage in Middleton-by-Wirksworth in Derbyshire.

It gives us an idea of Lawrence's financial situation at this time that he was grateful to have Ada rent the cottage for them at her own expense. For all the beauty of the Derbyshire cottage, Lawrence's spirits were lowered by his continuing poverty and dependency. In the last week of August he paid a short visit to the Carswells, who were staying in the Forest of Dean with their young son John. With them, Lawrence was more cheerful, but the underlying bitterness remained.

Lawrence received new call-up papers on 11 September 1918, and went for yet another military examination to a big schoolroom in Derby on 26 September. Once again he felt ridiculous, and had to force himself to remain composed. Describing Somers' similar experience in *Kangaroo*, he speaks of the 'slight lifting of his nose, like a dog's disgust. [He saw] that men were handled as if they were furniture, and determined no one should ever touch him in that way again, cursing those who had handled his private parts: their eyes should burst, and their hands should wither and their hearts should rot.'[27]

'I have one really passionate desire – to have wings, only wings and to fly away – fly away. I suppose one would be sniped at by anti-aircraft guns,'[28] Lawrence wrote to Amy Lowell on 5 November 1918.

Chapter 14

CAPRI AND TAORMINA

When peace came, the Lawrences' relief was muted by their own insecurity. In November 1919, a year after the end of the war, Lawrence was able to leave England, and he made for Italy. His humiliating wartime experiences had left him with a hatred both of people in general and of English society in particular. He was never to live in England for a long period again.

Frieda went to visit her parents in Germany in October. In *Kangaroo*, the parting of Somers and his wife Harriet on a similar occasion suggests there was a look of vindictive victory on her face. By now, Lawrence feared Frieda's triumph over him so intensely that he saw evidence of it in her every act. Frieda found her family in Germany sad and poor, and many of her childhood friends dead.

Although the Lawrences were short of money, Lawrence had the addresses of several people who would help him. In Florence he met the author Norman Douglas, whose frankness in acknowledging his own late-developing homosexuality impressed Lawrence, though he did not much like Douglas's friends. Frieda, arriving in Florence after a muddled journey in which her trunks were lost, soon characterised the city as a male Cranford.

The Lawrences set off for Capri, where Mary Cannan was now living, as was Compton Mackenzie, whom they had met in Sussex. Lawrence loved Capri's physical beauty, the gulf of Salerno and the little town with its jungle of streets and bustling Italian life. Frieda did not like Capri when they arrived – the island was too small, she observed, for all the gossip it contained. Still, she looked forward to bathing in the sea.

Compton Mackenzie's novels had made him a wealthy man, and

he adapted a patronising, amused manner towards Lawrence. Once, when he was taken up by Ford Madox Ford, Lawrence had imagined he might soon earn a great deal of money himself; he had been sadly disappointed. Even if he had been wealthier, however, he would have been unlikely to enjoy Mackenzie's sybaritic lifestyle. 'I hate those damned silk pyjamas you wear,'[1] he told him. In his autobiography Mackenzie retaliates with caustic comments on Frieda's calico under-wear, which he claims she showed him to illustrate Lawrence's dislike of extravagant finery.

Nevertheless, the two men spoke intimately about sex, though Lawrence's confessions were too earnest for Mackenzie's urbane temperament. While on Capri, according to Mackenzie, Lawrence was much preoccupied with the difficulty he and Frieda experienced in reaching orgasm at the same time: the innocence of this confession raised Mackenzie's eyebrows. For all Mackenzie's amusement, such a conversation is not the stuff of comedy; Lawrence was clearly anxious about his and Frieda's lovemaking. It seems likely that Frieda, her panoply of ideas from Gross still with her, had come to demand her own satisfaction, and that Lawrence resented her failure to find fulfilment in the way he thought she should; certainly hostility along these lines enters all his novels from now on. Everything we know about their relationship suggests that by now Lawrence was worried about his ability to bring Frieda to orgasm, and that his deepening resentment of her efforts to find sexual satisfaction interfered with his own love-making. If Mackenzie's memoirs, Literature in My Time (published in 1933), are to be trusted, Lawrence was horrified and depressed by his remark that, except for the two people concerned, the sexual act was basically comic. But Mackenzie is perhaps not an unbiased witness, as Lawrence offended him in 1927 with his story 'The Man Who Loved Islands', which made fun of his materialism.

Lawrence was bad-tempered and short of money, and after receiving a welcome cheque for £20 from Amy Lowell in February 1920, he wrote to thank her, irked by his continuing need for charity: 'Why can't I earn enough? I've done the work.'[2]

Lawrence was still on poor terms with John Middleton Murry, who was making a comfortable niche for himself in the literary world. In January 1919 he had been made editor of The Athenaeum, and Lawrence quarrelled with him over the rejection of his 'Adolphe', a charming essay about a pet rabbit, which he had particularly chosen as being unlikely to alarm anyone. Impoverished as he was, Lawrence saw the rejection as a betrayal.

He continued to feel affection for Katherine, but there are no rich, funny letters to her in 1919. In February 1920, when Katherine was alone and very ill with tuberculosis, Lawrence wrote accusing her of 'stewing in her consumption',[3] calling her 'a reptile' and hoping she would die. Katherine quoted from this letter when she wrote to Murry, who swore he would never have anything to do with Lawrence again, and promised to hit him as hard as he could across the mouth if ever he ran into him. Perhaps to increase his indignation, she added that Lawrence had called him 'a dirty little worm'. Katherine was proud of Murry's chivalrous anger on her behalf, but doubted his resolve and predicted that a time would come when he would forgive his old friend.

Lawrence's rage ironically arose in part from his knowledge that he was himself tubercular. And as Katherine's condition worsened he began to blame her for her illness. Perhaps he reasoned that disease could be kept at bay by inner vitality, and that those who succumbed did so through some fault of their own. And where else could the failure of vitality lie, given Lawrence's pattern of thought, but in the relations between the sexes? Lawrence was distressed by the fact that his own intimate relations with Frieda were unsatisfactory. Who managed them even worse? Only Katherine and Murry.

In February 1920 the Lawrences moved to a house named Fontana Vecchia in Taormina, a lovely old Sicilian town overlooking the sea. It was while he was living there that Lawrence wrote most of the marvellous poems collected in *Birds, Beasts and Flowers* in 1924. For all the squalor of Sicilian peasant life, the physical beauty of the island exhilarated him. But his emotional difficulties with Frieda continued.

At the Fontana Vecchia Lawrence once tried to choke Frieda in his rage. Frieda reports that he screamed at her, 'I am the master, I am the master!' to which she, gasping for air, was able to cry with some relief, 'Is that all? I don't care, you can be the master as much as you like.'[4] This desperation resonates through Lawrence's most important writing of this period. The poems are filled with his idiosyncratic observation of the world, an utterly original vision: Venice is seen as 'abhorrent, green and slippery'; the crevice in a peach or the inner fruit of a fig are heavily charged with female sexuality; the yellow-brown snake, sipping with his straight mouth from the water trough, is seen as one of the lords of this world. There is also often a querulous anger with Frieda. In 'Pomegranates', for instance:

> *You tell me I am wrong.*
> *Who are you, who is anybody to tell me I am wrong.*
> *I am not wrong.*[5]

The poems about animal sex are particularly disturbing. Lawrence writes with weird empathy of the copulation of a he-goat, who can never quite reach the quick of the 'goaty, munch-mouth Mona Lisa' he is mounting. Lawrence's advice to the goat –

> *Forget the female herd for a bit*
> *And fight to be boss of the world.*[6]

– has a quirky side-glance at his own obsessive needs. His description of tortoises copulating is even more intimately revealing, since he links their mating directly to human experience:

> *Why were we crucified into sex?*
> *Why were we not left rounded off, and finished in ourselves . . .*

And, later in the poem:

> *. . . The cross,*
> *The wheel on which our silence first is broken,*
> *Sex, which breaks up our integrity, our single inviolability, our deep silence*
> *Tearing a cry from us*
>
> *Sex, which breaks us into voice, sets us calling across the deeps, calling,*
> *   calling for the complement*
> *Singing, and calling, and singing again, being answered, having found*
> *Torn, to become whole again, after long seeking for what is lost,*
> *The same cry from the tortoise as from Christ, the Osiris-cry of*
> *   abandonment,*
> *That which is whole, torn asunder,*
> *That which is in part, finding its whole again throughout the universe.*[7]

What has happened to the joy that filled Lawrence's days in Gargnano? These poems do not suggest that his desire for Frieda has abated; much more that he has begun to detest the desire itself, which prevents him from feeling independent.

This is a theme which runs through the novel *Aaron's Rod*, which was also written in Sicily. The novel has passages of Lawrence at his best: descriptions of trams, barbers' shops and all the marvellous carelessness of Italian city life. The essential plot involves Aaron Sisson, a flute player who has left his wife and is now wandering about Europe looking for the writer Rawdon Lilly. Lawrence's own personality is divided between Aaron and Lilly, who in many ways resemble each other. Aaron's wife complains that 'He can't give himself; he always kept himself back,'[8] which is very much Frieda's complaint, and Lilly's wife has a voice even more recognisable as Frieda's: 'Because I hold you safe enough all the time you like to pretend you're doing it all yourself.'[9]

The novel is permeated by the sourness of Aaron's reluctance to love, as if a man was to be treasured as a gift and a woman was only the receiver of his 'sacramental spirit and body'. It is also filled with Lawrence's usual terror of powerful women. When men gather together they speak anxiously of their fear of being harried into submission. And when Aaron is welcomed into the bedroom of the Marchesa del Torre in Florence, he describes a resentment which may well arise from the Lawrences' own marital bed. Aaron is angry with his wife's sexual behaviour; she either wants him when he does not want her, or puts him off when he does. He particularly complains that she waits until his erection has subsided so that she can have the pleasure of arousing him, and that she only enjoys sex when she initiates it. When he is the initiator, she may give in, but is then only a passive participant.

If this is any indication of the way Lawrence conceived of lovemaking, one's sympathies go out to Frieda. Sex evidently had to be only when Lawrence wanted it, and his desire had to be enough in itself to arouse her. Aaron's resentment at being used as an implement for a woman's pleasure sounds close to Lawrence's own.

Rawdon Lilly has many of Lawrence's domestic skills, and when Aaron falls ill in his house, he is nursed in a way that recalls Lawrence's care for Murry at Greatham after Katherine's departure in

1915. There is no concealment of the homoerotic pleasure that Lawrence takes in describing that episode. Aaron's inability to recover from his 'flu is blamed on his bowels: to make them work, Lilly rubs his lower abdomen with oil. Lawrence says this is a well-known way in which mothers treat children whose bowels don't work, as if he remembered the custom from his own childhood. It may be so. At any rate, Lilly rubs Aaron's abdomen, buttocks and thighs – and presumably his sexual organs, though they are not mentioned – and afterwards Aaron feels better. Set as it is in a novel so pervaded by resentment of women, it would be hard to exaggerate the significance of the passage.

The anarchist bomb that destroys Aaron's flute makes a rather clumsy point about the destruction of his male potency; the 'rod' of the title is identified with both Aaron's flute and his penis throughout the book. It is only when Aaron plays music to himself that he can imagine how his flute, 'Aaron's rod', would blossom. His happiest moments are those when he can retire to bed at night alone.

The new political themes which enter this novel are not handled with particular subtlety. Between 1920 and 1922 there were riots all over Italy. Lawrence was in the country between the postwar breakdown of government authority and the civil war between socialists and fascists, though he wasn't there for the fascists' march on Rome in October 1922, nor for Mussolini's brutal consolidation of power. The anti-democratic ideas Lawrence voices are essentially those he had formulated during the war, including his preference for a natural aristocracy, although he does not make clear who the natural kings of the world should be. Rawdon Lilly's declaration at the end of the book that there is a need for 'profound obedience more important than the need for love'[10] is a vehement foretaste of the novels to come.

In Taormina Lawrence also wrote an introduction to Maurice Magnus's *Memoirs of the Foreign Legion*, which is related in a skewed fashion to the events and places he makes use of in *Aaron's Rod*. Lawrence first met Magnus, a cosmopolitan journalist who had once been Isadora Duncan's manager, in 1919 in Florence, where Magnus was much attached to Norman Douglas. Lawrence found him an intriguing figure, at once dapper and down-at-heel, and he was bewildered by Magnus's ideas about money. Lawrence, though usually impoverished, always managed to live on his income, and was shocked to discover that when Magnus travelled by train he went first class.

From Capri, Lawrence sent Magnus £5 of the money Amy Lowell had unexpectedly given him. This incautious act of kindness brought Lawrence an invitation by return to stay at the monastery of Monte Cassino on the mainland, where Magnus, a Catholic, had made a retreat, and was having some thoughts of becoming a monk. Lawrence accepted, though he sensibly decided not to take his chequebook with him. At Monte Cassino he read Magnus's account of his life in the Foreign Legion, which he thought poorly written, and soon found himself being followed about with the same tender, worrying affection that Magnus had turned on Douglas. Lawrence left the monastery after two days instead of the fortnight he had been expected to stay.

In Taormina, however, their connection was uncomfortably renewed a month later. Magnus appeared early one morning, claiming he had escaped from Monte Cassino with the police at his heels. Frieda disliked him on sight, and berated Lawrence for encouraging him. Lawrence did not invite Magnus to stay at Fontana Vecchia, though he did pay his hotel bill. Ironically, since both Lawrence and Frieda prided themselves on being able to distinguish the aristocracy from the despised bourgeoisie, it was not until after Magnus's death that Lawrence learnt he was of royal stock, being the illegitimate son of Kaiser Frederick III.

In November 1920, after staying in San Gervasio on the hills above Florence, Lawrence and Frieda heard that Magnus's attempts to live beyond his income had overwhelmed him in Malta. Two detectives had arrived with extradition papers, but he locked the door against them and ended his life with hydrocyanic acid. By then Lawrence had written about Magnus satirically as May, the smart and shady American theatrical manager in *The Lost Girl*, who tempts James Houghton to start the cinema which eventually ruins him. Now Magnus was dead, Lawrence was stricken by the thought that he might have saved the man's life with a little money, and had chosen not to do so.

By February 1920 there had been an upturn in Lawrence's finances. He had sold the American rights to *The Rainbow*, and was making arrangements with Martin Secker to bring out other books in England. From this he had been able to repay money he owed his agent J. B. Pinker, and even to send something to both his own father and to Frieda's mother. When Catherine Carswell sent him £50 out of a literary prize she had won he was able to burn the cheque. His situation was still precarious, but he knew he could have done more for Magnus. In that spirit, and to help placate Magnus's creditors in Malta, he began to prepare the *Memoirs* for publication.

The book did not appear until 1924, and was then attacked by Norman Douglas, Magnus's literary executor, who complained, with some unfairness, of Lawrence's ill-treatment of Magnus.

Chapter 15

TRAVELLING

In April 1921 Frieda left Lawrence behind in Taormina while she visited her mother, who was ill in Baden-Baden. Lawrence found the house very empty without her. He was continuously invited out by expatriate English acquaintances, but after a month of loneliness he decided to set out to join her; taking his time, however, and stopping with various friends on the way in Capri, Rome and Florence.

It was in Capri that he first met Earl and Achsah Brewster, two American painters who had lived all over Europe. By no means wealthy, though Achsah had a small income, they tried to live off their paintings and, being far less provident than Lawrence, were often short of money. Lawrence made fun of their gentle Buddhism, vegetarianism and yoga exercises, but they were to be close friends for the rest of his life.

Reunited in May, the Lawrences rented a house for two months near Baden-Baden, in the village of Ebersteinberg, where he wrote most of *Fantasia of the Unconscious*. This little book is an extension of 'Psychoanalysis and the Unconscious', an essay which was published by Seltzer in New York that year, and received enthusiastically by George Soule in the *Nation & Athenaeum*, though H. L. Mencken found it not merely bad but childish. *Fantasia of the Unconscious* is written in Lawrence's knockabout, letter-writing style; it is a mixture of nonsense and brilliant observation about the education of children, the Freudian unconscious and the relation of sexuality and human creativity. By now Lawrence had a wider knowledge of Freud, gained through his acquaintance with Dr David Eder and Barbara Low. David Eder had written articles about Freudian theory for the *New*

Age, and it was through him that Lawrence met Ernest Jones, the most noted exponent of Freud's theories in England, in 1916. Jones was well enough disposed to the Lawrences for Frieda to turn up at his flat that year begging refuge, 'since her husband was about to murder her'. Jones's sympathies may be gauged from his riposte: 'From the way you treat him I wonder he has not done so long ago.'[1]

Nevertheless, Lawrence had not been much attracted to Frieda's theories which placed erotic pleasure at the heart of human fulfilment. He was by now in no doubt that for men the creative impulse was more important than the sexual; about the creative impulse in women he does not concern himself. For all the confidence this suggests, in *Fantasia of the Unconscious* Lawrence is still worrying away at the disposition of power in the relation between men and women. He has rethought his attitude to his own childhood, is sure now of the importance of the father in the development of the child, and seems disposed to blame his own delicacy on an upbringing left in the hands of his mother: 'Now the father's instinct is to be rough and crude, good naturedly brutal with the child,'[2] he says approvingly. Much in the book recalls William Blake's horror of the cerebral repression of instinct, which Lawrence thinks is particularly a danger for women: 'Teach a woman to act from an idea and you destroy her womanhood for ever.'[3] He spells out again what he objects to in a woman who has become 'sexually self-conscious', and who is bound to run through a series of experimental roles which make her miserable:

> First she is the noble spouse of a not-quite-so-noble male; then a Mater Dolorosa; then a ministering angel . . . a Member of Parliament, or a Lady Doctor or a platform speaker; and all the while as a sideshow she is Isolde to some Tristan, or the Guinevere to some Lancelot or the Fata Morgana of all men in her own idea.[4]

To prevent these things happening, Lawrence recommends: 'Let her learn the domestic arts in their perfection. Let us even artificially set her to spin and weave. Anything to keep her busy, to prevent her reading and becoming self conscious.'[5] The chirpy style rather belies Lawrence's frame of mind, though we can believe him when he speaks of wishing to draw back from the continuous burden of relationships and be alone with his soul. He does imagine a gentle spouse at his side, but in his fantasy there is silence between them.

By the middle of July he and Frieda were ready to move south again. In Ebersteinberg Lawrence had felt excluded – he couldn't breathe, as he put it – by Frieda's close relationship with her sister Johanna.

The Lawrences now went to Florence, where they stayed in the large and empty flat of their friend Nelly Morrison. There they were visited by Mary Cannan, who by now rather bored Lawrence, and also by Catherine and Donald Carswell, who observed his lack of interest in Mary, but overlooked the fact that he made little attempt to see much of them either. Lawrence was unusually withdrawn, as if for a time he had lost all inner conviction.

When Lawrence and Frieda returned to Taormina in September there were other reasons for unhappiness. Secker's edition of *Women in Love* had appeared in May; mail waiting for them included a letter from solicitors representing Philip Heseltine, who had recognised himself in the portrait of the hysterical young artist Halliday (this threat frightened Secker into paying him £5 plus ten guineas' costs to settle out of court). There was also a collection of appalling reviews.

In *John Bull*, the influential reactionary magazine edited by Horatio Bottomley, W. Charles Pilley vilified *Women in Love* as a loathsome study of sexual depravity in a review headed 'A Book the Police Should Ban'. Not satisfied with this recommendation, Pilley said, 'Most of his characters are obviously mad. They do and say the sort of things for which living people are shut up in lunatic asylums.' Murry's review in the *Athenaeum* was equally uncomprehending; he wrote of swimming through 'five hundred pages of passionate vehemence, wave after wave of turgid, exasperated writing, impelled towards some distant and invisible end'. At least Ottoline had taken no legal action over her portrayal as Hermione; in the four years that had elapsed since she read the manuscript her rage had diminished, and she saw that legal action would bring more ridicule than satisfaction. And the moral climate of English opinion had changed in the years after the war; no charge was brought against the novel for obscenity.

Nevertheless, Lawrence might well have wondered whether any of his work would ever be properly valued. Now, in a new way, he depended on Frieda as an understanding and validating reader. Every day she had to read what he had written, see how closely it had come out of their daily life, and, crucially, prize what he had done. Lawrence was coming to loathe everybody else: publishers, reviewers, even agents. He longed to get away from Europe, and in October was writing to Earl Brewster of a plan to 'get a little farm somewhere by myself, in Mexico, New Mexico, Rocky Mountains or British Columbia'.[6] An opportunity to do so was about to come his way.

In January 1921 Lawrence and Frieda had visited Sardinia, and as a result of that trip Lawrence wrote *Sea and Sardinia* in the following months. This magical evocation of a harsh island and an ancient, isolated people gives incidental and charming pictures of Frieda as 'the queen bee', getting up grumpily in the early hours, or slogging along at Lawrence's side, which bring us close to an understanding of their relationship in that year. The Sardinian trip was uncomfortable; they had no money for anything other than the cheapest lodging and transport, they were often cold and hungry and the only food they enjoyed was the English bacon sandwiches Lawrence had made before they set off from Sicily. He had chosen Sardinia precisely because it had 'no history, no date, no race, no offering'. It was a way of going back in time, finding a people uncontaminated by modern life, and uncorrupted by what Lawrence had now come to dislike as the softness of Italian culture. He tried his best to make a virtue of the ugliness of the dilapidated Sardinian towns, and declared himself delighted that there were no tourist sights to see. He was irritable and impatient throughout the trip, and Frieda was often silly and bossy. Yet the book that emerged from this trip has a charm and an engaging honesty which make it one of Lawrence's best.

Sea and Sardinia brought Lawrence to the attention of Mabel Dodge Sterne, a wealthy American woman living at Taos, in New Mexico, who at once wrote to tell him about the American Indians and to invite him to live in New Mexico. With her letter she enclosed an Indian necklace for Frieda and a few leaves of desachey, a perfume which is supposed to make the heart light.

The Lawrences were alternately delighted and apprehensive about this offer: for some years Lawrence had thought of America as a possible country to live in, and in 1915 he had had every intention of taking up Frederick Delius' offer of a house in Florida. He wrote back to Mabel making practical enquiries about the cost of living, and she replied that the Lawrences would have all their expenses paid once they arrived in the United States.

Letters and cables reminding the Lawrences of Mabel's invitation continued over several months, and they continued to mull over the offer, as Lawrence wrote to Jan Juta, who had painted the illustrations for *Sea and Sardinia*: 'It is awfully cold here, the snow right down to Monte Venere and on Froza all sprinkled white – Etna a shrouded horror. I hate it when it's cold . . . I keep on with the Taos trip. If I'd been well enough, we'd have sailed from Bordeaux to New Orleans on the 15th of this month.'[7]

Lawrence wanted to leave Europe, but he was by no means sure he liked the idea of Mabel. Frieda was more enthusiastic, though she understood Lawrence's reluctance. 'Lawrence says he can't face America *yet*; he doesn't feel strong enough.'[8] The idea of sailing to America via the friendly Brewsters in Ceylon seemed a sensible compromise. In December 1921 Lawrence received £100 when the James Tait Black Prize was awarded to *The Lost Girl*, a novel begun in 1913, rewritten in 1920, and among his weakest. The money, however, was encouraging. In late January Frieda wrote to Mabel outlining their intended route to New Mexico, and they set sail from Naples on the *Osterley* on 26 February 1922.

The Lawrences' fellow-passengers saw him as thin and frail, and Frieda as a large German Hausfrau with voluminous clothes, almost motherly towards her highly-strung husband. Once, Lawrence had praised Frieda as 'a gushing woman'. Now she had become outgoing and gossipy to the point of garrulousness. Mrs Jenkins, a young Australian woman, was placed at the Lawrences' table. She was very friendly, and may well be the original of Victoria Callcott in *Kangaroo*. The Lawrences got on well with her: she had read and admired *Sons and Lovers*, and thought Frieda a model of Teutonic placidity. Lawrence stayed in touch with her when they got off the ship at Colombo in mid-March to visit Earl and Achsah Brewster, who were now living there since Earl was interested in studying Buddhism and the language of its earliest scriptures.

The Brewsters were staying in an old bungalow on a hilltop; sixty acres of forests came right up to the door. Lawrence was ill most of the time he was in Ceylon, and decidedly tetchy. He hated what he saw of the East and its casual oppression: 'When, frail as he was, he needed to be carried uphill through the heat, he simply could not allow a rickshaw boy to pull him, but got out and walked.'⁹ Earl Brewster commented on his more general ill humour: 'Lawrence began his life with us by saying, "I consider you truly my friends, therefore I shall tell you your faults!"' Even Brewster, who passed his mornings in a Buddhist monastery, found his sanguine temper ruffled.

Although he enjoyed the bazaars, and the grand festival of Perahera when Buddha's sacred tooth is taken out of the temple (the young Prince of Wales was there for the ceremony), Lawrence was no longer sure it had been wise to move so far away from Europe. 'So I am making up my mind to return to England in the course of the summer,'¹⁰ he wrote to a friend in Sicily on 30 March.

Lawrence did not write much in Ceylon, because he felt too ill to trust his impressions of the island: he could scarcely drag himself about in the heat. Nevertheless, he was revising his thoughts with fierce energy: he was now convinced, as he told Achsah Brewster, that his mother's self-denial was more blameworthy than his father's self-indulgence. He remembered with tenderness how his father had crept in at night hoping to escape his wife's notice, how he had been reviled by her and yet gently reassured his frightened children. Through his own physical frailty, he was beginning to respect his father's relish for living.

The Lawrences had decided to continue their journey towards Australia, rather than America. 'Heaven knows why: because it will be cooler, and the sea is wide ... Don't know what we'll do in Australia – don't care,' Lawrence reflected in a letter to Cynthia Asquith.¹¹ Australia was on the way towards San Francisco and Mabel, of course, and Mrs Jenkins offered them hospitality in Perth. 'We shall stay with the Jenkins for a time: if we don't care for that go on to Sydney. I am taking a ticket to Sydney as it only costs £6 more,' Lawrence wrote to Mountsier on 17 April. 'And then after trying Sydney and New South Wales, if I don't like that we shall go across the Pacific to San Francisco, and then I shall have to sit down and earn some money to take the next stride, for I shall be blued.'¹²

The Lawrences sailed from Ceylon on 24 April, some six weeks after their arrival, and they arrived in Perth on 4 May.

Australia felt like the end of the world.

After two days in Perth, looked after by Mrs Jenkins, they headed sixteen miles inland to Darlington to stay at a guest house run by Mollie Skinner. The countryside was so frighteningly empty of people that it seemed to Frieda to exist in a time before the creation of the earth; Lawrence saw it as a land where unborn souls lived.

Mollie Skinner was the daughter of an English captain in the Royal Irish Regiment who had spent her childhood in Britain; she had written a book, *Letters of a V.A.D.*, about her experience as a nurse in the First World War, and was forty-six when Lawrence met her. Mrs Jenkins had arranged with some excitement for Mollie to have a room ready for a famous author, but Mollie was not overwhelmed by her first impression of Lawrence. She 'hoped the little one with the red beard was not Lawrence . . . It was Frieda who had us at her feet first. She was beautiful, beaming.'[13] As so often, however, once Lawrence began to talk she was completely captivated.

Lawrence admired the freshness of Mollie Skinner's writing. In 1923 she was to become another of the women with whom he collaborated on a book: *The Boy in the Bush*. While he was in Perth Mrs Jenkins introduced him to other local intellectuals, and he was surprised and pleased to find that a few copies of his books, including *The Rainbow*, had reached the Book Lovers' Library in Perth. Nevertheless, the Lawrences sailed for Sydney after two weeks, arriving on 28 May.

Much as they loved their first sight of Sydney's beautiful harbour, the town was too expensive for them. So, the day after their arrival, they took a train with all their trunks south along the Pacific coast until they saw somewhere on the sea that looked attractive. They fixed on Thirroul, about fifty miles from Sydney; it was a mining township, little more than a collection of bungalows with corrugated-iron roofs and unpaved streets. There was no one they knew for thousands of miles around.

Meat was cheap, as was butter and fruit of excellent quality. Frieda rather liked their situation. It brought Lawrence and herself closely together; there were no hangers-on and admirers. She threw herself into the task of setting up home in their rented bungalow. Photographs of 'Wyewurk', as the bungalow had been named by earlier residents, show a surprisingly large and attractive building with a tiled roof, verandahs and large windows looking over the Pacific Ocean. Soon the Lawrences were taking up carpets, scrubbing floors and clearing the waste paper lying in the garden. Lawrence had already begun to dislike much of what he saw in Australia. The healthy extroversion of the people struck him as almost imbecile, and he felt that Australian society – with no aristocracy, no patronage, and little acquaintance with his work – was empty. While Frieda was attracted to the thought of staying in Australia, Lawrence wanted to move on to America.

An almost diary-like account of relations between Lawrence and Frieda in their two and a half months in Thirroul can be found in *Kangaroo*. Frieda, at forty-three, knew it was unlikely she would have children with Lawrence. The children from her first marriage were growing up far away from her, and she felt she had made a great sacrifice in loyally following Lawrence wherever he wanted to go. As she read his new work, she found his obsessions were becoming less sympathetic to her. Why should she accept the necessary subjection of a woman to a man?

Kangaroo is not one of Lawrence's better novels; there are lovely descriptions of bush and beach, but the claims made for his insight into Australian society seem exaggerated. Politically the book is fairly naive: the conflict between fascism and socialism has simply been transplanted from Italy. Lawrence does have important insights, however, into the connections between politics and sexuality.

Richard Lovat Somers and his wife Harriet are befriended by their neighbours Jack and Victoria Callcott. Through Jack, Somers is introduced to a militant organisation of World War veterans, the Diggers, based on respect for authority and discipline, and an opposition to democracy. The figure of the fascist leader 'Kangaroo', Ben Cooley, is implausibly built on the physical presence of Kot as Hebrew prophet and the war hero Sir John Monash as Australian notable. Cooley has a magnetic sexual attraction for Somers, and the activities of the Diggers have a strong homosexual component. It has to be said that the socialist leader, Willie Struthers, also exalts a Whitman-like love between comrades, but Somers finds Struthers repellent. While Kangaroo himself is both benevolently idealistic and kindly, his followers are not. Indeed, Jack Callcott is bitterly anti-Semitic: 'I hate the thought of being bossed by Jew capitalists and bankers,'[14] he remarks. This comment is far more disturbing than earlier instances of Lawrence's prejudice and this seems an appropriate place to consider how Lawrence's own anti-Semitism had developed.

On 16 June 1921, while travelling in Germany, Lawrence had written to Amy Lowell's companion Ada Russell that 'Nobody has any money any more except the profiteers, chiefly Jews.'[15] There were in fact very few affluent Jews in Germany in the Weimar Republic, and Lawrence did not meet them. The few Jews he had already met in England were fellow artists or thinkers. His Jewish publishers had treated him with great kindness, but this did not prevent him referring to William Heinemann as 'his Jewship', writing impudently to Thomas Seltzer, 'Are you a Jew?', and to Robert Mountsier: 'If Seltzer deals decently with me ... then I don't mind if he is a Jew and a little nobody, I will stick to him. I don't really like Jews.'[16] Although Harry Moore would like us to believe that such thoughts linked with fascist ideals have 'nothing in common with the Nazis',[17] they surely make a worrying pattern.

Lawrence was aware of his own prejudice, and was capable of analysing it as a kind of snobbery. In the same letter to Mountsier he observes that, for all that he dislikes Jews,

I like still less the semi-gentleman, successful, commercial publisher, who is always on the safe side: Duckworth, Methuen, Chatto, all that crowd. They, bourgeois, *are my real enemy. Don't be too sniffy of the risky little Jew. He adventures – these other all-right swine, no.*[18]

Observations formed on such a personal basis are clearly impossible to project into future circumstances.

In *Kangaroo*, Lawrence's intelligence, however, was troubled by a recognition of the sources of political excitement. When Kangaroo is shot at a political meeting, Jack Callcott beats out two men's brains, and afterwards makes an analogy between sex and violent aggression: 'There's *nothing* bucks you up sometimes like killing a man – *nothing*

... Having a woman's something, isn't it? But it's a flea bite, nothing, compared to killing your man when your blood comes up.'[19]

Most of the revolutions of this century have been misguided, but if Cooley's revolution had taken hold it would surely have been the most foolish of the lot. Lawrence's impatience with democracy is a hangover from his impatience with wartime England. Even Kangaroo admits to not caring what he stands for: 'I don't care, I tell you. Where there's fire there's change,' while Somers, and Lawrence, are tempted by a wish to cut clear of humanity altogether. One recalls the appalling image in *Women in Love* in which Birkin thinks with pleasure of the planet cleaned of its humanity and reduced to the plants and animals.

However, the novel is an excellent account of Lawrence's continuing battle with Frieda, who was incensed that he had begun to take a certain pride in his ability to live in isolation from society without noticing that it was she who made it possible. Harriet Somers, too, dislikes being given no credit for sustaining her restless husband. Rather like Harriet, Frieda had begun to resent the contrast between her husband's sweetness and gentleness towards everybody they met and the way he treated her.

In fact, Lawrence was in no danger of minimising his dependence on Frieda. He hated the situation. By now, apart from his life with her, he had nothing. If it was disloyal of him to want something else from life, he could not help it, and *Kangaroo* is an attempt to articulate that want. That it connects to his own homosexual longings is clear. In the 'Nightmare' chapter, where Lawrence makes use of his humiliating army medical examinations in Cornwall, he introduces a character based on his young farming friend William Henry Hocking. In naming this character John Thomas Buryan the vernacular meaning of John Thomas (penis) must surely have been in his mind, as it was when he titled a version of *Lady Chatterley's Lover* 'John Thomas and Lady Jane'. Kangaroo's own demand for Somers' love is embarrassing throughout most of the book, although there is considerable poignancy in his plea for it on his deathbed. Somers does not sleep well in Australia: his rest is full of dreams. Perhaps Lawrence too found the continent disturbed his nights. Somers dreams of a woman he loved 'something like Harriet, something like his mother',[20] who was bitter because she felt he had betrayed her great love. In his dream her face has some of the bloated quality of the madwoman who hangs over Jane Eyre in Rochester's house. The dream disturbs Somers deeply. When he wakes, shaking with horror, he repeats as the central insight in the dream: 'They neither of them believed in me.'[21] In a sense, Lawrence's mother had never believed in him. She had always felt that Ernest was the brilliant son, and for all her attachment to him, she never quite put the same faith in Lawrence. Perhaps Lydia simply had not dared show it, but Frieda had always been insistent about Lawrence's genius, most recently in Perth to one of the local literati who had criticised *The White Peacock*.

As ever, Lawrence is pitilessly accurate in *Kangaroo* about the spitefulness of marriage: Harriet is delighted to take the side of anyone who gets across her husband, as if to prove her own case, and when Somers is hurt by the hostility he has aroused, observes: 'You're never happy unless you're upsetting somebody's apple cart.' In Chapter Nine, 'Harriet and Lovat at Sea in Marriage', Lawrence tries to analyse what has gone wrong with the relationship of men and women, and posits three roles for a man: one as lord and master, which he confesses is out of date; another, where the husband is the perfect lover; and a third where he is a friend and companion. Lawrence contends that the current view of marriage demands the second of these alternatives. In a complicated metaphor he suggests that this can only lead to dashing the boat of marriage to pieces when storms come. At this point, the woman can either steer the boat into the vast and peaceful Pacific Ocean of lord-and-masterdom, or choose the dull grey Atlantic of perfect companionship. The craft cannot survive in the Straits of Magellan which lie between those oceans. There is some pathos in Lawrence's suggestion that the 'lord and master is not much more than an upper servant while the flag of perfect love is flying and the sea mother is on board',[22] as if all he wants is the name of captain, and the pleasant job of giving orders. The ship of Harriet and Somers, like Lawrence and Frieda's, had set out in the 'extremest waters of perfect love', and had hit foul weather. Having engaged in that nautical diversion, the text returns to the authentic voices of the daily marital struggle. *Kangaroo* is not a wise book, however intriguing; though there is an element of personal prophecy in Harriet's conclusion: 'I shall have to sail along, poor woman, till I see the end of him.'[23]

Meanwhile, Mabel Dodge Sterne continued to summon the Lawrences to New Mexico, and Lawrence was eager to leave Australia, for all his insistence on his enjoyment of isolation: 'We don't know one single soul – not a soul comes to our house. And I can't tell you how I like it. I could live like that forever and drop writing.'[24] The £50 fare to San Francisco, however, was not easy to find. On 18 July he was writing to Mabel: 'I still haven't got the money from Mountsier [his American agent] so we can't finally engage berths'. The royalty cheque was so delayed he had to borrow money from Arthur Dennis Forrester, an Australian acquaintance. On 11 August, three weeks after Lawrence completed *Kangaroo*, he and Frieda sailed from Sydney for San Francisco, travelling with a crowd of cinema actors and technicians, mainly Australian and French, whose champagne drinking, white faces and immorality Frieda found shocking.

Lawrence, who was so strident now in his opposition to the domineering female, was about to put himself under the protection of yet another powerful woman.

Chapter 16

NEW MEXICO

The Lawrences always travelled courageously; they arrived in San Francisco in September 1922 with less than $20 in their pockets. Fortunately, Mabel Dodge Sterne had telegraphed them their train fares to Lamy in New Mexico, 1200 miles to the east.

Mabel Dodge Sterne was the heiress to a banking fortune. Her first husband, Karl Evans, had been killed in a hunting accident in 1903; her second, the Boston architect Edwin Dodge, had taken her to live in a palazzo near Florence, and there she had set up a salon for artists and writers, and made friends with Gertrude Stein and Bernard Berenson. After her divorce from Dodge in 1912 she lived in New York, where she had a love affair with John Reed, author of the sensational account of the Russian Revolution *Ten Days that Shook the World*. Her circle of friends included Lawrence's patroness Amy Lowell and the dancer Isadora Duncan. When the Lawrences arrived in America her third marriage, to the Russian-Jewish painter Maurice Sterne, had recently ended in divorce, and she was living with Antonio Luhan, a handsome pueblo Indian.

Mabel met Lawrence and Frieda at the station in Lamy, and the two women assessed one another sharply. Frieda registered Mabel's turquoise and silver jewellery with the disdainful eye of a European aristocrat, but decided she had eyes that could be trusted. Mabel saw Frieda's size and vitality, and observed that Lawrence had to run to keep up with her. Lawrence himself struck her as fussy and distraught.

The plan was that Antonio would drive them across the Rocky Mountains to Taos, about 150 miles away. Unfortunately the car broke down not far from Santa Fe. Antonio, who knew little about cars, looked under the bonnet, and Frieda suggested that Lawrence might do something to help. When at last the car started again, Antonio blamed the mechanical failure on the malevolent emanations of a snake. Frieda habitually assessed people in sexual terms, and when she praised Antonio to Mabel that first day as 'a rock to lean on',[1] Lawrence shifted uneasily.

The breakdown meant it was impossible to reach Taos that day, and Mabel arranged for them to spend the night in Santa Fe with her friends the American poet Witter Bynner and his lover Willard 'Spud' Johnson. Bynner was an extremely wealthy man, four years older than Lawrence, who spent most of his life travelling and was now living in Santa Fe with the much younger Johnson. While Antonio was trying to park the car in the narrow courtyard he backed over a Sicilian cart panel which Frieda had sentimentally kept, and Lawrence burst out in rage with her for insisting they bring the thing with them from Taormina. He was tired from the journey and agitated by his new surroundings, and Frieda accepted the blame calmly.

This first meeting with Lawrence made an unfavourable impression on Bynner, to whom Lawrence made a gift of the cracked panel. He quickly decided that all the reports he had heard of Frieda being unworthy of Lawrence were stupidly mistaken, and from this time onwards he saw her as 'warm, wise, earthy womanhood', and thought her a better mate for a genius than the 'lion chasers' who tried to disparage her. His opinion of the belligerent genius himself was much improved next morning when he found that Lawrence had risen early and done all the washing up.

New Mexico delighted Lawrence as they drove north the next day. The beauty of Taos valley is astonishing: the Rocky Mountains tower above the desert plain, and when the sun shines the snow has a blinding purity. The weather can change in an hour from summer heat to lightning, ice and hail. It is no wonder that the Indians regarded the mountains as sacred.

Lawrence was less impressed by Mabel's ranch, although the adobe cottage she had provided for them was very comfortable. Mabel herself was attractive, if not exactly pretty, and about the same age as Frieda. The artist Georgia O'Keeffe described Mabel's 'small, square, determined body, bright grey eyes, and a soft melodious voice'.[2] In a letter to his mother-in-law, Lawrence noted that she 'looked young' and was 'very clever for a female'.[3] She was also exactly the kind of bossy and opinionated woman he frequently condemned.

Mabel was genuinely concerned about the welfare of the local pueblo Indians, although she had scandalised them by taking up with Antonio Luhan when he came to work for her as a carpenter. Her purpose in bringing Lawrence to Taos was to make their plight and their wisdom known to the world. As soon as the Lawrences had settled in, she arranged for Lawrence to go off with Antonio to see the ceremonies of the Apache Indians, while Frieda remained behind to gossip. The two women got on well. Frieda talked a great deal about her life with Lawrence, and Mabel encouraged her, enjoying Frieda's shrewdness about all matters relating to sex. Some of these indiscreet reminiscences found their way into *Lorenzo in Taos*, the memoir Mabel wrote after Lawrence's death. Mabel's main literary work can be found in her *Intimate Memoirs*. In these she explores herself candidly, admitting to an inner emptiness, and an insensate 'grabbing for things all through the years, to try and satisfy an unnameable hunger'.[4] Her narration is often repetitive, but she is observant, candid and sometimes witty. Speaking of her difficulties with John Reed, she remarks: 'We can't seem to live with the men who want to sit at home with us, and the men we want to live with can't sit at home with us.'[5]

There is something very persuasive in her account of Antonio Luhan's inner serenity and the enveloping kindness he brought to her. She claimed that Antonio had taught her how to love by exciting her compassion: 'When I saw Tony was hurt, something happened. I felt, for the first time in my life, another person's pain.'[6] Antonio was far from faithful, but this did not seem to disturb her. She chafed at his habitual silence, however. Mabel needed someone to talk with, and in Lawrence she thought she had found exactly what she wanted.

When Lawrence returned from his visit to the Apaches, Mabel explained her plan that they collaborate on a book about the plight of the Indians. Lawrence agreed, and began to go dutifully to her house every morning to help her write. To Achsah Brewster he reported apprehensively that the only trouble with their present situation was the *padrona*.

There was much to enjoy in Taos. Both Lawrence and Frieda learnt to ride, though Lawrence's horse cantered off with him on his first attempt, to Tony's amusement. By 22 September, Lawrence was writing sourly to Earl Brewster: 'Well, we are in the home of the brave and the land of the free. It's free enough out here, if freedom means that there isn't anything in life except moving *ad lib* on foot, horse, or motor car, across deserts and through canyons.'[7] On 29 September, however, he observed to Catherine Carswell:

> *Taos in its way is rather thrilling. We have got a very pretty adobe house, with furniture made in the village and Mexican and Navajo rugs . . . The pueblo is towards the foot of the mt., 3 miles off: a big, adobe pueblo on each side of the brook . . . Perhaps it is necessary for me to try these places, perhaps it is my destiny to know the world. It only excites the outside of me. The inside it leaves more isolated and stoic than ever.*[8]

Lawrence continued to do a great deal of the housework, though Frieda had learnt how to make cakes in Italy and by now enjoyed doing the washing. In the evenings, which they often spent with Mabel, Lawrence took control of all conversation, though his monologues sometimes ended in an argument with Frieda. Occasionally they played charades.

Lawrence began to collaborate on the writing of Mabel's *Intimate Memoirs* as he had with Helen Corke's 'The Saga of Siegmund'. At one point he sent her a note of the scenes for which he wanted her jottings, on subjects such as:

1. *The meeting with Lawrence*
2. *John [her son by her first marriage] and you in Santa Fe*
3. *How you felt as you drove to Taos*
4. *What you* wanted *here before you came*
5. *First days at Taos*
6. *First sight of Pueblo*
7. *First words with Tony*
8. *Steps in developing intimacy with Tony*
9. *Expulsion of M.*
10. *Fight with Tony's wife*
11. *Moving into your house*

He also appended a note: 'You've got to remember also things you don't want to remember.'[9]

Unsurprisingly, Frieda was infuriated by the growing closeness between Lawrence and Mabel. On one occasion, as they walked back to the Lawrences' cottage, where Frieda was hanging up the laundry, Mabel could see even at a distance how angry she was. She also registered her self-assurance, and for a time made herself scarce.

Mabel's memoir, *Lorenzo in Taos*, is an odd mixture of mysticism and shrewdness. Her perceptions of Frieda are far from hostile. What Frieda liked best, she saw, was to get on with what she wanted to do, while Lawrence wrote in the next room. She did not enjoy that exchange of inner feelings that women like Ottoline Morrell and Mabel, in many ways so different, craved more than any other intimacy, and she was determined Lawrence should not be party to any such exchange.

Nor did Frieda dislike Mabel; in fact, she even confided in her when she felt particularly isolated. One morning she tearfully complained: 'I cannot stand it ... He tears me to pieces. Last night he was so loving and tender with me, and this morning he hates me.'[10] According to Mabel, Frieda's unhappiness led her to consider leaving Lawrence and making a life of her own. Hearing this, Mabel seems to have suddenly begun to wonder if she herself wanted to take on such a difficult man.

Women often felt there was a special empathy between them and Lawrence, and Mabel was no exception. Although she was not interested in him sexually, she persuaded herself she was in love with him, and determined to 'seduce his spirit'. Tony was away a good deal (and indeed enjoyed sexual relations with a great many other women), and Mabel began to press for a closer relationship with Lawrence. She took to dressing pointedly in nothing but a loose housecoat and moccasins. Lawrence was well aware of her intense excitement in his presence. Once, when they were washing up and their fingers touched accidentally, he paused to explain that there was something more important than love, namely fidelity, which suggests some sexual arousal on his part; but otherwise there is little sign that he was drawn physically to Mabel. To reach her study he had to pass through her bedroom, and Mabel noted that he averted his eyes from the unmade bed as he did so.

On the strength of the rapport she felt she had with Lawrence, Mabel convinced herself that Frieda was the wrong woman for him.

She rashly said as much to Frieda, who retorted that she should try what it was like to live with a genius. Frieda did not see Mabel as a sexual challenge, yet letters she wrote after Lawrence's death suggest that she had felt insecure about Lawrence at that time:

Why was I such a fool and couldn't manage the situation, why did I doubt that he loved me? How wrong of me ... And I never denied Lawrence the ultimate freedom to choose another woman he liked better than me. There I was a fool, because when a real man has given his final allegiance to a woman, he has given it, and basta.[11]

Frieda in the New World needed attention as desperately as Lawrence once had. Mabel put her finger on the reason why Frieda never allowed the relationship between them to relax. When things were going smoothly, she was afraid of being ignored, so she gibed and insulted Lawrence until she had his furious attention. For his part, Lawrence abused her for her dirty cigarettes and fat belly, to the alarm of the numerous painters and writers who lived in Taos enjoying Mabel's protection. Frieda and Lawrence could often be seen arm in arm soon after these altercations – a pattern of behaviour which had not changed.

Mabel saw Frieda's manipulative control more clearly than her vulnerability. In her memoirs she admits it made her even more eager to dominate Lawrence herself. Frieda might have dismissed the idea that Mabel would be able to seduce him physically, but she had no intention of surrendering Lawrence's soul, and that was mainly what was in question.

Mabel thought the source of Frieda's power over Lawrence lay in the way he received his impressions of the world through her: Frieda may well have said something like that to her when describing her contribution to some of his books, such as *The Rainbow*. She may also have claimed some pages of *Sons and Lovers* as her own. Both women were extraordinarily open to each other about their feelings despite their rivalry.

While all this turmoil went on about him, Lawrence remained curiously passive. Mabel reports conversations in which he complained about Frieda's failure to understand him, and compared her German cast of mind unfavourably to the Latin. Considering the way he liked to express all his views with extreme vehemence, he may also have spoken, as Mabel claimed, about hating to feel Frieda's hands on him when he was sick. He had no intention of leaving her, however, and when Frieda finally told him how she felt about Mabel, he appeared at the ranch rather shamefacedly the next day to tell Mabel their morning sessions of work would have to come to an end.

After that break, Lawrence began to feel it was Frieda's job to keep Mabel at bay. As he drew away from her, Mabel pursued him with intimate letters, which he showed to Frieda. It was becoming difficult to go on living as dependants in a house provided by Mabel, and Lawrence's rage at the situation mounted. In November he wrote to Mabel not only to say how much he resented the way she was exacerbating the conflicts in his marriage, but to set out his own continuing faith in that marriage. 'I believe that, at its best, the central relation between Frieda and me is the best thing in my life.'[12]

There was some good news, however. As he wrote to Catherine Carswell on 17 December 1922, his books were selling well in America: '*Women in Love* is going now into 15,000. Why do they read me? But anyhow they do read me – which is more than England does.'[13]

In October, on a visit to the Lobo mountains to see Mabel's son John Evans, a sociologist, Lawrence and Frieda found two log cabins on the neighbouring Del Monte Ranch, seventeen miles from Taos, and decided to move there. Writing to Mabel to explain his decision, Lawrence acknowledged her generosity, but could not resist pointing out her failings, which he ascribed to her American background.

He thought that Mabel's wealth enabled her to command whatever she wanted; a power he particularly disliked in a woman. It meant that she could buy sex, which he felt had corrupted Tony Luhan. The arrangement between Tony and Mabel was in fact a very happy one, even though Tony had been excluded from the ceremonies of his tribe after he left his wife. He might have been attracted initially by expensive boots, tailored clothes, and the chance to drive a Cadillac, but he and Mabel shared a genuine affection, despite the fact that they had little to say to one another. Even after Lawrence had left Taos he continued to feel provoked by Mabel, and once exclaimed to Frieda that he could kill her.

In his portrait of Mabel as the wealthy Mrs Witt in 'St Mawr', written in 1925, Lawrence depicts a woman who thinks she can control everyone. Lewis, the groom to whom Mrs Witt proposes marriage, rejects her because he 'couldn't give his body to a woman who did not respect it'. This at first bewilders Mrs Witt, but Lawrence has Lewis spell out what he means by a lack of respect: 'Nothing in the world would make me feel such shame as to have a woman shouting at me or mocking at me, as I see women mocking and despising the men they marry.'[14] Mrs Witt lightly suggests that mockery is something a man must put up with sometimes, but Lewis goes cold and distant, and Lawrence accords him the victory. Lawrence did not on the whole find it difficult to accept help from wealthy patrons, but the combination of financial help with sexual overtures offended him deeply. A close relationship with Mabel would have made him feel he was selling himself, as Lewis had with Mrs Witt.

Mabel figures again as the American heroine of 'The Woman Who Rode Away', also written in 1925, who leaves her materialist husband to discover the savage customs of the Indians, and becomes a willing human sacrifice. The descriptions of the stony valley and the Indian village are exquisite; the sounds and smells of Indian life overwhelmingly convincing. Yet this is one of the most chilling stories Lawrence ever wrote, and one wonders how Mabel could have read it without hating the writer.

The unsophisticated women of the tribe are represented as having the feminine virtues Lawrence wants to see restored, while 'her kind of womanhood, intensely personal and individual, was to be obliterated again, and the great primeval symbols were to tower once more over the fallen individual independence of woman'.[15] The murderous end of the story, with the woman lying naked among near-naked priests, waiting for the sun to sink and a priest to kill her, is among the most barbaric Lawrence ever wrote. Kate Millett makes a convincing case that it is pornographic, with the supernatural maleness of the priests and the simultaneous purity of their lack of sexual feelings. She is struck by the sense in the story of maleness as something inhuman and cruel which has no truck with the female, and the way the sacrifice has nothing to do with sexual activity, which might gratify the woman. Perhaps it was possible for Mabel to tolerate the story because she suspected the true source of Lawrence's animosity was not herself but Frieda. One cannot but speculate that Lawrence had come to dislike female sexual gratification in his own life also, and that the story is a vindication of that dislike.

Isolated together once again in the two cabins they had rented high up in the Rockies on the Del Monte Ranch, Lawrence and Frieda made peace. The thin mountain air was healthy for Lawrence's lungs, but there were a great many chores to be done in the winter months. Lawrence and Frieda occupied one cabin, and luckily two Danish painters, Knud Merrild and Kai Gotsche, whom the Lawrences had met in Taos, were willing to spend the winter of 1922–23 in the other, and they shared the heavy work, which Lawrence was no longer fit enough to do on his own. Frieda was still impractical and usually idle, but for the time being in better mood: the boyish young Danes chopped wood and went to Taos to bring back supplies, and Lawrence in turn taught them to ride and to cook, and commissioned them to design dustjackets for several of his books. On the whole, the artists found it easy enough to get along with the Lawrences: they enjoyed Lawrence's friendship, though they sometimes took Frieda's side in arguments.

For all the relative placidity of Lawrence's life at this time, one incident is recorded in which he showed a savagery which almost brought him to blows with Merrild. Lawrence's Airedale bitch was in heat, and had gone off with another dog, ignoring Lawrence's commands. He attacked the dog with such fury that it ran to the Danes for protection, and Lawrence pursued and kicked it, yelling at it that it was a 'dirty, false bitch'. It was almost as if the dog's behaviour had activated other, more personal memories of betrayal. The incident is recorded in Lawrence's poem 'Bibbles', in which he writes with disgust of the creature who must 'always be a-waggle with love'. Lawrence saw nothing incongruous in belabouring the creature for following its natural sexual instincts.

Then when I dust you with a bit of juniper twig
You run straight away to live with somebody else,
Fawn before them, and love them as if they were the ones you had really
*   loved all along,*
And they're taken in.
They feel quite tender over you, till you play the same trick on them, dirty
*   bitch.*[16]

It seemed that to witness the power of female sexuality, even in a dog, touched Lawrence's raw spot. His puritanism was much in evidence at this time in other ways, too. He showed extreme moral anxiety when a pretty young girl, a friend of the Danes from Taos, hitchhiked up to see them and spent the night in the Danes' cabin.

In February 1923 Lawrence and Frieda received from Murry the news that Katherine Mansfield had died the month before. Lawrence and Katherine had always been close, even when they were most angry with each other. The previous July, when Katherine knew she was dying, she mentioned in a letter to Kot how much she would like to see Lawrence 'in a sunny place and pick violets'.[17] When she read *Aaron's Rod*, she felt 'as if the book was feeding me'.[18] One can see why. Lawrence's desperation for a separate, creative life was close to her own need to be less dependent on Murry's letters and visits during the separations made necessary by her disease. Murry had disappointed her and neglected her so often, yet she had invested him with all the tenderness of an ideal lover; it was as much to escape such dependency as anything that in the last year of her life she entered Gurdjieff's Institute for the Harmonious Development of Man, at Fontainebleau, which taught spiritual insights based on the mystical teaching of the East. While there she had thought of Lawrence a great deal, and had been pleased by his one-word postcard – 'Ricordi!' – from New Zealand, where his ship called on the crossing from Australia to America. She stated in her will that she wanted him to have one of her books, but the bequest was never honoured by Murry.

Katherine's death led Lawrence to mend the quarrel with Murry for the time being. 'Feel a fear where the bond is broken now,' he wrote to him. 'Feel as if old moorings were breaking all. What is going to happen to us all?'[19]

The news of Katherine's death had frightened Lawrence: 'I feel like the Sicilians. They always cry for help from their dead. We shall have to cry to ours: we do cry.'[20]

Chapter 17

OLD MEXICO

In the spring of 1923 Lawrence and Frieda set off to visit Mexico
City, where Witter Bynner and Spud Johnson were also taking a
holiday. They travelled with their usual exuberance, although
Frieda was disappointed in her first sight of the capital: she enjoyed
herself in the poorer markets, trying to pick up bargains among the
stolen goods. Bynner records her beaming with pleasure at every
interesting new sight they discovered. And though Lawrence found
Mexico City alien, it excited him. They took short trips out of the city
to neighbouring towns such as Cuernavaca and Xochimilco; they
visited a ruined monastery, and took a trip on a barge, upon which
Frieda lolled 'like Cleopatra', as Bynner describes her, eating chicken
mole.[1] They visited Diego Rivera, on a scaffold, working on one of
his frescoes. Lawrence thought most of Rivera's paintings ugly, and
insisted that his socialist ideals were not Mexican but imported.

Witter Bynner's declaration that, apart from neurotic females, most
people (including himself) detested Lawrence, makes him an unreliable witness, and his accounts in *Journey with Genius* of his own
cleverness in dealing with Lawrence verbally are often tiresome. But
his sympathy with Frieda (she reminded him of delicious home-made
bread) makes his observations of the Lawrences' relationship at this
time useful.

Bynner had never liked the way Lawrence treated Frieda. His
mother, whose opinion he perhaps overly valued, had commented
during a brief visit to New Mexico on Frieda's unnatural submissiveness; now he saw that whenever Lawrence was restless, he took it
out on his wife. Once, after shouting at her to take a cigarette out of
her mouth, he added: 'There you sit with that thing in your mouth

and your legs open to every man in the room! And then you wonder why no decent woman in England would have anything to do with you.' Frieda, breathing hard, said to Bynner: 'I have to put up with him but I do not answer him.'[2] Lawrence's rudeness in referring to Frieda's failure to find acceptance in circles to which he had gained entry left her uncertain what to do. After such incidents, Spud Johnson simply looked away in embarrassment. Bynner's account of these savage quarrels is reinforced by Frederick Leighton, an acquaintance who supervised the teaching of English in American schools. 'Never before or since have I heard a human being, in educated society, repeatedly release such a flow of obscene vile abuse on his wife (or on anyone) in the presence of comparative strangers as Lawrence did on Frieda.' In fairness, he added, 'Nor, I must admit, have I heard such apparently uninhibited response.'[3]

Something decisive happened to Lawrence and Frieda's relationship in Mexico. It was as if Frieda had begun to realise the damage Lawrence's irritability was inflicting on her. She certainly persuaded Witter Bynner that she could no longer cope when Lawrence attacked her in front of other people, and confided to him, 'If I answer him, it's worse. If I don't answer him, that's bad too but it's the best I can do. So I sit and stare at him like a silly dummy and people think that what he says is true.' With some pathos, she added: 'I can't be so dumb when he quotes me all the time in his books.'[4] She wondered if Lawrence, in his illness, could not bear to see her so healthy. Bynner was convinced that Lawrence resented her greater physical and psychological health. He believed that Lawrence was incapable of having anything but a deep love/hate relationship with women, and suggested that Frieda find ways of compensating herself for his spleen. He thought she should take the initiative and be aggressive first, and records a triumphant example of her doing so when at table with Idella Purnell Stone, who edited a quarterly poetry magazine, *Palms* in Chapala, and her father.

He was passing her a plate of napkin-wrapped tortillas, and cordiality reigned, when, with no relevancy and no warning, she blazed at him, 'Stop it, Lorenzo! You're impossible! I won't have it. You can hold your silly tongue and behave yourself. Had you been born to manners, you might have some! . . . I won't have you making an idiot of yourself with

your nasty tongue and letting Hal's friends see what a poor fish you are.'
There was a dead silence ... Lawrence sat stunned, wordless, while
Frieda stole at me a look of victory.[5]

Lawrence made no reference afterwards to Frieda's onslaught. On
another occasion, however, Idella Stone remembers Lawrence saying
to Frieda, 'Don't be so stupid. I should slap you for that,' and Idella
herself saying, 'Shall I slap him?'[6]

It was in Mexico City that Lawrence saw the bullfight which he
was to use in *The Plumed Serpent* to such brilliant effect. He was badly
affected by the experience. He loathed the brutality of the spectacle
and the amusement of the spectators, and yelled at them in Spanish.
Frieda's equanimity was less affected, and she tried to persuade Lawrence that the bull at least was beautiful, but when Lawrence insisted
on leaving, she went with him. Afterwards he was so disgusted with
Johnson and Bynner for staying that he praised her as a finer spirit.
It was Lawrence who had needed to leave the bullfight, rather than
Frieda: Kate Leslie in *The Plumed Serpent* experiences a fusion of both
their reactions.

In April, Lawrence and Frieda went to Guadalajara, and rented a
house with a patio on Lake Chapala. Here the problems of the society
around them began to impinge. The Mexican revolutions of 1911 and
1920 had brought some social progress, but the unstable regimes and
civil wars that succeeded them had left a society verging on chaos.
Marauding bands were active in the area, and the Lawrences sometimes had to sleep with an armed guard outside their bedroom door.
Nevertheless, Lawrence wrote every morning, while Frieda swam in
the lake. They found Chapala enchantingly beautiful, even though by
21 April 1923 Lawrence was writing to Knud Merrild, one of the
Danish artists who had lived with them on Del Monte Ranch: 'I've
had about enough of this country and continent.'[7] It was there that
Lawrence began to write *The Plumed Serpent*, his novel in praise of
brute masculinity. The novel has had its advocates, and its reputation
grew during the 1970s, with the spread of the drug culture and the
interest in the work of such writers as Carlos Castaneda. Today the
falseness of the book's exoticism seems too obvious, its fantasy too
dangerous.

Bynner and Johnson were living in the nearby Hotel Arzapalo, and the four often ate together. At Chapala they heard that Mabel had married Tony Luhan, which surprised Lawrence, who had seen no signs of the commitment he associated with marriage.

In Mexico the relationship between Lawrence and Frieda was at its worst. One night, after Frieda had gone to bed, Lawrence was fulminating to Bynner against Murry's exploitation of the dead Katherine Mansfield in publishing her letters and journals posthumously. Frieda, woken by the sound of his voice, came in sleepily and took out a box of photographs to show Bynner. This exasperated Lawrence, and when Frieda began looking at some pictures of her children, he was 'out of his chair like a rattlesnake', according to Bynner, and snatched them and tore them across.

Journey with Genius, in which Bynner describes these quarrels, was published in 1953 when Lawrence's reputation was reaching its height, and it was received with suspicion. Nevertheless, for all the bias and the emphasis on such scenes in the book, Bynner is clearly recording a new stage in the long, battling marriage: for the first time, Frieda began to think of leaving Lawrence, not merely as a gesture, but for her very survival.

Frieda had determined to return to London, and Lawrence decided not to go with her. His American royalties had improved their financial situation, which made it possible for them to make separate plans, and they left New Mexico in July with these in mind. Frieda wanted to see her children; Lawrence did not want to go back to Europe, and planned instead to go to Los Angeles where the Danes were then living. There was a loose arrangement that Frieda would rejoin him by October.

From 20 July 1923 the Lawrences spent a month at his American publisher Thomas Seltzer's cottage in New Jersey, and planned to visit the Brewsters, who were living at that time in New Haven, Connecticut. But they were too distracted and angry with one another to do so. Nor did they take up Amy Lowell's invitation to visit her for a few days in Boston.

As he saw Frieda off on the steamer from New York on 18 August, Lawrence was already wondering whether he ought not to have gone to Europe with her; but something inside him made it impossible. Frieda was also in two minds, and asked him to come with her there and then, without any baggage. Lawrence refused. On the quay they had one of the worst quarrels of their lives, and when they parted both were angry, and felt the separation was permanent. After the ship had sailed, Frieda felt calmer, and sent Lawrence a wifely cable, repeating her wish that he should join her in England. He was not willing to do so, though as Catherine Carswell drily puts it, 'no doubt he was glad of the cable'.[8] After seeing Frieda off, Lawrence wrote, 'I ought to have gone to England. I wanted to go. But my inside self wouldn't let me.'[9]

Just how close he came to accepting a final separation from Frieda at this time is clear in a letter he wrote to her that November. Even as he agrees to return to Europe, he makes it clear that he is aware of the gap between them: 'I am glad if you have a good time with your flat and your children. Don't bother about money – when I come we'll make a regular arrangement for you to have money if you wish. I told you the bank was to transfer £100 to you.'[10] The penultimate sentence suggests Lawrence envisaged a new separation of his and Frieda's finances.

Chapter 18

FRIEDA AND MURRY

F rieda had not seen her children for four years. Her son Monty was now at Oxford, and his attitude to her was still reserved. Elsa, too, who was now twenty, was still conscious of her mother having abandoned her. But her younger daughter Barbara, now eighteen, had always been curious about her. In 1989 she suggested that she was closer to Frieda than the others because she had so often been rebuked in her childhood for being just like her. While Lawrence and Frieda were in Sicily, Barbara had written them an enchanting letter from her uncle's vicarage in Great Mapleshead, to which she had been banished from St Paul's School for drawing pictures of nudes and passing them around during Algebra. In 1923 she was studying at the Slade School of Fine Art in London, and Frieda easily established a relationship with her.

Frieda stayed for some time with Kot, with whom she had enjoyed a friendly correspondence after their initial mutual distrust, and then moved on to an old house in Hampstead, where she lived on the floor below Catherine and Donald Carswell. The house belonged to Catherine's brother, who lived on the top floor.

Frieda hinted to Dorothy Brett, who lived nearby, that she and Lawrence might have split up permanently. And Brett noticed that Frieda had a constant visitor: John Middleton Murry. Brett was close to Murry herself at the time, although, as Lawrence was later to gibe at her, Murry did not find her sexually attractive. Lawrence himself had asked Murry to look after Frieda a little, as she would be all alone. Murry, who was living in Brett's house, was still recovering from Katherine's death, and speaking of his grief to anyone who would listen. He had always been attractive to women, and Frieda found him an agreeable and personable companion. She began to enjoy her stay in London.

Meanwhile, Lawrence was making a bad job of living without her. The accounts of his wandering make sad reading: he seems to find no peace. Kai Gotsche, one of the Danish artists from Del Monte, was travelling with him. They watched the total eclipse of the sun with a group of artists in Santa Barbara, California; then they travelled down to Guadalajara together at Lawrence's expense. On 22 October Gotsche recorded: 'Why even before he got out here, he said he didn't like to go to Chapala without Frieda (he is longing for her) . . . As he lives now, he only writes in the morning, and the rest of the day he just hangs around on a bench or drifts over to the market place.' By 25 October Gotsche was writing, 'I am avoiding Lawrence as much as possible at present, because, considering all things, he is really insane as he is now.'[1] They were supposedly looking for a ranch where they might settle, but Gotsche was relieved that they could find nothing suitable. 'It would be too difficult to live with a man like L. in the long run. Frieda is at least an absolute necessity as a quencher.'[2]

Gotsche could see that Lawrence feared Frieda might have gone for good. He could no longer bear to be alone, and wrote to Frieda insisting that she yield to him and return to America. This was looking more and more unlikely: she needed to recapture her sense of herself, which she had lost in the long years of battling with Lawrence. And by now she was more than a little in love with Murry.

Murry returned her feelings, but all his accounts of this period are tinged with evasion: to himself, he justified his involvement with Frieda by her assurance that her relationship with Lawrence was at an end. As he put it long afterward, 'She had had enough of Lawrence in his Mexican moods and, in fact, she had left him. She felt – rightly enough – no more loyalty to him.'[3]

Frieda found Murry enormously attractive, according to Catherine Carswell, because he 'was somebody',[4] and because the *Adelphi*, which he now edited, was an important literary magazine. Murry was convinced of Lawrence's genius, although he had done little enough to promote his work. He wrote urging Lawrence to return to England in spite of his wartime humiliations, and even suggested that he was only running the *Adelphi* as Lawrence's lieutenant. Some part of the attraction he felt for Frieda came from her relation to Lawrence. Murry was in a vulnerable state emotionally. He felt guilty about his selfish treatment of Katherine, who believed he had abandoned her; he was enshrining her memory in his own work, and in the process exploiting her tragic early death, as Aldous Huxley suggested in his portrait of Murry as Denis Burlap, the sententious literary editor who writes articles about his dead wife Susan in *Point Counter Point*.

When Frieda set off to visit her mother in Baden-Baden in September 1923, Murry decided to travel with her. He had an excuse for doing so, since his friend T. S. Eliot's wife Vivien was suffering from a mental disorder, and Murry had promised to consult a specialist in Freiburg about her condition.

Murry and Frieda travelled together as far as Freiburg. It is hard to be certain of the degree of intimacy they established on the journey. Murry admits they fell in love, but claims that they restrained themselves from becoming lovers. Frieda, he said, wanted them to stay on together in Freiburg, and 'I wanted it terribly. The idea of our sleeping together, waking in one another's arms, seemed like heaven on earth … And Lawrence had been horrible to her in Mexico – something really had snapped between them. So I felt free to take Frieda, or thought I did; but when it came to the point, I didn't.'[5]

Even if Murry did reject Frieda's invitation to stay on with her in Freiburg, that does not mean they were not lovers before then. Kot and Catherine Carswell seem to have assumed that they were, and Kot quarrelled with Frieda about her journey with Murry when she returned to England.

Both Frieda and Murry had an eye to a prying posterity and were clever at covering their tracks. In his memoirs, Murry claims he refused to sleep with Frieda out of loyalty to Lawrence. This is possible, although Frieda was very much the stronger character, and Murry had passively allowed himself to be seduced in the past, by Katherine among others. Letters that passed between Murry and Frieda many years later, which suggest a happy intimacy, are inconclusive. Murry wrote on 27 May 1946:

You know I am not trying to flatter you, my dear, when I say that she [his fourth wife Mary Gamble] reminds me of you more than of any other women I have known. Anyway, with her I have come into full possession of a knowledge which you alone came near to teaching me: what I call the knowledge of the innocent Eve.[6]

However, Murry was briefly Frieda's lover in the year after Lawrence's death, and his recollections of 'those moments of blessedness when I lay beside you'[7] could well refer to that time.

In 1951, when Frieda was seventy-two, Murry wrote recalling their journey together in 1923:

You gave me something then that I needed terribly: as it were opened a new world to me. And I sometimes wonder when I think of that journey of ours to Germany together, and we wanted each other so badly, whether I was not a fool in feeling (or rather, thinking) that it would have been disloyal to Lorenzo.[8]

This letter is ambiguous enough; what Frieda gave him may have been no more than the knowledge that he was desired; the refusal he implies could refer to setting up a permanent relationship.

When, in July 1953, Murry read Witter Bynner's book about his travels with Lawrence and Frieda in Mexico, with its evidence of the collapse of their marriage, he regretted once again that he had lacked the courage to accept Frieda's invitation. Had he known how things really were between them, he said, he might have taken the risk. He was then happily married to Mary Gamble, but he felt he had to write to Frieda, partly to tell her of the complete physical fulfilment he was enjoying, and partly to let her know that he and Mary never quarrelled. 'And, in my inmost soul, I believe it would have been the same between me and you, you and me, if I had had the courage in 1923.'[9] One may well speculate as to whether such a peaceful relationship was what Frieda would have wanted, but it was not what she chose when she was offered it again after Lawrence's death. Whether or not they ever consummated their desire for one another, Murry made Frieda feel she was released from the selfless attachment Lawrence had demanded of her in Mexico.

While Frieda's relationship with Murry was developing, Lawrence continued to miss her acutely. From Guadalajara he wrote miserably to his mother-in-law that Frieda did not understand that a man had to be a bit of a hero as well as a husband, and that if 'Frieda finds it such hard work to love me, then she should have a rest from it'.[10] He had decided that he no longer needed love from her, but strength; the strength to fight the world, which is the quality he always defined as maleness.

Lawrence was working on the story about the Australian bush which Mollie Skinner had sent him. He had offered to help her rewrite it, saying the book could then appear under their joint names. She cabled him delightedly to say he should do what he thought fit with the manuscript. Lawrence introduced some of his own recent experiences – for instance, of riding. In his unhappiness, it may have been that bringing Mollie Skinner's scenario to life was as much as he was capable of. The manuscript became *The Boy in the Bush*. Mollie liked the title, but wept when she saw how extensively Lawrence had changed her book. 'You may quarrel a bit with the last two chapters,' Lawrence wrote to her on 3 March 1924. 'But, after all, if a man really has cared, and cares for two women, why should he suddenly shelve either of them? It seems to me more immoral to drop all connection with one of them than to wish to have two.'[11] The book came out to excellent reviews, and Lawrence made sure that Mollie Skinner received royalties from it until his death.

When Frieda returned to London from her German trip, Murry, Koteliansky and other friends insisted she telegram Lawrence to urge him to come to England. She regretted the telegram as soon as it was sent, though whether because she felt she should have gone to join him in Mexico as she afterwards claimed, or whether she wanted to continue to enjoy her freedom, is not entirely clear. Lawrence's coolness incensed her, as she wrote to Kot in December 1923: '*Why* can't he say he will be glad to see me? Always a misery and a pain! It makes me *sick!*'[12]

She was outspoken to Kot about her side of the marital quarrel. 'When you say Lawrence has loved me, I have loved him a thousand times more,'[13] but was still unwilling to concede that the world was right to regard him as the more important figure, even if 'I grant you in the world of men Lawrence *is* and I am *not*.'[14] For his part, Lawrence had faced up to his own helpless dependence upon her, and capitulated. In a postscript to a letter to Mabel Luhan on 8 November 1923, he confessed he had decided to return to England: 'I shall give in once more in the long fight.'[15] He arranged a berth on a boat for England.

At the same time he generously paid for Kai Gotsche to return to Denmark.

Lawrence arrived in England at the beginning of December, and Frieda, Murry and Kot met him at Waterloo station. Murry has described the 'greenish pallor' of Lawrence's face on that occasion. It was not altogether due to his illness: Lawrence already felt he had made a mistake, and wished he had insisted on Frieda returning to Mexico to join him. He saw at once that a new relationship had been established between her and Murry, and may well have guessed from his knowledge of Frieda that it had gone further than the 'chumminess' Catherine Carswell mentions.

Lawrence's story 'The Borderline', written in 1924, suggests there was a sense of strain whenever Murry came to call. The hero, Anstruther, is a red-headed army officer clearly intended to represent Lawrence: his wife is the daughter of a German baron, and after Anstruther's death she marries a man with many of the worst characteristics of Murry. Anstruther returns as a ghost to avenge himself and give his widow more sexual pleasure than she had received from his puny rival. Lawrence believed that what made Murry so attractive to women was that knowing and insinuating sexuality which pleasured the female more than asserting the male – precisely the opposite of what Lawrence wanted to offer.

Almost as soon as Lawrence had unpacked his Indian trophies – including a belt of plaited horse hair, a snow leopard skin and a Mexican vase he gave to Catherine Carswell – his spirits plunged into gloom. He found England ugly. To Witter Bynner he wrote of the 'yellow air', and said he was 'perfectly miserable, as if I was in my tomb'.[16] Murry might have made what he came to call his 'great renunciation', but the signs of the spell he had cast over Frieda were visible to Lawrence.

Even if he had not had so cruel a personal reason for disliking Murry at this time, Lawrence would have been disappointed in him as a literary ally. For all Murry's declarations to Frieda of his undying admiration for Lawrence, his recent public utterances had been extremely hostile. His review of *The Lost Girl* in the *Athenaeum* in 1920 had been entitled 'The Decay of Mr Lawrence', and in August 1921 he had described *Women in Love* as 'sub-human and bestial'. Whatever his intentions in starting the *Adelphi*, there was little sign in the magazine of the influence of Lawrence's ideas. All in all, Lawrence began to long to be back in New Mexico.

Frieda's own emotions were confused, but she put the possibility of leaving Lawrence for Murry out of her mind. Other aspects of her life were improving. Her younger daughter Barbara met Lawrence for the first time and approved of him, though she noticed his fragility and his high-pitched voice with its residual Midlands accent. Secretly she preferred Middleton Murry, who was more like the people she was used to, but she saw something solid and good in Lawrence. At least she now found it easy to forgive her mother for going off with him.

The reconciliation between Lawrence and Frieda was an uneasy one. Dorothy Brett now became hospitable to Lawrence's circle, and on Christmas Day 1923 she gave dinner in her small Queen Anne house in Hampstead to Frieda and Lawrence, Murry, Kot and Gertler. One day in January 1924 when Lawrence and Frieda were sitting in her rooms, Lawrence began to dominate the conversation, as he liked to. Frieda, tired of being reduced to a listener, attacked him, accusing him of wanting to make a god of himself. Lawrence picked up a poker and smashed some cups and saucers, saying, 'Beware, Frieda, if you ever talk to me like that again, it will not be the tea things I smash but your head.' He then gave a little nervous laugh, took Brett's hand and added, 'Frieda should not make me so angry.'[17] The chemistry between Lawrence and Frieda had not been changed by his realisation of his need for her, or by her discovery that she could be happy away from him.

By now, after a rather dismal trip to Paris and another visit to her mother in Baden-Baden, Frieda was almost as depressed as Lawrence by Europe. She had made her point. She had proved to herself that she could force Lawrence back to her; that he could not survive without her. Literary London no longer charmed her; she was restless; she even felt some relish at the thought of returning to Taos. She wrote from Baden-Baden to Mabel on 10 February 1924: 'I want to be in Taos by the end of April – We never saw the spring there and I want to see that – and I don't see why with some good will on all sides we shouldn't live near each other.'[18] At the beginning of March she was ready to go back to America with Lawrence.

Once this was decided, Lawrence's spirits rose, and he arranged a celebration at the Café Royal. They hired an ornate room and invited Brett, Catherine and Donald Carswell, Mary Cannan, Murry, Kot and Mark Gertler to dine there. After toasts to the departing couple, Lawrence ordered port, though it was not a drink that agreed with him, and asked each of his friends in turn whether they would agree to accompany him back to New Mexico so that a community with the old ideals of Rananim could be established. Frieda watched remotely, almost scornfully. Gertler, who had been fairly silent all evening, made a noncommittal reply; Kot and Donald Carswell both agreed to go in principle. Mary Cannan returned a flat, sensible no. Dorothy Brett said she would go, as did Murry. Catherine Carswell had neither the money nor the freedom from domestic responsibilities and said as much.

This bizarre episode has been reported by several of those present, but Murry and Catherine Carswell disagree about the key words spoken. Murry claims that he said: 'I love you, Lorenzo, but I won't promise not to betray you.'[19] Catherine records something rather more incriminating: 'I have betrayed you, old chap, I confess it . . . In the past I *have* betrayed you, but never again. I call you to witness, never again.'[20]

Whether the betrayal Murry had in mind related to Frieda, or his failure over the years to take Lawrence's part as a writer with sufficient force, is not clear. Soon afterwards, Lawrence fell forward without a sound, vomiting and striking his head on the table. It was a sad end to the occasion. Lawrence was ashamed of vomiting in public; he was an abstemious man and had never done such a thing before. In the morning, however, he had recovered a sense of humour.

Over the next few years, Lawrence was to urge Murry to wash away his preoccupations with Jesus and Judas as if they were slime. He disliked being identified with Jesus, and thought of Murry's identification with Judas as 'the brokenhearted lover' who 'was the only one of the disciples who understood Jesus' as pathological.

When Lawrence and Frieda sailed for America on 5 March 1924, the only one of their friends to accompany them was Dorothy Brett.

Chapter 19

ONCE AGAIN IN THE NEW WORLD

They arrived in New York in the middle of a blizzard. Lawrence was not disposed to like the city in any weather, and a supper at the Waldorf Astoria with Thomas Seltzer gave him no pleasure. They took a train west to Santa Fe, from where they crossed the snow-covered Rocky Mountains by stagecoach, and arrived in Taos on 11 March. At first they stayed on Mabel's ranch, where the Lawrences were given a guest house and Brett a studio, and they ate in the main house with Mabel, who was mild-tempered and disposed to be generous. She wanted to give the Lawrences a mountain ranch two miles above Del Monte, and when Frieda saw Lawrence was reluctant to accept such a gift, she accepted it herself, giving Mabel the manuscript of *Sons and Lovers* in exchange. This was a bargain for Mabel, since the neglected ranch was not worth much more than a thousand dollars, while Lawrence's growing reputation meant the manuscript was worth three or four thousand. (Mabel later used the manuscript to pay her psychoanalyst's bill.)

Kiowa, as Lawrence named it, was 160 acres of unfarmed land, covered in pine trees, with a few log cabins. With the help of three Indians and a Mexican carpenter, the Lawrences set about rebuilding three of the cabins: one for themselves; one, with room for little more than a bed, which Brett used, and one which could become a guest cabin for Mabel.

Living so high up in the Rockies delighted Lawrence, for all the harshness of the life. He loved the wilderness in which he now found himself, and the breathtaking view of snowcapped mountains. He bought several horses and a cow, taught Brett to ride, and began to take an interest in the rites and ceremonies of the Navajo Indians, which he witnessed in August on a trip through New Mexico and Arizona with Mabel and Tony Luhan. Lawrence admired the wild red landscape and the animistic Navajo religion which permeated the Indians' lives so intensely.

Frieda loved the ranch, which was the first secure home she had owned since running away from Weekley. Lawrence milked the cow, and Frieda made butter in a little glass churn. They kept chickens, and made their own bread. But Frieda soon began to find Brett an irritant: she was so uncritically devoted to Lawrence that Frieda once offered her half a crown if she would contradict him. The offer was not taken up. For her part, Brett took a sly delight in the continuing marital arguments, in which Lawrence's voice would become shrill and Frieda became violent and rude. For all her impatience with Brett, Frieda occasionally turned to her as an ally. Once, in front of Lawrence, she told her that Lawrence was much stronger than she was, though he did not look it: 'Sometimes I think he is mad; when he is in one of his rages, I am frightened of him.'[1]

Noting this in her memoir written in 1933, Brett suggests that most of the Lawrences' arguments were still about male superiority, but she once overheard Frieda accusing Lawrence of still being drawn to Mabel.

Mabel, in turn, was annoyed by Brett's presence, seeing her as yet another person who stood between her and Lawrence, preventing her from being able to talk to him alone. She thought Brett arrogant and offputtingly English, and made fun of her deafness, her brass ear-trumpet and her liking for girlish diminutives. Brett was no match for the assured Mabel, whom she laconically describes as a woman who was born bored.

Brett pulled her weight in rebuilding the cabins, and worked hard carrying stones: she was happy enough, particularly when she and Lawrence spent whole days riding together, usually in silence, because she was still shy, and Lawrence was conscious of her deafness.

When the cabins were finished, Lawrence began writing again in the mornings, while Frieda lay about and smoked. Brett helped eagerly with all the household chores, chopping wood for Frieda's stove and carrying water from the stream. At the same time, without irony, Lawrence frequently castigated her for her aristocratic background, which meant, he said, that she could know nothing about work, and nothing about life as he had learnt from watching his mother. Lawrence always felt ambiguously about the aristocracy; describing Brett in a letter of 3 June to the painter Frederick Carter, he could not resist mentioning that she was the daughter of Viscount Esher.

On Kiowa Ranch, Brett was very much the Cinderella. When Mabel arranged a trip into the desert for two weeks to witness the Hopi snake dance, Brett was excluded. She did not complain. She and Lawrence spent many hours together; so many indeed that she once overheard Frieda shouting at Lawrence that he was only interested in talking to Brett. Probably it was not Brett's conversation Lawrence valued, but she was extremely useful to him. She was happy to type out everything he was writing, beginning with 'The Woman Who Rode Away'. Frieda came to see her as an even more dangerous rival than Mabel.

Recording this time in her memoir, Brett relished all Frieda's absurdities, particularly when she mouthed 'Lawrentian' views. Once, when cantering along on a large horse, she spoke of the wonder of feeling the great thighs of the animal moving underneath her. To this Lawrence retorted 'Rubbish!'

Lawrence loved both Kiowa Ranch and the landscape in which it was set; he enjoyed the chores of living there, and was particularly adept at making bread. In the evening, he sometimes read aloud to Brett and Frieda from his writing of the day, and especially relished performing a violent passage from 'St Mawr'. Nevertheless, he began to find the demands of three women on his attention oppressive. One of the three cottages on Kiowa Ranch was supposed to be reserved for Mabel and Tony, but she felt that Lawrence was never pleased to see them arriving. He was proprietorial about his land, the only land he had ever owned, and resented it when Tony shot a porcupine there. For all her generosity, Mabel irritated Lawrence, and he once exclaimed to her: 'I can't stand a certain way you walk.'[2]

That Brett and Mabel were passionate rivals for Lawrence is suggested by a strange incident. Brett had often cut Katherine Mansfield's hair, and offered to cut Mabel's when she said that she disliked the local hairdresser. In Brett's version, a sudden movement of Mabel's head led to the scissors biting into something soft: Mabel's ear. In Mabel's version, Brett was panting with excitement as she snipped, and deliberately cut off the tip of Mabel's ear. Mabel claimed that she was so interested by Brett's sadistic impulse that she forgot to be indignant.

Among Mabel's arty protégés at Taos was Clarence Thompson, a university graduate who had spent two years at Harvard and had some claims to be a writer. Tall, blond and arrogant, he was openly homosexual, and was much attracted to Lawrence. On one occasion, according to Mabel, Clarence and Lawrence planned to ride off into the desert together. When Mabel told Frieda this with bated breath, however, Frieda only laughed and was quite confident that if they did, Lawrence would be back inside a week.

Mabel organised a dance in her big studio in May 1924. Lawrence did not much enjoy dancing, but when Brett, who had drunk a great deal of brandy, asked him to dance, he agreed. At this point Mabel's and Brett's accounts of the episode differ wildly, though it is clear that the drunken Brett and Lawrence bumped into many other people on the dance floor, including Mabel and Clarence, and that Frieda and Clarence disappeared together, to everyone's consternation.

What Frieda and Clarence talked about while they were alone is uncertain, but Mabel claimed in her memoirs that Frieda told Clarence that Lawrence intended to kill Mabel. Lawrence, without any evident sign of malice, left Mabel with the manuscript of 'The Woman Who Rode Away' when he, Frieda and Brett set off back to Kiowa the next morning. There were certainly aspects of Mabel's behaviour that Lawrence disliked. In a letter to her of 5 June 1924 he wrote: 'I only wanted to sit still and be still on Saturday evening . . . I wish to heaven you would be quiet, and let the hours slip by.'[3] He hated both the undignified dancing and the atmosphere of license and self-indulgence which surrounded Mabel, and had begun to conceive a murderous hostility for her personality and her way of life; the quarrel did not, however, prevent Lawrence and Frieda travelling with Mabel and Tony to Arizona to see the Hopi snake dances in August.

In September, Lawrence heard that his father had died at the age of seventy-eight. The news filled him with an oppressive sense of his own mortality, and as the weather began to worsen with the approach of autumn, Lawrence wanted to go further south to protect his chest, which was once again becoming raw.

When the Lawrences, accompanied by Brett, set off for Mexico City again in mid-October, they had £303 in their English bank account, and more than $2000 in Chase National Bank. Lawrence's books were beginning to earn substantial royalties in America, and the years of grinding poverty at least were over. But neither Lawrence nor Frieda felt physically well. Brett recorded with some glee that at the Mexican Consulate Frieda was taken for Lawrence's mother because of her girth and size.

On 20 October in Mexico City Lawrence had a brief meeting with Somerset Maugham, whom he regarded thereafter as 'narrow gutted'[4] and disagreeable, mainly because Maugham, who had a terrible stutter, had asked his secretary to deal with Lawrence on the telephone. And there was another débâcle when Lawrence, who was supposed to speak at the PEN club in Mexico City, failed to show any understanding of the fervent patriotism of Mexico in those days.

On 8 November the Lawrences and Brett moved further south, to Oaxaca, which was as primitive as Chapala had been. Lawrence and Frieda lived in the house of Padre Edward Rickards, an English priest, while Brett stayed at the Hotel Francia. Nevertheless, Brett and Lawrence spent more time in each other's company than Frieda would have liked, often riding out into the desert to sketch together.

Frieda still resented Brett, who came to see Lawrence every day as he began to rewrite *The Plumed Serpent*. She saw that Brett had no emotional life other than Lawrence, and one day she flared up at him and insisted that Brett be sent back to the ranch.

Lawrence thought Frieda's jealousy was foolish, and in a letter to Brett Frieda showed that she knew as much herself by stating that the relationship was like that of a spinster with a curate. Nevertheless, Lawrence wrote obediently to Brett on 9 January 1925: 'You, Frieda and I don't make a happy combination now.'[5]

One might speculate as to the kind of friendship Lawrence had been expecting when he asked Brett to cross half the world to throw in her lot with him. Frieda always hated those sexless relationships which were Lawrence's counterpart to her own earlier infidelities, and she was determined to drive off Brett as hurtfully as possible. She wrote: 'Lawrence says he could not possibly be in love with a woman like you – an asparagus stick.'[6]

That Lawrence did indeed prefer shapely women can be made out from Mabel's memoir, in which he is reported as saying that he liked Frieda to dress in clothes waisted as his mother's had been, even if they are out of fashion. Frieda herself had long since passed a fashionable shape of any period, however, as the remarks of the Mexican consular official confirm.

Lawrence told Brett in a letter of 26 January 1925 that he no longer wanted her friendship. Indeed, he had begun to wonder if it was possible to have a friendship with any woman unless she had a vital relationship of her own with someone else. Brett duly accepted her dismissal and departed before the end of January for the Kiowa Ranch.

Two weeks later, writing to her there, Lawrence's tone was harsh. He said that he felt much better now that she had gone, and claimed that her presence had been making him ill, adding: 'Your friendship with Murry was spiritual – you dragged sex in – and he hated you ... between you and me there is no sensual correspondence ... You like the excitement of sex in the eye, sex in the head ... It is an evil and destructive thing.'[7]

Brett must have felt humiliated and rejected. To defend herself against the charges Lawrence had levelled against her, quite as much as to satisfy her sexual impulses, she began a liaison with a married Indian named Trinidad who worked on the ranch. When he learnt of this, Lawrence dismissed Trinidad. This suggests a rather curmudgeonly jealousy, though Lawrence did continue to disapprove of all forms of promiscuity. His version of the episode went into the story 'The Princess', written that year, in which Brett becomes Dollie Urquhart, a repressed aristocratic spinster who rides off into the forests with Romero, a hot-blooded Mexican. Lawrence gives a rather unkind account of Brett's attempt to overcome the feelings of sexual inadequacy that his and Frieda's letters must have engendered in her. After seducing Dollie, who fails to respond, white men kill Romero for sleeping with a white woman.

It was while living in Oaxaca that Lawrence wrote the lovely opening chapter of *Mornings in Mexico*. He also rewrote his second version of *The Plumed Serpent*.

The Plumed Serpent is Lawrence's most desperately written book; he had to force himself to finish it, and was ill once he had done so. It tells the story of Kate Leslie, a forty-year-old widow, who comes to

Mexico to find deliverance and undergoes a profound transformation there. She falls under the spell of the Mexican Indian Cipriano's 'ancient phallic mystery' and of Ramón, 'the living Quetzalcoatl' himself. The novel begins with Kate's revulsion at the blood and violence of the bullfight, but by the time she has gone upriver, the whole world is soaked with blood. The most hideous act of male violence in the book is the ceremonial killing of a gang who attack Ramón. Cipriano himself stabs them to the heart, and then the bodies are taken into the church for ceremonies from which all women are excluded. Crucially, Kate has to learn to regard sex as being for her lover's pleasure, not her own; she must learn to abandon her own desires, and practise passivity and submission. When Cipriano feels she is approaching orgasm, he withdraws from her: 'When in their love, it came back on her, the seething electric female ecstasy, which knows such spasms of delirium, he recoiled from her.'[8] It is impossible to miss the personal element in this fantasy. Lawrence's complaint against Frieda is reaching its last stage: 'By a dark and powerful instinct he drew away from her as soon as this desire rose again in her, for the white ecstasy of frictional satisfaction, the throes of Aphrodite in the foam. She could see that to him it was repulsive.'[9]

Lawrence is describing a repulsion which is surely linked to his own often-repeated reluctance to be made use of to give pleasure to a woman. He invents a situation where the hatred of being used as a woman's servant in this way is legitimised to the point where a man can refuse to continue any sexual act which seems to reward her more than it does him. It is not until *Lady Chatterley's Lover* in 1928 that we reach the fullest analysis of these feelings; here we can observe that in asking his heroine to lie still and forgo her own pleasure the excuse is offered that male gratification connects to a more primitive and wiser world. In *The Plumed Serpent*, the phallic mystery Kate allows herself to become part of is more than a recognition of the need to serve her husband, which Lawrence had insisted on in *Kangaroo*; now she agrees to dispense with her own orgasm in the sexual act. This assertion arose not from Lawrence's greed for masculine power, but from a pathetic need to be bolstered in his own weakness.

There is a certain clarity in the trajectory of Lawrence's thought. He had moved from a resistance to powerful mother figures at the time of *Women in Love* to Lilly's insistence that woman 'must submit,

but deeply, deeply submit . . . A deep unfathomable free submission'
in *Aaron's Rod*.[10] In *Kangaroo* he had looked in vain for maleness in a
man's world. Cossetted and enclosed in Taos, or isolated in a hut in
the wild Rockies, Lawrence knew little of America, but his hatred of
democracy had increased as he observed the vulgar society surround-
ing Mabel Luhan. He had already imagined her ritual murder in 'The
Woman Who Rode Away'. Now in Oaxaca, with Frieda as stubbornly
unsubmissive as ever, he fantasised that Mexico and the Indians could
effect a cure for the ascendancy of modern womanhood.

When he finished the book, Lawrence's stamina appeared to give
out and he fell seriously ill. On 2 February 1925 he went down with
malaria and typhoid; he also had a near fatal tubercular haemorrhage,
which left him gasping for breath with blood gushing from his mouth.
At that time there was no cure for tuberculosis. Even if there had
been, Lawrence would have been reluctant to enter a sanatorium, as
he always refused to admit he had the disease.

But Lawrence knew how ill he was. He told Frieda that he expected
to be buried in a local cemetery. She tried to laugh him out of it,
saying the place was far too ugly, but she was sick with fear. That
night he told her, 'If I die, nothing has mattered but you.'[11]

Frieda had one of the qualities of an excellent nurse: she had no
fear of catching the disease herself. In this emergency she did what
she could to ease Lawrence's pain by putting hot bags of sand against
his painful chest. He survived, but he had been close to death, and he
knew it. In his story 'The Flying Fish', he wrote so vividly of the
parching fevers that racked his body that he could never bring himself
to finish it.

At the end of February, when Lawrence was well enough, they
struggled to Mexico City, where he was put to bed for another three
weeks. He was examined by Dr Sidney Uhlfelder, head of surgery at
the American Hospital, who pronounced in Lawrence's presence: 'Mr
Lawrence has tuberculosis . . . Take him to the ranch; it's his only
chance. He has TB in the third [most severe] degree. A year or two
at most.'[12] They set off for Kiowa but were stopped at the U.S.
border. Because of American fears of tuberculosis, anyone entering the
country had to produce a certificate stating they were free from the
disease. In an attempt to disguise his tubercular appearance Lawrence
had put rouge on his cheeks, but the border officials treated him with

an arrogance that recalled his medical inspections during the war. Only the intervention of the Secretary of the American Embassy in Mexico City persuaded the officials to make an exception in Lawrence's case.

Lawrence was frail and tottery when he arrived back at Kiowa Ranch, but he was happy to be out of Mexico. As so often, he transferred to the place he had been in all the responsibility for the pains he had suffered there. In Taos it was brilliantly sunny, though a log fire was needed to warm the cabin. Lawrence recovered a little, but some things had changed forever. Frieda had no intention of allowing Brett, who was living nearby, back on the ranch, and Lawrence wrote to her that it would be best for them to go their separate ways.

The dream of Rananim was over. As autumn came, the Lawrences decided to return to Europe.

Chapter 20

THE RETURN

With some difficulty, as Seltzer was facing bankruptcy, Lawrence collected $3000 in royalties from his American publisher on his way through New York. He felt sorry for Seltzer, but things were worse for many people: they left New York at midnight on 21 September 1925 for England, where there were a million and a quarter unemployed, receiving a wretched dole.

In October they visited Lawrence's two sisters, staying in Ada's house in Ripley, just outside Derby, but the weather was bleak, and Lawrence did not like returning to the region, though he noted that his sisters' homes were opulent in comparison to those of his childhood. He found Emily was becoming rather stolid: she and her husband had got on badly since he had come back from the war, and Lawrence tried to play the peacemaker between them; but he saw in Ada something of a physical resemblance to himself.

Frieda's younger daughter Barbara, who visited them in Ripley, observed that Ada adored her brother, and had manifestly never forgiven Frieda for taking him away. She also saw how out of place her mother looked in Ada's house. Lawrence treated Barbara with affection, and was characteristically certain that he knew what was best for her. In London earlier that month Barbara had introduced them to the man she intended to marry; Lawrence did not approve of him, because he feared he would not have enough energy for 'the fight that every man knows he has to make against the world'.[1] Lawrence himself had always been willing to take on the whole world for Frieda, and he had ferociously protective instincts. When Lawrence and Frieda asked Barbara to remain overnight in Ripley, she returned shamefaced from a telephone call to the friend of her father's she was staying with and explained that permission had been refused. Lawrence sprang up white as a sheet, protesting furiously against the 'mean, dirty little insults'[2] Frieda had had to endure over the years.

Returning to London ten days later, the Lawrences were invited to literary parties, including one in honour of the novelist Margaret Kennedy, and visited old friends. Lawrence's illness was still very apparent. Yvonne Kapp, a friend of Catherine Carswell, noted his wasted figure and Frieda's bulk, and found the contrast reminiscent of the species who mate by the tiny male fastening on to the back of an enormous female.

Frieda never treated Lawrence like an invalid and, for all her wish to sustain Lawrence by her strength, she continued to let him do the household chores. When they entertained the author William Gerhardie (whom they had met at the party for Margaret Kennedy), he was surprised to find it was Lawrence who cooked and served the meal. For all Lawrence's frailty the general pattern of their relationship had not changed. Even their quarrels continued. Gerhardie observed that Frieda was snubbed by Lawrence when she tried to join in the conversation, and was told she was being too intense. Frieda retorted with spirit, 'If I want to be intense I shall be intense, and you go to hell.'[3]

That autumn Lawrence saw Middleton Murry for the last time. Murry had married Violet le Maistre, an assistant on the *Adelphi*, in the summer of 1924. She was very delicate, and was expecting their second child. The Murrys were living in Dorset, and when the Lawrences declined an invitation to visit them there, Murry came by himself to see them in London. He may have hoped to see Frieda again, but she kept out of the way when the two men met. Lawrence was as cantankerous as ever, and Murry could not help wondering what would have happened to him if he had thrown up his whole life and gone off with Lawrence to New Mexico. Nevertheless, they parted amicably enough. Lawrence suggested that Murry might like to visit them when they had found somewhere to live in Italy, but showed no interest in taking a house near the Murrys in Dorset.

After a brief visit to a now a markedly older Baroness von Richthofen in Baden-Baden, Lawrence and Frieda hurried south towards Italy.

It was his English publisher Martin Secker who had recommended Spotorno, just west of Genoa, to Lawrence, and there they rented the Villa Bernarda, a pink house on a hill, which belonged to the wife of Angelo Ravagli, a lieutenant of the Bersaglieri in Savona.

The first time Ravagli showed them the house was on the Italian Queen's birthday, and he was in dress uniform. He was so smart with his gay plumes and blue sash that Lawrence insisted Frieda come and take a look at him. The sight of Angelo Ravagli in uniform made quite an impression on her, as Lawrence could hardly fail to notice. Ravagli was something of a ladies' man, despite the fact that he was married and had three children. Frieda was twelve years older than Ravagli, and more than a little overweight, but she was still energetic and good-humoured, and had not lost that 'genius for life'[4] which Lawrence had identified so long ago.

On his next visit, to attend to the smoking stove, Ravagli was in workman's overalls. He climbed on the roof to help Lawrence fix the chimney, and Lawrence noted that he would be a very useful man to have on their Kiowa ranch. This was prophetic, for Ravagli was to become Frieda's husband after Lawrence's death, and lived with her on the ranch until her death.

Ravagli began to visit Spotorno every weekend, and took English lessons with Lawrence. On the few occasions they met, Lawrence got on well with Ravagli's wife, who taught Italian and French at a school in Savona. Frieda flirted with Ravagli. He was smaller than her, but well-proportioned and graceful; as an officer, he reminded her of her father. In a letter to Brett, Frieda playfully confessed the attraction she felt: 'We have a nice little Bersaglieri officer to whom the villa belongs. I am thrilled by his cock feathers; he is almost as nice as the feathers!'[5]

Lawrence sensed Frieda's interest in Ravagli, and their conflict continued unabated, as Barbara soon observed when she came to visit in December. Barbara got on well with Lawrence, who taught her Italian, but he could not help trying to enlist her sympathy against her mother. As part of a campaign to make Barbara see his side of things, he attacked Frieda for smoking too many cigarettes, eating too much, or expressing her own muddled versions of his ideas. He also complained, with crafty flattery, that Frieda lacked Barbara's simplicity, and needed to feel she was important, thus echoing Ottoline Morrell's diagnosis made ten years earlier.

Barbara was more exhilarated than shocked by the Lawrences' quarrels, even when she was awakened one morning by loud bumps from their bedroom and found Frieda in tears, and Lawrence sitting glum and pale on the end of the bed. She had inherited her mother's spirit, and was unafraid of taking Lawrence on when she thought him unjust. One evening at dinner, Lawrence turned on Barbara and claimed that her mother did not love her and could not love anybody. 'Look at her false face,'[6] he said, then flung a glass of red wine at her. Barbara was furious, and shouted, 'My mother is too good for you . . . it's like pearls thrown to swine.' After Frieda had fled to her room, Barbara asked Lawrence if he cared for her. Lawrence said, with a malicious expression since he had no respect for Frieda's artistic talent, 'It's indecent to ask . . . Haven't I just helped her with her rotten painting?'[7]

These outbreaks of hostility were fuelled by Lawrence's tubercular fevers; they may also have been exacerbated by his virtual impotence. It is impossible to know with any certainty about the date of the onset of this condition, but Richard Aldington said that Frieda began to complain about it in 1926. Aldington suggested that she might have been doing so to justify her own later infidelity with Angelo Ravagli, but even though he tells the story with some hostility, he was probably reporting Frieda truthfully. It is unlikely that, in his illness, Lawrence would have had the energy he once did, and Frieda continued to be both healthy and passionate.

Into this febrile atmosphere came Frieda's older daughter Elsa, and Lawrence's sister Ada, in February 1926. This precipitated a painful crisis. Responding to Ada's ready affection and sympathy, Lawrence began to complain about Frieda to her. Ada, who had noticed Frieda's interest in Ravagli, felt both maternal and possessive, which meant in practical terms keeping Frieda away from Lawrence. One night when Frieda went to his room, she found it locked against her, and discovered that Ada had the key. Presumably Lawrence had given her permission to keep Frieda out. Frieda, at any rate, assumed as much, and responded to the gesture as if it had been Lawrence's. It was the only time he had really hurt her; or so at least she claimed in her memoir. As a result, she hardened her heart against him, and soon afterwards she began her affair with Ravagli. For the moment she moved with Barbara and Elsa into a hotel, leaving the field to Ada.

Ada went back to England after a fortnight, but Frieda did not return to look after Lawrence. He set off on his own, ill as he was, on an aimless kind of wandering, as bleak as his adventures in California and Mexico in 1923. After a time he decided to visit the Brewsters in Capri. Dorothy Brett was also staying there. Although she saw how unhappy he was, Compton Mackenzie's wife Faith observed that Brett was delighted at the chance of having Lawrence to herself for a time.

Brett showed Lawrence a painting she had done of him as Christ, but it left him weary and bored. Occasionally he reflected that he and Brett were 'the only two left . . . everyone else has gone over to the enemy',[8] but there was no question of her adoration compensating him for the loss of Frieda. They took walks together around Ravello, and Lawrence slept and rested a great deal, but he was obviously very depressed. Frieda was far from asking him to go back to her. One of her letters, which Brett saw sticking out of his pocket, was a 'cruel, hard letter'[9] according to Achsah Brewster, which upset him very much.

Towards the end of her life (she died in her nineties in Taos), Brett claimed that Lawrence came to her hotel room in Ravello one night and got into her bed. Although some things about the account have the ring of truth, notably Brett's admission of 'an overwhelming desire to be adequate',[10] the story could well be an invention. It seems unlikely that Lawrence, who had never found Brett sexually attractive, would have tried to break out of his lifelong fidelity at a time when he was almost certainly impotent even with Frieda. Desperation, however, may lead to strange behaviour, and Lawrence was feeling altogether abandoned and wretched. According to Brett's account nothing much happened: Lawrence got up after a short time, saying it was no good, and left her devastated and bewildered.

Her company had, in any case, begun to pall. When she was summoned to appear at the English Consulate in Naples for the American visa she needed to return to Taos, she offered to stay near at hand rather than go back to New Mexico, but Lawrence showed only boredom at the prospect. At last, in late March, Frieda began to write more mildly, though far from humbly. She and her daughters had gone back to the villa and were extremely happy together, walking under the almond trees or lying in the sun. Sometimes Barbara went off to look for subjects to paint. And Ravagli came to the villa and flirted with both mother and daughters. Lulled by this tranquillity, Frieda relented a little, but she was not amused when Lawrence sent her a drawing of Jonah about to be swallowed by the whale, with the inscription, 'Who is going to swallow whom?'

Lawrence confided to Brett that he did not know what to do. 'I may go back to Frieda soon; she is quieter now, more friendly. I can't tell. Her last letter was so much better.'[11] But when Lawrence wrote announcing his imminent return, Frieda was in two minds about having her idyll come to an end.

Lawrence always maintained that Frieda's daughters were instrumental in bringing about the reconciliation because, after living with Frieda for a few weeks, they had begun to sympathise with him. Unlike Lawrence, though, Elsa and Barbara could handle their mother easily. They encouraged her to make herself look nice when she went to meet him at the station, and over the following weeks Lawrence noted with some gratification that 'her children are very fierce with her, and fall on her tooth and nail. They simply won't stand for her egotism for a minute: she is furious, then becomes almost humble with us all. I think they've taught her a lesson.'[12] Two and a half weeks after their reunion, in April 1926, Lawrence decided to leave the Villa Bernarda (and Angelo Ravagli), and take the girls to Florence on their way home to England. The lease was in any case about to expire on the villa. The Lawrences moved first to Florence, and then to the Villa Mirenda in the Tuscan hills near Scandicci, at the suggestion of Arthur Wilkinson, an eccentric red-bearded socialist whom Lawrence and Frieda had met in Florence. It was the last house Lawrence was to live in in Italy. This was not the end of Frieda's interest in Ravagli, however, and Lawrence knew as much.

Chapter 21

THE VILLA MIRENDA

T he Villa Mirenda was seven miles outside Florence. It had no electricity or running water and little furniture; the linen was coarse and the beds hard, and the cooking had to be done on a charcoal stove. Nevertheless, the Lawrences' apartment's six rooms were large, and were on the top floor. Arthur Wilkinson and his family lived below. From the windows Lawrence and Frieda could see pine forests, olive groves and cypress trees. And the rent was low. The Lawrences took the place for a year, and stayed for two. They still lived economically on about £300 a year. Lawrence had even made a few investments in America, though these were to suffer in the Wall Street crash in 1929.

Lawrence loved the Tuscan landscape, and the human hands that had made it with such care. He made good friends with the families who worked on the farm attached to the Villa Mirenda, particularly Giulia, a sixteen-year-old girl who came in to look after the house, and Pietro, who drove a little pony to Scandicci when Frieda wanted to go there. At Christmas time they delighted the local children by having a huge tree and holding a feast for more than twenty people.

Lawrence did the usual chores, and read, but wrote very little: he believed that forcing himself to finish *The Plumed Serpent* in Mexico had taxed his health, and the book's unfavourable reviews that spring discouraged him from making such an effort again. To a friend he wrote: 'I don't feel much like doing a book of any sort. Why do any more books? There are so many, and such a small demand for what there are.'[1]

He finally put an end to his friendship with Middleton Murry. Murry, who had written to him in January with some unkind comments about his essay 'Reflections on the Death of a Porcupine', wrote in the spring of 1926 for permission to use another essay, 'Blessed are the Powerful' in the *Adelphi* without payment, but as 'the gift of one man to another'. Telling a friend of this, Lawrence added, 'To which I can only say, as one writer to another, I will give you nothing, paid for or unpaid,' and dismissed Murry as 'an incorrigible worm'[2] from now on.

That summer was very hot, and the Lawrences travelled north; partly to avoid the heat, and partly to visit Frieda's mother for her seventy-fifth birthday. This time Lawrence hated Baden-Baden. His mother-in-law's age and infirmity reminded him of his own precarious hold on life, and he raged at the number of old women in the spa town whose wish for life was still so strong. In a later letter he wrote, 'They don't mind who else dies. I know my mother-in-law would secretly gloat, if I died at 43 and she lived on at 78.'[3]

At the end of July, Lawrence paid a two-month visit to England which was to be his last. He and Frieda rented a small flat in Chelsea, to which Frieda invited her son Montague. The long separation from her children had come to an end. Even Monty was now ready to accept Lawrence; he put out a friendly hand as soon as he saw him, and acknowledged later what a profound impression Lawrence had made on him. Lawrence and Frieda visited Catherine Carswell in Hampstead and made a few new acquaintances, including the novelist Louis Untermeyer, whom Lawrence took against, in part because of his competitive style of conversation, but also because he was a Jew. Lawrence's pattern of thought continued to share certain features with fascist ideology, notably his dislike for democracy, his longing for an elite leadership, and his nostalgia for a primitive world of traditional relationships. Some of the letters he exchanged with Rolf Gardiner, an English farmer who pioneered Land Service Camps for Youth (intended to bring young people closer to agriculture, folk dance and folk history), confirm how close he was coming to an idealisation of rural work: 'I will try to come to England and make a place ... where one can begin – and from which hikes, maybe, can branch out ... You are doing the right things, in a skirmishing sort of way. But unless there is a headquarters there will be no continuing.'[4]

At the beginning of October 1926 the Lawrences returned to the

Villa Mirenda. Lawrence was by now far too ill to have any sexual relationship with Frieda, and he must have speculated about whether her involvement with Angelo Ravagli continued. He wrote to his English publisher Martin Secker that he intended to do no more than 'bits of things'. Nevertheless he still had one important book to write: *Lady Chatterley's Lover*.

Just before the end of June 1927 Ravagli sent a telegram to the Lawrences at the Villa Mirenda to say that he would soon be in Florence on duty, and suggesting they meet. The Lawrences agreed to celebrate the reunion at a restaurant in Florence. Lawrence kept his suspicions to himself on that occasion, but soon afterwards Ravagli came to call on them at the Villa Mirenda without notice. This time, Lawrence questioned him closely about the official business he said had brought him to the neighbourhood. Lawrence's mistrust was only dispelled, according to Ravagli, when he produced a letter ordering him to give evidence at a court martial.

It is unlikely Lawrence was much reassured. Ravagli had been promoted to captain, and was as lively and amusing as ever. During his visits Frieda laughed more than she had for some time. Lawrence, whose insights into people were more than commonly penetrating, understood well enough what was happening.

When Frieda's daughter Barbara came to visit them at the Villa Mirenda in 1928, she saw that Lawrence had a new and extraordinary tolerance for Frieda's selfishness. Frieda found nursing Lawrence exhausting, and he seemed to accept that she needed holidays by herself, and had the right to do as she liked when she was away from him. As he said to Barbara, sadly: 'Every heart has a right to its own secrets.' When Barbara went back to Alassio, where she was staying in a pensione, Frieda accompanied her before going off on her own, almost certainly to a rendezvous with Ravagli.

This is the context in which Lawrence completed *Lady Chatterley's Lover*. He sat out under the trees to write it, drawing for his portrait of Lady Constance Chatterley on his tenderest memories of Frieda in their early days together. At the same time he took up painting again with enthusiasm. Aldous Huxley's wife Maria had turned up at the Villa Mirenda with four large canvases, and Lawrence painted directly on to them in oils without making any preliminary sketches.

Lawrence wrote *Lady Chatterley's Lover* in three different versions between October 1926 and March 1928, knowing it was unlikely ever to be accepted for publication by any English or American publisher: after his experience with *The Rainbow*, he had little doubt that a charge of licentiousness would be brought against it. So it was that he decided to bring it out privately. Norman Douglas, he knew, was bringing out his own books with the Florentine bookseller and publisher Pino Orioli in this way, and Lawrence thought he would do the same, as Orioli had no anxiety about being prosecuted. Lawrence was prepared to risk his own money, and hoped to earn back 90 per cent of the proceeds by selling the book to people he knew would be interested. It was not a bad scheme. The first edition of 1000 copies was printed in July 1928. Lawrence not only suggested a list of people who might purchase a copy, he also drafted a business-like letter to acknowledge cheques, and arranged for friends such as Enid Hilton, Koteliansky and Richard Aldington to post copies of the book inside England. The novel, which was to make him more money than any other, did so well that Lawrence needed to bring out a second edition. By this time, however, the contents of the book were known. The American authorities put a stop to its importation, and by February 1929 the English Customs and Excise were confiscating copies and William Joynson-Hicks, the Home Secretary, was speaking against it in the Commons. By writing a book he intended to speak for tenderness between men and women rather than promiscuity, Lawrence found himself regarded as a pornographer.

Lady Chatterley's Lover is in several ways Lawrence's sexual autobiography, for all that it is told through the sensibility of Constance Chatterley (unmistakably based on Frieda), and not only because Mellors, the gamekeeper on the Chatterley estate, resembles Lawrence in being working class, well educated and assured. Sir Clifford Chatterley, too, whose war wound makes it impossible for him to have sexual relations with his wife, is in a situation which reflects Lawrence's own at the time of writing; by 1928 he was too ill to make love to Frieda, and he guessed she was betraying him with Angelo Ravagli. The novel, a better one than is commonly recognised, is an analysis of his own sexual experience.

The book opens with sisters Hilda and Constance Reid, whose frankness and modernity recall Frieda and her sisters; they have their love affairs and take sexual pleasure in them, but from the outset

Lawrence criticises the way they do so. He suggests they already have a habit of 'holding themselves back' so that any lover would climax first, the aim being to 'prolong the connection and achieve her orgasm and crisis while he was merely her tool'.[5] If Frieda had confessed to such actions with her previous lovers, it was clearly not something to which Otto Gross had had any objection, but it does recall Lawrence's unease about female sexual behaviour in his earlier books. In this novel it is a symptom of the modern diseased female sensibility.

The portrait of Connie Chatterley is nevertheless one of the most delightful Lawrence ever drew of a woman. She resembles Frieda in her early days with Lawrence. When Mellors puts his hand on her body lying on the bed it is described as being like a Gloire de Dijon rose, as Frieda's had been long ago in Lawrence's poem.

Clifford Chatterley is not, of course, a portrait of Lawrence; he represents an old and dying class whose impotence is for Lawrence symbolic of all that was wrong with England after the war. Yet he has his own inner world, and if he is 'much too hurt in himself' to be close to anyone, he is still ambitious. Since the war he has turned himself into a writer.

At first Connie helps him as much as she can with this work. 'It was as if all her soul and body and sex had to pass into these stories of his.'[6] As owner of a huge estate, Clifford has no need to earn money, but he craves recognition. Connie wonders a little over his wish 'to be known as a writer, a first class modern writer', but she is proud to be part of the enterprise. As she puts it to herself, 'Clifford and I together we make twelve hundred a year out of writing ... Wring it out of the thin air!', a feeling which Frieda experienced at Lawrence's side. And perhaps, like Connie, Frieda too saw literary ambition as 'display'. For Frieda had never been seduced by the 'bitch goddess of success' as Lawrence calls it, though she was to enjoy the reflection of it well enough after his death.

When the writer Michaelis comes to stay, Clifford is impressed by his literary success. Michaelis's characterisation is the weakest in the book. He is supposed to be Irish, though neither his name nor his behaviour suggests it. The Armenian novelist Dikran Koujoumdjian (Michael Arlen), whom Lawrence knew, has been suggested, not very convincingly, as a model. Michaelis bears more resemblance to Middleton Murry in his cleverness, his childlike quality and the sadness which prompts compassion in women. Lawrence may also have believed that Murry was often used sexually, as Michaelis is. But that would not explain the European name. It seems likely Lawrence was also thinking of Ravagli.

What Michaelis objects to in Connie's sexual behaviour sounds like the voice of resentful figures such as Aaron Sisson in Lawrence's earlier novels: 'You couldn't go off at the same time as a man, could you? You'd have to bring yourself off! You'd have to run the show.'[7] This also recalls Compton Mackenzie's reported conversation with Lawrence about his anxiety over simultaneous orgasm. For her part, Connie is innocently astonished that her lover does not want her to have her own satisfaction.

In imagining how a woman of health and vitality relates to her impotent husband as he taps away at a typewriter, Lawrence can hardly have failed to have Frieda's relation to himself in mind. Clifford Chatterley believed in marital fidelity rather as Lawrence did, but he no longer thought sex was crucial. Lawrence too felt that he and Frieda were still bound together, even though their sexual life was over, and might have thought, as Clifford does: 'What does it matter? It's the life-long companionship that matters ... We have the habit.'[8] Lawrence himself was a much sicker man than Clifford, however. He has Connie observe that when Clifford is not working, his constant talking to her is a burden, and she prefers to be alone. This is reminiscent of Mabel Dodge Luhan's observation in New Mexico that Frieda liked life best when Lawrence was working in another room and she could get on with her own things.

Lawrence, of course, still thought sex was important, and it is in Mellors' relation to Connie that we have his most mature thoughts on the matter. To a large extent, he makes Mellors' history his own. Mellors is an impressive figure. In the final version of the book he has a good education, only falling into broad Derbyshire when he chooses to do so, and has been a lieutenant in the army. He is touched with desire mixed with tenderness for Connie when he sees her crying. When they first make love, all the activity and excitement is his; she does not even strive for an orgasm of her own. He is kind and gentle with her and it is rather a surprise to find that, like earlier Lawrence heroes such as Paul Morel, he hates being kissed on the mouth.

When Mellors describes the women in his past, we can recognise Jessie Chambers and Helen Corke easily enough. We can also recognise Lawrence himself, who wanted 'a woman who wanted it'. His savage account of the marriage to Bertha Coutts is another matter. Mellors behaves to Bertha rather as Lawrence did to Frieda at first, taking her breakfast in bed and happy to find her so interested in sex. But then, 'She got so she'd never have me when I wanted her, never ... And when I had her, she'd never come off when I did. Never.'[9] Once again, rather as Michaelis complains, a woman begins to 'wriggle and shout' until she manages to reach orgasm. As Mellors puts it, 'She sort of got harder and harder to bring off, and she'd sort of tear at me down there, as if it was a beak tearing at me ... I told her about it, I told her how I hated it.'[10] Bertha Coutts couldn't lie still and let Mellors 'work the business'.[11] She could only feel sensation in her clitoris, 'the top of her beak, the very outside top tip that rubbed and tore'. When Lawrence's critical esteem was at its height, this account was thought to contrast morally with Mellors' experience with Connie; by implication, readers might imagine Frieda as Lawrence's ideal sexual partner. But these problems are so closely related to those described in *Aaron's Rod* that one can only assume they derive from Lawrence's own experience with Frieda.

In Connie, Mellors is glad to find a woman who can have an orgasm, as he puts it, 'naturally'. This does not prevent him from taking her in sodomy, thus using her for his own sexual pleasure, despite his fulminations against the 'lesbian' passions of women who need stimulation of the clitoris. Lawrence either does not know, or ignores, the fact that the clitoris is as decisively the centre for female pleasure as the penis of which it is the counterpart. His persistent denunciation of the need for clitoral stimulation is, to say the least, puzzling.

Nor is it clear why he had become tolerant of sodomy. When Sir Clifford's helper Mrs Bolton describes Bertha Coutts' return to Mellors, she claims that Bertha recounts the 'filthy things' Mellors did to her when they were married. It seems likely that these included sodomy – Connie certainly thinks so. Even Sir Clifford feels that 'If a man likes to use his wife, as Benvenuto Cellini says "in the Italian fashion", well, that is a matter of taste.' Lawrence clearly did not extend the same tolerance to the female need for clitoral stimulation.

'Tenderness' was an early title of the novel, and Lawrence was much preoccupied both by what this could mean, and what it should not. Mrs Bolton, who becomes half mistress, half foster-mother to Sir Clifford, fondly remembers her dead husband: 'The touch of him. I've never got over it to this day, and I never shall. And if there's a heaven above he'll be there, and will lie up against me so I can sleep.'[12] This is a moving description of the tenderness between men and women Lawrence had in mind. Connie too wishes to be held with tenderness, and through it has the first orgasm she has not had to work to produce in herself. At the same time, Lawrence's own frailty made him fear becoming like Sir Clifford in his illness, a child to Mrs Bolton, kissed all over 'as a mother kisses a child'.

Chapter 22

LAST THINGS

One afternoon in early July 1927 Lawrence had another serious haemorrhage. He had been gathering peaches in the garden of the Villa Mirenda and came inside to rest. Suddenly Frieda heard him calling to her in a strange, gurgling voice. When she ran in to him, he was lying on his bed. As she wrote: 'He looked at me with shocked eyes while a slow stream of blood came from his mouth ... Be quiet, be still, I said. I held his head, but slowly and terribly the blood flowed from his mouth.'[1] All she could do was hold him and try to keep him still until a doctor came. The doctor could do nothing more than give him a coagulant and a little reassurance. After this terrifying episode Frieda nursed Lawrence day and night for six weeks.

In August, when Lawrence had recovered a little, they decided to leave the Italian heat for the mountains. Frieda's sister Johanna was on holiday in Irschenhausen in Bavaria, and Lawrence and Frieda found 'a Grimms' fairy-tale wooden house', as Barbara described it, in Villach, about six miles away. Lawrence rested as well as he could. No medicine could save him, and in the opinion of Dr Hans Carossa, a Bavarian poet who was also a doctor: 'An average man with those lungs would have died long ago. But with a real artist no prognosis is ever sure. There are other forces involved.'[2]

Johanna (now Frau Krug) was staying on the edge of Ossiachersee, and Frieda enjoyed going to swim there. Lawrence didn't mind being left alone while she did so. Ill as he was, he didn't need constant nursing. The Lawrences spent January and February 1928 with Earl and Achsah Brewster in Switzerland; first at St Nizier near Diablerets, which they had chosen since it was where the Huxleys were staying.

Aldous Huxley had first met Lawrence in Ottoline Morrell's circle at Garsington in 1915, and was then inclined to mock his tirades. Nevertheless, he was drawn to him, and he and his wife Maria visited the Lawrences often after 1926. The thin air of the Alps was beneficial for the tubercular, but Lawrence was by now too ill for it to be of any help. He had difficulty breathing, and coughed so badly at night that the owner of the hotel in which they were staying asked them to leave. The Brewsters and Frieda tried to conceal the reason from Lawrence, but they had to move on.

Lawrence's sister Emily and her daughter Margaret came to visit him at Gsteig in Switzerland in August. It was a gloomy experience for Lawrence, who reflected in a letter to Enid Hilton, the daughter of his old Eastwood friend Willie Hopkin: 'I am really not "our Bert". Come to that, I never was.'[3] Emily was from a past that no longer had much resonance for him. Some parts of it remained vivid, however, and in the same letter he speculated: 'Wonder what Alice Dax thought of our Lady C.' She would certainly have had a chance to read it, since Enid had hidden several copies of the novel in her long knickers and so smuggled them into England after a visit to Italy; thereafter she helped Lawrence with English distribution.

Lawrence, Frieda and the Brewsters went from Gsteig to Baden-Baden, where they strolled around the pretty streets and took the waters. Lawrence had taken against the Villa Mirenda since his haemorrhage there, and they decided to give it up.

Meanwhile, Lawrence made peace with an old friend. He had heard that Lady Ottoline Morrell was seriously ill, and in May 1928 he wrote to her in the hope of a reconciliation. It was twelve years since she had broken with him over her portrayal in *Women in Love*.

Cheered by her friendly reply, he wrote again. He admitted gently that the portrait of Hermione, which she had found so hurtful, was not altogether like her, and more importantly, that she 'has moved men's imaginations, deeply, and that's possibly the most a woman can do'.[4] Lawrence's acknowledgement of Ottoline's generosity, her uniqueness and her role in his imaginative life healed the rift between them. Reflecting on his own situation, he ascribed his illness to his inability to be tough or selfish enough for his own good. He knew he was neither tough nor selfish with Frieda.

Frieda and he were on the move again. Lawrence at first stayed in

Strasbourg with the Brewsters, while Frieda went to Italy to move their possessions out of the Villa Mirenda, then he travelled to Port-Cros, a French island just off the coast from Toulon, to stay with Richard Aldington. The conditions there were rough, though not uncomfortable, and he spent most of his days in a bed or a deck-chair, waiting for Frieda to join him. But Frieda's trip took longer than expected. She had used the opportunity of returning to Italy to renew her affair with Angelo Ravagli, who was now stationed in Trieste.

Aldington reports that Frieda returned from this trip with a heavy cold, which immediately infected Lawrence. Thereafter Lawrence, who either knew or guessed the reason for Frieda's delay, referred with heavy irony to her 'Italian cold'.[5] As Aldington wrote of Lawrence at Port-Cros: 'How utterly lonely he was, how utterly he depended on Frieda, how insanely jealous of her he had become.'[6]

One might question whether Lawrence's jealousy was 'insane'. He seems to have been exceptionally permissive to Frieda at this period. In one sense he had little choice: he was too ill to force a quarrel upon her, and he understood Frieda too well to expect her to live only as his dedicated nurse. He accepted her behaviour, even though he always disliked promiscuity. Lawrence hated Aldington's sexual behaviour and his casting off Dorothy Yorke for Brigit Patmore while Lawrence was under the same roof at Port-Cros.

The stay at Port-Cros was a bleak time. Lawrence argued with Aldington about the first part of *Death of a Hero*, the war novel Aldington was writing, which Lawrence disliked intensely; also about his own portrait as Mark Rampion in Huxley's novel *Point Counter Point*, of which Lawrence wrote to William Gerhardie on 14 November, just before leaving Port-Cros: 'I refuse to be Rampioned. Aldous' admiration for me is only skin deep.'[7] And he also had to read the worst of the attacks on the privately printed *Lady Chatterley* in Horatio Bottomley's reactionary magazine *John Bull*, headlined 'A Landmark in Evil'. The common reaction to the novel, as Lawrence put it, was 'superior disapproval, or slightly mingy, narrow gutted condescension'.[8] The Lawrences left Port-Cros for Bandol in the south of France in November, staying at the Hôtel Beau Rivage, where Katherine Mansfield had once lived, until March 1929. That winter Lawrence was often too weary to talk, but he continued nevertheless, with exemplary courage, to prepare for death: to furnish his 'ship of death', as he put it, using an image he had drawn from his exploration of Etruscan life in his walks about the central Italian towns of Tarquinia and Volterra with Earl Brewster in April 1927.

In approaching death, he set out his quintessential response to the world. He was writing the poems that would be collected in *Pansies*, and liked to look at the sea and be quiet and happy. 'It is lovely to be alone,' he wrote to Ottoline Morrell, 'especially when the sun shines.'[9] Visitors often distressed him. His sister Ada came in February 1929. She was now more than forty, and depressed Lawrence with a sense of all the Midlands life behind her, and something in her which he recognised as 'the result of having been too "pure", and unphysical, unsensual'.[10]

Lawrence was by now so ill that he could hardly remember not having a sore chest or a cough. Nevertheless, when they left Bandol, the Lawrences went separate ways – Lawrence to Paris, and Frieda to visit her mother in Baden-Baden.

Lawrence wanted to arrange for a Paris publication of *Lady Chatterley*. He hoped to interest Sylvia Beach, who in 1922 had published James Joyce's *Ulysses*, but failed to do so, perhaps precisely because she had already published a banned book. Nevertheless, he was able to arrange a new popular edition with the American Edward Titus, and this came out the month after he left Paris. For part of March Lawrence stayed at the Hôtel de Versailles, but he spent just over a week at the Huxleys' at Suresnes, to the west of Paris. Mark Gertler, who was also visiting the Huxleys then, remarks that Frieda was hardly pinned to his side after she arrived from Baden-Baden. He was aghast at the state of Lawrence's health, and reported that in Frieda's absence they managed to get him to a doctor. Frieda generally abetted Lawrence's reluctance to put himself in medical hands.

Aldous Huxley, who had no illusions about Frieda's fidelity, understood the situation well: 'Lawrence was, in some strange way, dependent on her presence, physically dependent, as one is dependent on the liver in one's belly, or one's spinal marrow. I have seen him on two occasions rise from what I thought was his death bed, when Frieda, who had been away, came back from a short absence.'[11]

After Frieda's return this time, she and Lawrence went to visit the wealthy playboy Harry Crosby and his wife Caresse, at the Moulin de Soleil, their house just outside Paris. Lawrence's story 'Sun' had been published by Harry Crosby's Black Sun Press in 1928. 'Sun' is a prefiguring of *Lady Chatterley's Lover*. Maurice, the husband in the story, is exhausted by earning money for his narcissistic wife Juliet. While walking through the fields completely naked, Juliet sees a peasant who is aroused by her, and wonders whether to meet him for an hour and bear his child. In the unexpurgated version, which Crosby published, Juliet chooses instead to submit to the 'little frantic penis' of her husband.

One day, while Lawrence sat with his collar up and a shawl tucked round his knees, Frieda played gramophone record after gramophone record. Eventually he could stand it no more, and broke one over her head. Caresse Crosby recalled the incident in her autobiography *The Passionate Years*, and observed that Frieda particularly loved Bessie Smith singing 'Empty Bed Blues'.

Harry Crosby tried to arrange for Lawrence to meet James Joyce, but Joyce made an excuse to avoid the encounter. His reaction to *Lady Chatterley* had not been favourable, and he expressed astonishment that lyrical passages should be used to make propaganda for 'something which, outside DHL's country at any rate, makes all the propaganda for itself'.[12] Lawrence had been even more uncharitable in private about *Ulysses*, which he insisted to Brett and Frieda in New Mexico was a dirty book. Joyce and Lawrence were two of the greatest living writers in the English language, but one cannot imagine they would have got on together.

Yet again, the Lawrences planned to move south. Lawrence had wanted to explore Spain for some time, but Frieda was not attracted to the country; they decided on Majorca, leaving Paris on 7 April. Once they reached the island, where they stayed in a small hotel, Lawrence took against it: though he found the landscape resembled Sicily, he disliked the dead, staring eyes of the peasants. When a woman looked at him with what he thought was sexual invitation, he was conscious of his lack of response. Frieda, for her part, had her bottom pinched on the tram.

While they were on Majorca, Lawrence received a letter from Murry. He had heard rumours that Lawrence was dying, and offered to come and visit him. Lawrence rejected the offer brusquely, saying: 'The me that you say you love is not me, but an idol of your own imagination,'[13] and claiming that there was an instinctive repugnance between their two kinds of animal.

In one of the poems in 'More Pansies', gathered together by Aldington and published as *Last Poems* after Lawrence's death, Lawrence wrote:

> *A man wrote to me: We missed it, you and I.*
> *We were meant to mean a great deal to one another;*
> *but we missed it.*
> *And I could only reply:*
> *A miss is as good as a mile,*
> *mister.*[14]

On Majorca, Frieda broke her ankle after bathing. She had looked ashore and seen an officer on horseback, resplendent in his uniform, staring at her. Becoming nervous of his intent gaze, she scrabbled over the rocks and twisted her foot in a hole. The pain was agonising. The officer gallantly put his horse at her disposal, but Lawrence sensibly preferred for her to be taken to the hospital by car.

Their weeks in Majorca were peaceful, even sleepy, but Lawrence suffered another attack of malaria, which discouraged them from renting a house on the island.

Although Frieda's broken ankle was still giving her great pain, she was well enough to travel to London for an exhibition of twenty-five of Lawrence's paintings which opened on 14 June at the gallery of Dorothy Warren, a niece of Ottoline Morrell. Lawrence had first met Dorothy at Garsington in November 1915. Now she ran an important gallery which had given Henry Moore his first one-man show in 1928. Lawrence was initially a little suspicious of her intentions, but she had both energy and courage. To coincide with the exhibition, the Mandrake Press, whose founder P. R. Stephenson co-edited the mildly pornographic London magazine *Aphrodite*, brought out a privately printed edition of *The Paintings of D. H. Lawrence*, for which Lawrence wrote an introduction. Lawrence had found painting an enjoyable change from writing *Lady Chatterley*, and he had always had a talent for it (his schoolfriend Mabel Collishaw thought him more talented as a painter than as a writer). Nevertheless, his paintings are not overwhelmingly impressive. Many of the women look like idealised versions of Frieda, many of the men bear a resemblance to Lawrence, and great prominence is given to sexual organs. Lawrence told Earl Brewster: 'I put a phallus, a lingam as you call it, in each one of my pictures somewhere . . . I do this out of positive belief that the phallus is a great sacred image: it represents a deep, deep life which has been denied us, and still is denied.'[15]

The paintings are fairly primitive in technique. Lawrence took a lively interest in the paintings of Cézanne, about whom he was to write excellently in his 'Introduction to These Paintings' in the catalogue to the Warren Gallery exhibition, yet there is no trace of his influence, or that of any other modern painter, in Lawrence's work. He seems to have been affected chiefly by the Etruscan tomb paintings he had seen when touring around Italy with Earl Brewster. Like *Lady Chatterley's Lover*, with which his painting was exactly contemporary, Lawrence's paintings portray a pastoral world made tender by the memories of the love he had once known with Frieda. Both the book and the paintings were created at a time when this kind of love was altogether denied to him, and his conscious aim was to make people see the beauty of what they had been taught to regard as obscene.

Inevitably, given the notoriety Lawrence had recently attracted over *Lady Chatterley*, the supposed indecency of the paintings aroused hostile reviews. A private complaint by the publisher Grant Richards was made on 27 June in a letter to the superintendent of Bow Street police station, and on 3 July the *Evening Standard* insisted the issue be tackled.

Nevertheless, in some respects the exhibition was a success. In three weeks, more than 13,000 spectators came to see it, most of them no doubt attracted by the salacious reputation Lawrence now enjoyed. The police, too, had been alerted to the 'obscenity' of the work by the reviews. On 5 July, after delicately waiting for the Aga Khan to view the exhibition, police entered the gallery and confiscated thirteen of the paintings.

Dorothy Warren wanted to fight the case, and Augustus John and others were willing to testify that the paintings had artistic merit, but Lawrence simply wanted to rescue his work. He had vivid memories of the burning of the remaining copies of *The Rainbow* in 1915, and wrote to Dorothy Warren: 'I think it's a mistake to want to go to High Court. What to do? prove the pictures are not obscene? but they are not, so how to prove it? ... No, no, I want you to accept the compromise. I do not want my pictures to be burned, under any circumstances and for any cause.'[16] The paintings were later shipped to Taos where, after Frieda's death in 1956, Angelo Ravagli was to sell them to Saki Karavas, the owner of the Hotel La Fonda in the town square.

In early July Lawrence, in a bitter mood, visited the Huxleys in their small house at Forte dei Marmi on the Italian coast. He was too ill to bathe in the sea, and could only wander about, according to Huxley, very tired and breathing with difficulty. Huxley could not persuade him to consult a doctor. Instead, Lawrence set off to visit *Lady Chatterley*'s publisher Pino Orioli in Florence, and while there he had another serious haemorrhage.

Orioli, panic-stricken to see Lawrence looking close to death, called a doctor and telegraphed to Frieda, but Lawrence wasn't finished yet. When Orioli asked him what Frieda would say when she found him in such a condition, Lawrence pointed to a bowl of peaches and said wryly, 'Do you see those peaches in the bowl? She will say "what lovely peaches", and she will devour them.'[17]

When Frieda did arrive from London on 13 July she behaved much as Lawrence had predicted. She was at her most exuberant, full of her anger with the police over Lawrence's paintings. She had received all the honours of a celebrity in Lawrence's stead, being treated 'like the Queen of Sheba'. The Aga Khan had given a dinner for her, and suggested the pictures might be exhibited in Paris.

Notwithstanding Frieda's evident ability to enjoy life in his absence, Lawrence made a surprising recovery. They could still relate tenderly, though in a letter to Ottoline Lawrence remarked rather wistfully: 'Old people can have a lovely quiescent sort of sex, like apples, leaving the young quite free for their sort.'[18] Lawrence was only forty-three, but he knew he was coming to the end of his strength.

Frieda was a long way from being satisfied with any such quiescence, but the very evidence of her continuing vitality helped to keep Lawrence going. As Richard Aldington reflected later, only a woman such as Frieda, 'with her health, strength, good looks, vitality and self confidence', could have endured the life they had together. Lawrence had not the least desire to have Frieda founder with him. He would have regarded her grieving and withering at his bedside as a kind of suicide. When, nine months after meeting Lawrence, Harry Crosby killed himself and his mistress in a New York apartment, Lawrence was appalled: 'That's all he could do with life, throw it away. How could he betray the great privilege of life?'[19]

It is hard to know how Lawrence bore his last years so finely. His letters are persistently cheerful; not optimistic, perhaps, but betraying little pain at the prospect of confronting death. 'It will be poetry,' Lawrence had said long ago to Jessie Chambers, and perhaps he was right. It is in the poems that we hear his innermost thoughts as he contemplates the world around him, knowing he must die, and that Frieda already has a life without him. 'Be careful then, and be gentle about death/ For it is hard to die,'[20] he counsels mournfully in 'All Souls' Day'. He consoles himself with an intense perception of beauty:

> *Not every man has gentians in his house*
> *in soft September, at slow sad Michaelmas.*[21]

He turns to the intense blueness of 'Bavarian Gentians' as an epiphany, imagining their dark brilliance as a torch with which he can enter the blackness about to enfold him. The phenomenal world gave him a sense of such lyric beauty that in 'Pax' he was able to write:

> *All that matters is to be at one with the living God,*
> *to be a creature in the house of the God of Life.*

> *Like a cat asleep on a chair*
> *at peace, in peace*
> *and at one with the master of the house, with the mistress*
> *at home, at home in the house of the living,*
> *sleeping on the hearth, and yawning before the fire.*[22]

These are religious, but not Christian poems: Lawrence did not return to the consolations of Christianity. He opposed the antisensual nature of Christianity even at the end of his life in the story 'The Man Who Died'. In a letter to Earl Brewster he gives a slangy account of it:

> *I wrote a story of the Resurrection, where Jesus gets up and feels very*
> *sick about everything, and can't stand the old crowd any more — so cuts*

out – and as he heals up, he begins to find what an astonishing place
the phenomenal world is, far more marvellous than any salvation or
heaven – and thanks his stars that he needn't have a mission any more.[23]

To believing Christians, the story would obviously be blasphemous. Jesus, whom Lawrence calls 'the man', wakes from the tomb and regrets his sacrificial mission. In the course of the story, particularly through a sexual experience with a priestess of Isis, he renounces his own teaching and becomes a man of the flesh rather than the spirit. The story makes it abundantly clear that Lawrence did not approach his death with the hope of another world.

The poem 'The Ship of Death' is much more than an act of mourning for Lawrence's own extinction. It opens in autumn 1929, when 'death is on the air like a smell of ashes', and portrays death as a journey from physical life towards spiritual peace:

> *Build then the ship of death, for you must take*
> *the longest journey, to oblivion*
> *And die the death, the long and painful death*
> *that lies between the old self and the new.*
>
> *Already our bodies are fallen, bruised, badly bruised*
> *already our souls are oozing through the exit*
> *of the cruel bruise.*
>
> *Already the dark and endless ocean of the end*
> *is washing in through the breaches of our wounds*
> *already the flood is upon us.*
>
> *Oh build your ship of death, your little ark*
> *and furnish it with food, with little cakes, and wine*
> *for the dark flight down oblivion.*[24]

In Baden-Baden, where the Lawrences repaired on 16 July, Lawrence corrected the proofs of *The First Lady Chatterley*, which was mild enough for Secker in Britain and Knopf in America to risk publishing. It was the first draft of the novel, which Lawrence had concluded on 8 March 1927, and had then rewritten and extended twice more. Much less explicit than the final version with which we are most familiar, it has some charm, particularly in its portrait of the amusing and likable gamekeeper, Parkin.

Frieda's mother was ill and frail, and she and Lawrence, usually such good friends, were irritable with one another. There were a great many minor irritations for Lawrence that Christmas. Compton Mackenzie, who had recognised himself as Cathcart, the materialistic and patronising figure in 'The Man Who Loved Islands', blocked Heinemann's proposed edition of the story and Lawrence was denied his £300 advance.

Lawrence continued to have little medical care, though on a visit to the Bavarian Alps he did try a quack cure with arsenic, which unsurprisingly made him feel a good deal worse. He and Frieda rented the Villa Beau Soleil in Bandol in the autumn of 1929, and the Brewsters rented a house nearby to help look after him. Lawrence could do little work, and tired easily, particularly when he had visitors. He was extremely emaciated, and even Frieda no longer had the power to revive him. Andrew Morland, Mark Gertler's physician and future head of the Department of Chest Diseases at University College Hospital in London, went out to see Lawrence and reported that he had obviously been suffering from pulmonary tuberculosis for ten or fifteen years, and that his general condition was poor. He had little appetite, and refused to follow a strict regime of rest. It was Morland who persuaded Lawrence to enter a sanatorium. When Lawrence left Bandol for the Ad Astra Sanatorium in Vence in the Alpes Maritimes a few miles above Cannes, on 6 February 1930, Frieda knew it was a defeat for both of them. She had always resolutely refused to treat him like an invalid, he to admit to his disease. Now they had both given in.

Lawrence tore up many of his papers before he left, and Frieda helped him pack. The long train journey from Antibes to Toulon was exhausting, and when they arrived Lawrence could barely walk. Friends of Barbara drove them from Toulon to Vence.

At first Frieda was relieved to have Lawrence under proper care; she stayed at a nearby hotel, and visited him in the sanatorium every day. After nine days she returned briefly to the Villa Beau Soleil to pack up.

Lawrence liked the view from his balcony, and in the sanatorium produced a last piece of writing: an essay about the artist Eric Gill. What he found valuable in Gill was his assertion that a man could exist in freedom as long as he did what he liked to do during his working life, and what was required of him in his spare time. That seemed to Lawrence a profoundly wise distinction.

Lawrence continued to have visitors, including Aldous Huxley and his wife Maria, who saw that his life, which had gone on for much longer than might have been expected, was now guttering to an end. H. G. Wells was an unexpected visitor; also the Aga Khan and his wife, who both remained interested in Lawrence's painting. Lawrence was dying, and Frieda knew it. Now she often stayed at the sanatorium overnight, although sometimes he was irritable, and once told her 'your sleeping here does me no good'.[25] The words hurt her and she went away to weep, but when she returned he said, with some of his old humour, 'Don't mind. You know I want nothing but you, but sometimes something is stronger than me.' When Frieda stayed overnight, she could hear the coughing of the sanatorium's patients, and once a little girl in the next room called out, 'Mama, Mama, je souffre tant.' Frieda was glad Lawrence was too deaf to hear it. Barbara, who had come to help her mother, was often a better companion to Lawrence in these last days. Lawrence was not above letting Frieda know this. To the end he used one woman against the other, once telling Barbara, for instance: 'It isn't often I want your mother, but I do want her tonight to stay.'[26] On another occasion he said to her: 'Your mother does not care for me any more; the death in me repels her.'[27]

Lawrence was beginning to dislike the sanatorium, and to feel he would be better off in a house. Frieda rented the Villa Robermond in Vence, as it was too late to make any medical difference. Shakily, Lawrence prepared to move to his new home on 1 March. Frieda had to help him dress and put his shoes on, which he normally insisted on doing for himself. She took him by taxi to the house, where he collapsed on the bed, exhausted. She slept on a couch in the same room where he could see her.

The next day was Sunday, and he asked her not to leave him. She sat by his bed and read. By tea time he had a temperature and, seeing his tortured face, Frieda collapsed in tears, almost for the first time in his presence. He told her not to cry, and she stopped. Then he asked for morphine, and Aldous and Maria Huxley, who had come to visit, went to find a doctor. Frieda described their last moments together: 'After a little while he said: "I am better now, if I could only sweat I would be better . . ." and then again "I am better now." The minutes went by, Maria Huxley was in the room with me. I held his ankle from time to time, it felt so full of life, all my days I shall hold his ankle in my hand.'[28]

At ten o'clock that night, 2 March 1930, aged forty-four, Lawrence died.

Chapter 23

AFTERMATHS

L awrence was buried in Vence on 4 March 1930. There was
no service, but flowers were thrown into the grave. As Frieda
put it, 'We buried him simply, like a bird.'[1] The Huxleys,
Achsah Brewster and Frieda's daughter Barbara were among the few
assembled friends.

The obituaries of Lawrence were largely hostile, though E. M.
Forster described him in the *Listener* as 'the greatest imaginative novelist of our generation'.[2] Frieda was left with a tangle of problems.
Lawrence's books had begun to earn money, but he had not made a
will, which meant that Frieda was entitled only to the interest on the
£4000 he had left, and had no prima facie right to either his manuscripts or his paintings. Letters of administration had been granted to
his elder brother George, who was supported in the legal action to
ensure the administration of the estate remained in the family by his
sister Emily. After a time Ada, shocked by what she had observed
earlier of Frieda's relations with Ravagli and disliking the pressure
Frieda's solicitors tried to bring on her, joined the rest of the family
to oppose Frieda's right to inherit Lawrence's property.

Frieda was surely right to think Lawrence would have been angry
if she simply allowed his family to get away with such a claim. She
determined to fight, even though Aldous Huxley advised her not to
go to court, observing to a friend that, 'Since L. is no longer there to
keep her in order, she plunges about in the most hopeless way.'

The hearing in the Probate Court in London did not take place
until 3 November 1932. Frieda asked that the letters of administration
granted to George should be revoked. At one point, as Frieda's
lawyers tried to paint a harmonious picture of the Lawrence marriage,

she is said to have leapt from her seat to cry, 'But that's not true – we fought like hell!'[3] Whatever Lord Merrivale, who was judging the case, thought of Frieda, the decisive evidence was given by Murry. He testified that he and Lawrence had made similar wills in Buckinghamshire in 1914, leaving everything to their wives. Murry convinced the court by producing his own document. Frieda won the case, and of the £4000 in cash she received, she generously gave £500 each to George, Ada and Emily. Ada, however, wanted nothing more to do with this sister-in-law of whom she morally disapproved.

Less than a month after Lawrence's death, Murry and Frieda had a brief affair in the south of France which, according to Murry, showed him for the first time what fulfilment in love really meant. Frieda, however, preferred Angelo Ravagli, and after a few weeks Murry returned to England. Ravagli was, of course, married, but the success of her court action gave Frieda enough money to buy him out of the army, and he left his wife and three children to be with her. She placated Signora Ravagli with a financial settlement in 1933.

Frieda's daughter Barbara collapsed soon after Lawrence's funeral. It was thought she had tuberculosis of the bone, and her back had to be put in plaster; but it was clear that her mind was also disturbed, and by July she was in the throes of a complete nervous breakdown. Barbara had been nursing a dying man; she had watched her mother take up with both Murry and Ravagli soon afterwards. In her delirium she called out, 'My poor mother, her child is dead,' but whether she was thinking of Lawrence or herself is unclear. She also mumbled incoherently about her violent hatred of Frieda. She can still remember trying to run away from the Villa Robermond, where Lawrence had died.

Frieda's treatment of Barbara's state of mind was decidedly eccentric. She still shared Otto Gross's belief in the all-purpose restorative power of sex, and decided that this was what was needed to heal her daughter. She arranged for the handsome garden boy, Nicola, to spend several nights with Barbara, but the doctor came to hear of it, and put a stop to the 'treatment'. Barbara recalls the episode with a kind of stunned resignation. Her son-in-law, the writer Al Alvarez, maintained that it was Barbara's knowledge of Frieda's affair with Murry, followed by her pursuit of Ravagli, that actually caused her collapse. It seems likely that the opprobrium which had been heaped on Frieda's name in her father's house during Barbara's childhood was reactivated by this behaviour. It is hard to see how her feelings for her mother could have been anything other than ambivalent. Even now, Barbara remembers the strength of Frieda's determination to have Ravagli, and recalls her own observation of considerable reluctance in him. She clearly found that disturbing, but she had a spiritual toughness that made her as much a survivor as Frieda. She now lives with her daughter Ursula in Tuscany.

Lady Ottoline Morrell, who once again had been in friendly correspondence with Lawrence in his last year, received the news of his death 'as a great blow'.[4] In his letters he had always been reticent about his own health, while showing great concern for hers. Ottoline had never agreed with Bertrand Russell's opinion that *Lady Chatterley's Lover* was a masterpiece. She could not like the book, and was amused when Lawrence wrote to suggest that she would have benefited from a more robust attitude to the body in her youth. She could not feel: 'If a man had been able to say to you when you were young and in love, an' if tha' shits, an if tha' pisses, I'm glad, I shouldna want a woman who couldna shit nor piss – surely that would have been a liberation to you, and it would have kept your heart warm.'[5] Fortunately, Lawrence also sent her his poems, which she thought amongst the finest things he had done, and was able to write and tell him so.

Ottoline was kinder to Frieda after Lawrence's death than she had been earlier in their acquaintance, though she was often amused by her. Frieda once turned up at Ottoline's house in Bedford Square dressed in fuchsia and crimson. She was uncharacteristically humble then, and Ottoline felt sorry for her. She also liked her honesty. Frieda confessed that she had been sleeping with Murry while waiting for Ravagli to get his divorce. In spite of their former difficulties, Ottoline found herself admiring Frieda's energy and enterprise, and the two women saw a great deal of each other in the two years following Lawrence's death – though Ottoline criticised Frieda for her treatment of Barbara, and Frieda's style always grated on her. Other visitors to Bedford Square might sign her book neatly, but Frieda recorded each return with a big, flourishing signature, and jokey words such as 'Here's Frieda – yet again.' On the whole, Ottoline was relieved when Frieda announced in 1933 that she was off to live on the Kiowa Ranch with Angelo Ravagli. By then, Ottoline was able to recollect

Lawrence's violence to his wife in the war years with some percipience:

> No one who did not know him intimately in the years 1914–1917 could ever know what Lawrence suffered from having all his most sensitive and tender feelings and affections violated by the woman who after all was his fate, and to whom he was bound . . . But the more I think about him the more clearly do I see that he was violent because he was afraid. He had a great fear, and like a frightened dog he could dash out from his kennel and bark and bark. He needed a kennel to run back to, and this is what Frieda was for him.[6]

Frieda adored Ravagli, who almost certainly made her sexually happy in the ways that Lawrence had disapproved of. And they were able to live together without quarrelling. In 1931, Frieda wrote that Ravagli was 'so human and nice with me and real, no high falute, but such a genuine warmth for me – I shall be all right . . . We have been fond of each other for years and that an old bird like me is still capable of real passion and can inspire it too seems a miracle.'[7] Ravagli was not an intellectual, but he looked after the affairs Frieda put into his hands competently and honestly. He was kinder to her than Lawrence had been, and though it shocked her friends to see it, she was much happier with him, even though she could not fail to be aware, as time went on, that he continued to be a womaniser. Saki Karavas was a good friend of Angelo, who often came into Taos to drink with him. He confirmed the rumours that Angelo was still a ladies' man, and that Frieda knew this and apparently did not care. Frieda's daughter Barbara disliked Angelo, and thought he had married Frieda for her money, but this seems unlikely. The Kiowa Ranch was not luxurious, and Angelo had to work quite hard to look after Frieda there. In any case, Frieda had no difficulty in dealing with Angelo's requests for money. While he was visiting his family in Italy in December 1937, she wrote to him with astonishing good humour and firmness: 'You think I ought to give you more money. If I were rich, yes, but I am not and I don't think it's reasonable. I know there is only $120 a month, but think of the money we spend. Going to South America and Boston and Hollywood. We spend quite a lot of money. But you don't think of that.'[8] He and Frieda only married on 31 October 1950, when it looked as though Angelo would otherwise be deported from America. The effect of this marriage was to ensure that half of Lawrence's very considerable estate went to Ravagli – and his first family, to whom he returned after Frieda's death.

It was Angelo Ravagli who brought Lawrence's ashes to Taos. In 1935 he went to Vence and arranged to have Lawrence's body disinterred and cremated, then brought the urn across the Atlantic, sorted out the difficulties of getting it through customs, and took it to Lamy, where Frieda met him. In the confusion of their meeting it seems the urn was left behind on the railway platform, and the loss was only discovered when they were already twenty miles away. This was not the only piece of black comedy associated with Lawrence's remains. Mabel Luhan, still living nearby, wanted the ashes for herself, and determined to steal them from the chapel Ravagli had built for them on Kiowa Ranch. When Frieda heard of this (from Brett, who was living and painting nearby in a new cabin high up under the pink rocks of the Del Monte Ranch), she had the urn cemented into the altar.

The creation of what was effectively a shrine to Lawrence's memory was appropriate enough as his reputation grew: Frieda found she was much celebrated for her connection to him, and people began to make pilgrimages to see her. Mabel Luhan was not pleased to discover Frieda had set up a rival court in the neighbourhood of Taos. She also conceived a dislike for Ravagli, and pointedly did not invite him to her parties (Frieda seems to have gone without him). Brett shrewdly observed of Frieda: 'Her frustration at not being the magnet (while Lawrence lived) was appeased when she became the magnet.'[9]

According to Harry Moore, Brett's cabin was close enough to Frieda's to enable her to see when Frieda and Ravagli had visitors. If they looked interesting she would go down and meet them. After the fiasco over the ashes (and perhaps in revenge for Brett's telling Frieda of her plans), Mabel asked Brett to leave. When Brett refused, she had her pitched out by the police.

Almost every intimate of Lawrence was moved to write an account of him. In 1931 Murry's *Son of Woman* was the first to appear. It was an attempt to see Lawrence's ideas entirely in terms of his psychological difficulties, although it always treated him with respect as a serious and important artist. Huxley called the book a slug's eye view, and it made Frieda so angry that she burnt her copy, and sent Murry the ashes in a cardboard box. It is easy to see why Frieda was so incensed. Murry presented *The Rainbow* mainly as the history of Lawrence's sexual failure, and intimated the source of the 'blind beakishness' of Bertha Coutts as clearly as he prudently could in 1931. Nevertheless, he has some persuasive insights into the 'heat of the struggle, the anguish of humiliation'[10] that Lawrence felt in his quarrelling with Frieda: 'Need so naked as that must inevitably pass into hate.'[11] Crucially, his attack is on a Lawrence who fantasises aggressive maleness just because he lacks it. Murry knew Lawrence found killing even a porcupine difficult, and comments of 'The Woman Who Rode Away': 'This imaginative self-persuasion that human sacrifice is lawful in a man who is so tender that only by an immense effort he can bring himself to shoot the vermin on his ranch, is a sickening perversity.'[12] In the same way he questions the implied basis of Lawrence's approval in 'St Mawr' of Lou's words: 'I don't hate men because they're men, as nuns do. I dislike them because they're not men enough: babies and playboys.'

Frieda's *Not I, But the Wind*, published in 1934, is the most freshly written of all the memoirs, and vividly recalls Lawrence's voice and presence. Reading it, one feels all the enjoyment of life that kept Lawrence and Frieda together. She describes the happiness of their life together, beginning in Beuerberg: 'We had very little money, about fifteen shillings a week. We lived on black bread that Lawrence loved, fresh eggs ... I didn't want people, I didn't want anything ... I could now flourish like a trout in a stream or a daisy in the sun.'[13]

Far from attempting to cover up their disagreements, she appears to revel in the way Lawrence mocked her impracticality, or lectured her on the wastefulness of throwing a pair of shoes with a broken heel into the river. Of worse quarrels, she remarks: 'What does it amount to that he hit out at me in rage when I exasperated him, or mostly when the life around him drove him to the end of his patience? I didn't care very much.'[14]

The book contains many letters from Lawrence, not only to Frieda but also to her mother and sisters, and the Lawrence who emerges is charming and brave. Her autobiographical fictions in *Frieda Lawrence: The Memoirs and Correspondence* (published in 1961), however, present a more sanctified portrait, which as her life proceeded and Lawrence's fame spread across the world, she liked to embellish.

Brett wrote her memoir *Lawrence and Brett* in 1933, casting it in the form of a letter to Lawrence. It moves informally from her first encounter with Lawrence in 1915, to her life in New and Old Mexico, and ends with a section about her time with Lawrence in Capri. She records whatever she remembers without apparent criticism, for instance Lawrence reading a violent episode of 'St Mawr' with such relish that Frieda is horrified, or the way he angrily chops off the head of a broody hen. Always placatory to Lawrence herself, there is some poignancy in her account of Frieda's rages alongside her own acceptance of Lawrence's casual rudeness. For the rest of her life (she died in her eighties) Brett was often consulted about Lawrence and enjoyed telling tales of him.

Jessie Chambers had not been in touch with Lawrence for nearly eighteen years when she read of his death in the paper. An affectionate letter Lawrence had written about Haggs Farm to her younger brother in 1928 had been kept from her for fear of making her unhappy:

Whatever I forget, I shall never forget the Haggs – I loved it so ... Oh, I'd love to be nineteen again, and coming up through the Warren and catching the first glimpse of the buildings. Then I'd sit on the sofa under the window, and we'd crowd round the little table to tea, in that tiny little kitchen I was so at home in ... Whatever else I am, I am somewhere still the same Bert who rushed with such joy to the Haggs.[15]

In 1915 Jessie had married John R. Wood, a farmer's son and a teacher like herself. She continued to teach until Wood came back from the war in 1919. Thereafter she looked after her husband.

Writing to Helen Corke shortly after Lawrence's death, Jessie said she had not even known Lawrence was ill, and asked for any details Helen might have about his life. Helen had been out of touch with Lawrence since 1913, but she sent Jessie details of his last months. Jessie replied: 'Of late, this last year or so, I have been conscious of a growing desire to write to him ... I had such a feeling that the business between us was not finished ... When I remember how despairingly he used to tell me he could not do without me in his artistic life, I feel terribly guilty.'[16] She told Helen she had read none of his books apart from *Twilight in Italy* and 'some short stories, which I thought utterly unworthy of him'.[17] However, her correspondence with Emile Delavenay confirms that she went on to read *Women In Love* and very probably others.

When in 1933 Helen Corke sent Jessie a copy of her recently published 'Lawrence and the Apocalypse' Jessie wrote again rather drily; she thought the essay had more to do with Helen's interests than with the Lawrence she had admired most when he was 'dealing with the immediate and the concrete'.[18] Jessie disliked Lawrence when he tried to write about abstract ideas, and in that her instincts seem sound. Yet there is perhaps an element of wishful thinking in her insistence that Lawrence's life was painful. She clearly wanted to believe he had made a mistake in rejecting her, and that life had paid him out for that. Jessie still felt that Lawrence had been driven into a tormented egoism because he had been prevented from loving her by his mother, and that that was why he looked only for the animal–female elements in women. For herself, she admitted her feelings for Lawrence had not changed in spite of, as she put it, 'other deep affection'.[19]

Jessie had once tried to set down her thoughts on the relationship in the form of a novel, *Eunice Temple*, which she subsequently destroyed. Now, under the pseudonym 'E. T.', she wrote a memoir of her early life with Lawrence. *A Personal Record*, published in 1935, is probably the best account of Lawrence as an adolescent and a young man. Jessie's memoir gives details of the way she and Lawrence grew to be close friends, the books they read together, the life of the mind they shared, and the way she encouraged his writing. She also describes what she saw of Lawrence's home, and her knowledge of Lydia's hostility to their friendship. There is so much pain in the account of their conversations after Lawrence told her he could not love her that it is easy to understand why her brother David said he could hardly bear to read the book.

In 1940, when she met Helen Corke again, Jessie was bent and heavy. She had suffered a severe stroke the previous year, and was recovering from a nervous breakdown; she was also a little deaf.

Helen recognised her only with difficulty. They went to a crowded café to talk, but Helen found it impossible to make contact with her; at length she decided with pity that Jessie resented the shabby neglect of *A Personal Record* by the press, and saw Helen, comically, as a representative of the commercially successful literary world. Although Helen's best book, *D. H. Lawrence's Princess*, a cool and lucid memoir of Jessie, was only put out in a very small edition in 1951, she published an autobiography as well as novels, including *Neutral Ground* (1933), her version of Lawrence's attempts to woo her away from her grief over her lover's suicide. She lived into her nineties, frequently invited by universities and literary societies to speak about her memories of Lawrence, and travelling to the Lawrence conference in Taos in 1970. Jessie Chambers was dead before the end of the Second World War.

Louie Burrows, who had been badly hurt by her broken engagement to Lawrence, went on working as a schoolteacher. She was an exceptionally beautiful young woman, and must have had suitors, but she did not marry until her fifties. For many years she continued to live with her parents in Quorn, where she became headmistress of the Church of England school. She visited Lawrence's grave at least twice in the five years he was buried in Vence.

Lorenzo in Taos, Mabel Luhan's idiosyncratic record of Lawrence's time in New Mexico, appeared in 1932. Frieda had earlier won Mabel's enmity by criticising a draft of the book as 'small beer' and recommending she try again. Like her four volumes of *Intimate Memoirs*, the writing is unabashed, often vulgar, and sometimes embarrassingly mystical, but it is also as direct as a personal letter. She begins with her reading of *Sea and Sardinia*, and her intense 'willing' of Lawrence to accept her invitation to Taos, and thereafter gives a frank account of her battle to secure Lawrence for herself, and details her resentment both of Frieda and, eventually, Brett. After reading *Lorenzo in Taos* Frieda wrote to her: 'No, Mabel, we were all *more* than that, I know we were.' A letter from Lawrence dated 21 May 1926 (which Mabel includes in the book) suggests that Lawrence encouraged her to publish her earlier *Memoirs*: 'Put your fight into the publishing of your book, and let *people* alone.'[20] Mabel, who claimed to have much more manuscript information which she was keeping under wraps, died in 1962.

Catherine Carswell's memoir of Lawrence appeared in 1932. *The Savage Pilgrimage* begins with their first meeting, but also describes the years when she and Lawrence were only in touch by letter. She writes in a clear, dry voice which is nevertheless passionately loyal. She saw his marriage with balance and understanding, and her most critical remarks are directed against Middleton Murry, whom she judged treacherous, both personally and in his treatment of Lawrence's work. Catherine's husband Donald was killed in an accident in wartime London, and she herself died in 1946.

One of the few of Lawrence's acquaintances who did not write about him is Alice Dax. She wrote a remarkable letter dated 23 January 1935 to Frieda after reading *Not I, But the Wind*. In a way the letter is as impressive as Jessie Chambers' memoir, and it shows an astonishing generosity of spirit:

> *'The Wind' nearly broke my heart with sadness and with gladness and with other conflicting emotions. And I was grateful to you – really grateful . . . I was never meet for him and what he liked was not the me I was but the me I might have been . . . Unlike you, I could never quarrel with D. H. . . . the probable truth being that I felt unsure of him and feared to lose him, whilst he in turn I suppose equally unsure of me, rarely quarrelled with me, but when he became extremely angry would turn and walk out . . . He needed you. I remember so well his words: – 'You would like Frieda – she is direct and free, but I don't know how you would get on together . . .' You had, without a doubt, all the things that he needed, and his sensitive soul knew it without an inventory.[21]*

We know little of Alice Dax's life after her time with Lawrence. She took great joy in the child she conceived with her husband when she returned to him. In her 1935 letter to Frieda she claimed the child 'would never have been conceived but for an unendurable passion which only *he* had roused and my husband had slaked'.[22] She and her husband emigrated to Australia in the 1950s.

Frieda wrote gratefully to Lady Cynthia Asquith after Lawrence's death: 'How you helped us in the past and what a good friend you were,' but Lady Cynthia had moved away from Lawrence since their close friendship during the First World War. He sent her a copy of *The Lost Girl* in 1921, but she did not acknowledge it, and when he took tea with her in October 1925 it was their first meeting in six years. He found her a little abstracted, and when he wrote to her afterwards from Italy, he observed that she had seemed rather cross.

In his last letter to Lady Cynthia a few weeks later, Lawrence mentioned the novel he was working on, *Lady Chatterley's Lover*, and suggested she might not care for the book. 'I'll have a few leaflets sent to you. But if you're afraid of blushing when it's too late, just put them on the fire.' It is unlikely that Cynthia ever read the book, or visited the exhibition of Lawrence's paintings in London in 1929. They did not meet again. Nevertheless, in *Remember and be Glad*, a book of her memoirs published in 1952, there is a fine essay on their friendship.

Of all Lawrence's women, Frieda was the only one who finally mattered to him, and he would not have grudged the fame that came to her as his reputation grew. She did not change her style of life or her dress; the American artist Georgia O'Keeffe gives a marvellous description of her as she was in 1934: 'I can remember clearly the first time I ever saw her, standing in a doorway with her hair all frizzed out, wearing a cheap red calico dress that looked as though she had just wiped out the frying pan with it. She was not thin, not young, but there was something radiant and wonderful about her.'[23] In the twenty-odd years Frieda lived in Taos after Lawrence's death, she entered into correspondence with Lawrence scholars from all over the world, stressing perhaps too frequently how happy Lawrence's life with her had been, yet with a pugnacity which always had its own charm. Among her correspondents was the critic F. R. Leavis, a passionate admirer of Lawrence, to whom she politely wrote that his book *D. H. Lawrence: Novelist* would be useful in explaining Lawrence to the world. She took him a little to task however: 'You say I was not maternal, I think I was, and not intellectual, but I was not dumb either, and thought things out for myself. Nobody seems to have an idea of the quality of Lawrence's and my relationship, the essence of it.'[24]

Frieda was ill with a virus in the spring of 1955, and never quite got over it; Ravagli believed she may have had a stroke. On 17 July 1956, soon after his return from one of his visits to Italy, she began to complain of pains which she took to be indigestion. One evening Ravagli heard a strange noise from her room; Frieda had fallen out of bed, her right side paralysed and her mouth twisted. She never recovered. With her death on 10 August 1956, her part in the Lawrence story came to an end.

Lawrence's books have continued to be widely read, even though there have been fluctuations in his reputation. An important contribution to the high standing his work enjoyed in the fifties was the critical support of F. R. Leavis, both as a lecturer at Cambridge University, and through his influential journal *Scrutiny*. In *D. H. Lawrence: Novelist*, Leavis argued that there was much in Lawrence's work which had the same moral concern to be found in George Eliot. He attended to the text of Lawrence's novels as if they were poems, and his close reading of the 'felt life' of Lawrence's prose influenced a generation of teachers both in universities and schools.

In 1960, the Home Office's decision to prosecute Penguin Books for the planned publication of the unexpurgated *Lady Chatterley's Lover*, under the 1959 Obscene Publications Act, which allowed literary merit to be taken into account, brought a stream of eminent witnesses to the book's defence. These included E. M. Forster, the poet Cecil Day-Lewis, Richard Hoggart, the Bishop of Woolwich, and a number of distinguished literary women, among them Helen Gardner (Reader in Renaissance Literature at Oxford University), Joan Bennett (Lecturer in English Literature at Cambridge) and the celebrated writer Dame Rebecca West. All agreed that Lawrence was a writer of the highest calibre, and were eager to rebut the charge that the novel would 'deprave and corrupt'. Some placed him in the great Puritan tradition. F. R. Leavis did not appear.

The case may well have been decided in the minds of the jury as early as the prosecuting counsel Mervyn Griffith-Jones's question in his opening address: 'Is it a book you would wish your wife or your servants to read?' Perhaps, simply, the time for the book had arrived. At any rate, *Lady Chatterley's Lover* was declared not to be obscene, and thereafter sold in enormous numbers.

Feminist comment on Lawrence grew through the seventies as sexually liberated women began to question the way in which they had been conditioned to see themselves, and identified Lawrence as part of the patriarchy they wanted to resist. Germaine Greer, Betty Friedan, and even Shere Hite (in her report that established the vaginal orgasm was a myth) played a part in this. Kate Millett's *Sexual Politics* (1972), a serious historical analysis of twentieth-century attempts to reverse women's emancipation (including Nazi and Soviet models), examined the writing of Henry Miller and Norman Mailer alongside key works of Lawrence. Her case against Lawrence as a writer of pornographic and murderous fantasies was extremely influential. However, there are new uncertainties in the feminist movement: Erica Jong, Betty Friedan, Germaine Greer and Kate Millett have recently modified their positions dramatically, and this, together with the growing 'men's movement' has been hailed as a sign that the tide has turned against feminism, perhaps because of an economic climate of work shortage, which often sends women back to their traditional roles.

In 1984 the publication of *Mr Noon* by Cambridge University Press brought to light a piece of Lawrence's work which had disappeared for nearly fifty years, and awakened a new curiosity about his marriage which went beyond an interest in gossip. In 1912 Lawrence hoped that a new generation would learn to understand him enough to read him gratefully. It is the task of our generation to learn to read him again with compassion.

NOTES

Introduction

1. I am, however, indebted to to Margaret Storch, *Sons and Adversaries: Women in William Blake and D. H. Lawrence* (University of Tennessee Press, 1991), for her use of the work of Melanie Klein
2. DHL to Katherine Mansfield, 5 December 1918, James T. Boulton (ed.), *The Letters of D. H. Lawrence* (6 volumes, 1979–91), Vol 3, p. 302
3. *Women in Love*, pp. 270–1
4. Quoted in Geir Kjetsaa, *Dostoevsky* (1987), p. 200
5. *Lady Chatterley's Lover*, p. 281

Chapter One: Mother

1. Edward Nehls (ed.), *D. H. Lawrence: A Composite Biography*, Vol 3 (1959), p. 564
2. *Phoenix II.*, pp. 592–3.
3. *Sons and Lovers*, p. 44
4. ibid, p. 46
5. DHL to Rachel Annand Taylor, Boulton, *Letters*, Vol 1, p. 190
6. *A Collier's Friday Night*, p. 109
7. Taped interview with D. E. Gerrard, Nottingham County Library
8. 'Jimmy and the Desperate Woman', *Complete Short Stories* (1963), p. 621
9. DHL, 'That Women Know Best', Bancroft Library, University of California, Berkeley
10. *Sons and Lovers*, p. 45
11. ibid, p. 64
12. *Fantasia of the Unconscious*, p. 126

Chapter Two: Bonds

1. Nehls, *Composite Biography*, Vol 1, p. 8
2. ibid, p. 29

3. ibid, Vol 3, p. 578
4. DHL to Edward Garnett, 19 November 1912, Boulton, *Letters*, Vol 1, p. 477
5. *Sons and Lovers*, p. 176
6. Boulton, *Letters*, Vol 1, p. 477
7. George Neville, *A Memoir of D. H. Lawrence*, p. 89
8. Boulton, *Letters*, Vol 1, p. 190
9. *Fantasia of the Unconscious*, p. 126

Chapter Three: Jessie

1. Nehls, *Composite Biography*, Vol 1, p. 51
2. Taped interview, op. cit.
3. Quoted in John Worthen, *D. H. Lawrence: The Early Years, 1885–1912* (1991), p. 108
4. Compton Mackenzie, *My Life and Times, Octave Five* (1966), p. 168
5. *The White Peacock*, p. 257
6. 'E. T.' (Jessie Chambers), *D. H. Lawrence: A Personal Record* (1935), p. 28
7. Nehls, *Composite Biography*, Vol 3, p. 591
8. ibid, p. 592
9. Chambers, *A Personal Record*, p. 57
10. ibid, p. 111
11. Lydia Lawrence to Lettice Berry, 11 July 1910, quoted in Worthen, *The Early Years*, p. 160
12. Chambers, *A Personal Record*, p. 66
13. ibid, p. 186
14. ibid, p. 163
15. *Sons and Lovers*, p. 227
16. ibid, p. 228
17. Chambers, *A Personal Record*, p. 133
18. ibid, p. 131
19. *Sons and Lovers*, p. 242
20. Quoted in Chambers, *A Personal Record*, p. 139
21. ibid, p. 138
22. Notes by Lewis Richmond, Nottingham County Records Office
23. Quoted in Moore, *Priest of Love*, p. 149
24. Boulton, *Letters*, Vol 1, p. 126
25. Quoted in Moore, *Priest of Love*, p. 149
26. E. W. Tedlock (ed.), *Frieda Lawrence: Memoirs and Correspondence* (1964), p. 246
27. Postcard from DHL, September 1912, Boulton, *Letters*, Vol 1, p. 457
28. Tedlock, *Frieda Lawrence*, p. 246
29. Quoted in Worthen, *The Early Years*, p. 369

Chapter Four: Schoolteachers

1. Chambers, *A Personal Record*, p. 175
2. DHL, 'An Autobiographical Sketch', in Harry Moore and Warren Roberts (eds.), *Phoenix II*, p. 593
3. Boulton, *Letters*, Vol 1, p. 153
4. *Sons and Lovers*, p. 351
5. Neville, *A Memoir*, p. 86
6. Boulton, *Letters*, Vol 1, p. 157
7. *The Collected Poems of D. H. Lawrence* (edited by V. de Sola Pinto and F. Warren Roberts), p. 87
8. Quoted in Worthen, *The Early Years*, p. 255
9. *Collected Poems*, p. 99
10. ibid, p. 116
11. Chambers, *A Personal Record*, p. 109
12. Boulton, *Letters*, Vol 1, pp. 285–6
13. ibid, p. 362
14. *Collected Poems*, p. 98
15. ibid, p. 65
16. Boulton, *Letters*, Vol 1, p. 173
17. Chambers, *A Personal Record*, p. 109
18. Nehls, *Composite Biography*, Vol 2, p. 705
19. Chambers, *A Personal Record*, p. 175

Chapter Five: Son and Lover

1. *Collected Poems*, p. 106
2. Boulton, *Letters*, Vol 1, p. 192
3. DHL's introduction to Edward McDonald, 'A Bibliography of D. H. Lawrence', *Phoenix II*, p. 232
4. Quoted in Worthen, *The Early Years*, p. 141
5. Chambers, *A Personal Record*, p. 117
6. Boulton, *Letters*, Vol 1, p. 49
7. *Phoenix II*, p. 300
8. Letter from Aubrey Waterfield to Robert Calverley Trevelyan, quoted in Lina Waterfield, *Castle in Italy* (1961)
9. Quoted in Jeffrey Meyers, *D. H. Lawrence* (1990), p. 65
10. Chambers, *A Personal Record*, p. 184
11. Boulton, *Letters*, Vol 1, p. 193
12. ibid
13. ibid, pp. 190–1
14. ibid, pp. 285–6
15. ibid, p. 303
16. ibid, p. 243

17. ibid, p. 178
18. Chambers, *A Personal Record*, p. 191
19. Quoted in Moore, *Priest of Love*, p. 191

Chapter Six: Frieda

1. Robert Lucas, *Frieda Lawrence* (1973), p. 12
2. Frieda Lawrence, *Not I, But the Wind* (1934), p. 5
3. ibid, p. 4
4. ibid, p. 5
5. Boulton, *Letters*, Vol 1, p. 383
6. ibid, p. 384
7. ibid, p. 389
8. ibid, p. 390
9. ibid, p. 392
10. ibid, p. 393
11. Frieda Lawrence, *Not I, But the Wind*, pp. 179–80
12. Boulton, *Letters*, Vol 1, p. 404
13. ibid, p. 406
14. *Collected Poems*, p. 205

Chapter Seven: The Wanderers

1. *Collected Poems*, p. 204
2. *Mr Noon*, p. 183
3. Boulton, *Letters*, Vol 1, p. 441
4. Quoted in Worthen, *The Early Years*, p. 412
5. *Collected Poems*, p. 211
6. Boulton, *Letters*, Vol 1, p. 403
7. *Collected Poems*, p. 217
8. ibid, p. 249
9. Boulton, *Letters*, Vol 1, p. 440
10. *Collected Poems*, p. 212
11. Boulton, *Letters*, Vol 1, p. 421
12. ibid, p. 429
13. ibid, p. 409
14. ibid, p. 403
15. *Mr Noon*, p. 327

Chapter Eight: Gargnano

1. Frieda Lawrence, *Not I, But the Wind*, p. 97
2. ibid, p. 68

3. ibid, p. 52
4. Boulton, *Letters*, Vol 1, p. 479
5. ibid, p. 449
6. ibid, p. 470
7. ibid, p. 486
8. Quoted in Lucas, *Frieda Lawrence*, p. 97
9. ibid
10. Frieda Lawrence, *Not I, But the Wind*, p. 52
11. ibid, p. 56
12. Boulton, *Letters*, Vol 1, p. 538
13. Chambers, *A Personal Record*, p. 217
14. Helen Corke, *D. H. Lawrence's Princess* (1951), p. 31
15. ibid
16. Boulton, *Letters*, Vol 1, p. 527
17. Chambers, *A Personal Record*, p. 221
18. Quoted in Meyers, *D. H. Lawrence*, p. 134

Chapter Nine: The Widening Circle

1. Frieda Lawrence, *Not I, But the Wind*, p. 61
2. Quoted in Moore, *Priest of Love*, p. 237
3. Boulton, *Letters*, Vol 1, p. 119
4. Dorothy Brett, *Lawrence and Brett* (1933), p. 17
5. Quoted in Claire Tomalin, *Katherine Mansfield: A Secret Life* (1987), p. 96
6. Frieda Lawrence, *Not I, But the Wind*, p. 61
7. John Middleton Murry, *Reminiscences of D. H. Lawrence* (1933), p. 21
8. Constance Garnett to Edward Garnett, 1 April 1913, quoted in Richard Garnett, *Constance Garnett: A Heroic Life* (1991), p. 273
9. David Garnett, review of *The Letters of D. H. Lawrence*, edited by Aldous Huxley, in *The Saturday Review of Literature*, 1 October 1932
10. Constance Garnett to Edward Garnett, 28 June 1913 (Eton)
11. Boulton, *Letters*, Vol 2, p. 111
12. *The Journal of Katherine Mansfield*, p. 61
13. Boulton, *Letters*, Vol 2, p. 111
14. Nehls, *Composite Biography*, Vol 1, p. 215
15. ibid, p. 216
16. ibid, p. 218
17. Constance Garnett to Edward Garnett, 31 January 1914, quoted in Richard Garnett, *Constance Garnett*, p. 282
18. Constance Garnett to Edward Garnett, 5 February 1914, ibid, p. 281
19. Boulton, *Letters*, Vol 2, p. 151
20. Quoted in Richard Garnett, *Constance Garnett*, p. 283
21. David Garnett, review of *The Letters of D. H. Lawrence*, op. cit.

Chapter Ten: Passionate Friends

1. Quoted in Miranda Seymour's forthcoming biography of Lady Ottoline Morrell
2. Boulton, *Letters*, Vol 2, p. 109
3. Lady Cynthia Asquith to Mary Charteris, 19 February 1915 (Apperley Papers)
4. C. A. Hankin (ed.), *The Letters of John Middleton Murry to Katherine Mansfield* (1983), p. 40
5. Boulton, *Letters*, Vol 2, p. 339
6. *The Trespasser*, p. 30
7. Richard Aldington, *Portrait of a Genius But* . . . (1951), p. 169
8. Lady Cynthia Asquith's journal entry for 21 June 1915, as quoted in her essay on DHL in *Remember and be Glad* (1952), p. 140
9. Boulton, *Letters*, Vol 2, p. 337
10. Asquith, *Remember and be Glad*, p. 140
11. Quoted in Robert Gathorne-Hardy (ed.), *Ottoline at Garsington 1915–18* (1974), p. 78
12. Michael Holroyd, *Lytton Strachey*, pp. 600–1
13. Boulton, *Letters*, Vol 2, p. 431
14. Quoted in Gathorne-Hardy, *Ottoline at Garsington*, p. 37
15. ibid, p. 78
16. Catherine Carswell, *The Savage Pilgrimage* (1932), p. 41
17. Boulton, *Letters*, Vol 1, p. 503
18. Carswell, *Savage Pilgrimage*, p. 18
19. Boulton, *Letters*, Vol 2, p. 479
20. ibid, p. 29
21. ibid, pp. 234–5

Chapter Eleven: The War

1. Boulton, *Letters*, Vol 2, p. 212
2. ibid, p. 222
3. ibid, p. 225
4. ibid, p. 263
5. ibid, p. 82
6. ibid, p. 277
7. Quoted in Seymour, forthcoming biography of Ottoline Morrell
8. ibid
9. ibid
10. Bertrand Russell, 'Portraits from Memory: D. H. Lawrence', reprinted in Russell's *Autobiography* (1968), p. 115
11. Boulton, *Letters*, Vol 1, p. 503

12. ibid, Vol 2, p. 371
13. ibid, Vol 1, p. 424
14. ibid, Vol 2, pp. 37, 39
15. ibid, p. 660
16. ibid, Vol 3, p. 44
17. ibid, Vol 4, p. 46
18. Quoted in Meyers, *D. H. Lawrence*, p. 130
19. Boulton, *Letters*, Vol 3, pp. 136–7
20. *The Rainbow*, p. 29
21. ibid, p. 63
22. ibid, p. 64
23. ibid, pp. 78–9
24. John Middleton Murry, journal entry, quoted in Antony Alpers, *The Life of Katherine Mansfield* (1980), p. 170
25. Katherine Mansfield to Harold Beauchamp, 15 December 1914, V. O'Sullivan and M. Scott (eds.), *The Collected Letters of Katherine Mansfield*, Vol 1, p. 142
26. Hankin, *Murry/Mansfield Letters*, p. 63
27. Quoted in Nicola Beauman, *Lady Cynthia Asquith* (1987), p. 167
28. Boulton, *Letters*, Vol 2, p. 429
29. Quoted in Miranda Seymour's forthcoming biography
30. Carswell, *Savage Pilgrimage*, p. 41
31. ibid

Chapter Twelve: Cornwall

1. Aldington, *Portrait of a Genius But . . .*, pp. 172–3
2. Boulton, *Letters*, Vol 2, p. 571
3. ibid, p. 564
4. Frieda Lawrence, *Not I, But the Wind*, p. 77
5. Boulton, *Letters*, Vol 2, p. 533
6. O'Sullivan and Scott, *Mansfield Letters*, Vol 1, p. 264
7. Nehls, *Composite Biography*, Vol 1, p. 377
8. Katherine Mansfield to S. S. Koteliansky, O'Sullivan and Scott, *Mansfield Letters*, Vol 1, p. 263
9. Boulton, *Letters*, Vol 2, p. 526
10. ibid, Vol 3, p. 302
11. Katherine Mansfield to Beatrix Campbell, 4 May 1916, O'Sullivan and Scott, *Mansfield Letters*, Vol 1, p. 261
12. Katherine Mansfield to Lady Ottoline Morrell, May 1916, ibid, p. 292
13. ibid
14. Quoted in Seymour, forthcoming biography of Ottoline Morrell
15. Murry, *Reminiscences*, p. 73
16. Boulton, *Letters*, Vol 2, p. 623

17. ibid, p. 645
18. Quoted in Tomalin, *Katherine Mansfield*, p. 154

Chapter Thirteen: Infidelities

1. Boulton, *Letters*, Vol 2, p. 610
2. *Kangaroo*, p. 243
3. ibid, p. 245
4. Carswell, *Savage Pilgrimage*, p. 76
5. ibid, p. 74
6. ibid, p. 75
7. ibid, p. 92
8. Boulton, *Letters*, Vol 2, p. 642
9. *Phoenix II*, pp. 106–7
10. Quoted in J. C. Stevens, *Lawrence at Tregerthen* (1988), p. 33
11. Boulton, *Letters*, Vol 2, p. 115
12. Tedlock, *Frieda Lawrence*, p. 360
13. Boulton, *Letters*, Vol 3, p. 180
14. ibid
15. *Women in Love*, p. 229
16. ibid, p. 377
17. ibid, p. 388
18. ibid, p. 269
19. ibid, p. 270
20. ibid, p. 505
21. Boulton, *Letters*, Vol 3, p. 215
22. ibid, p. 312
23. ibid, p. 41
24. Gathorne-Hardy, *Ottoline at Garsington*, p. 128
25. Boulton, *Letters*, Vol 3, p. 302
26. Lady Cynthia Asquith, journal entry for 25 November 1918
27. *Kangaroo*, p. 283
28. Boulton, *Letters*, Vol 3, p. 295

Chapter Fourteen: Capri and Taormina

1. Quoted in Compton Mackenzie, 'Memories of D. H. Lawrence', in *Moral Courage* (1962), pp. 107–8
2. Boulton, *Letters*, Vol 3, p. 475
3. Murry destroyed the letter. What we know of it is quoted in Boulton, *Letters*, Vol 3, p. 470
4. Tedlock, *Frieda Lawrence*, p. 341
5. *Collected Poems*, p. 278
6. ibid, p. 382

7. ibid, p. 364
8. *Aaron's Rod*, p. 56
9. ibid, p. 101
10. ibid, p. 336

Chapter Fifteen: Travelling

1. Vincent Brome, *Ernest Jones: Freud's Alter Ego* (1982), p. 103
2. *Fantasia of the Unconscious*, p. 49
3. ibid, p. 85
4. ibid, pp. 85–6
5. ibid, p. 87
6. Boulton, *Letters*, Vol 4, p. 95
7. ibid, p. 158
8. ibid, p. 163
9. Nehls, *Composite Biography*, Vol 3, p. 127
10. Boulton, *Letters*, Vol 4, p. 218
11. ibid, p. 234
12. ibid, p. 228
13. Nehls, *Composite Biography*, Vol 3, pp. 136–9
14. *Kangaroo*, p. 108
15. Boulton, *Letters*, Vol 4, p. 38
16. ibid, Vol 3, p. 547
17. Moore, *Priest of Love*, p. 427
18. Boulton, *Letters*, Vol 3, p. 547
19. *Kangaroo*, p. 352
20. ibid, p. 109
21. ibid, p. 189
22. ibid, p. 188
23. ibid, p. 317
24. Nehls, *Composite Biography*, Vol 2, p. 157

Chapter Sixteen: New Mexico

1. Mabel Dodge Luhan, *Lorenzo in Taos* (1932), p. 46
2. Quoted in Laurie Lisle, *Portrait of an Artist: A Biography of Georgia O'Keeffe* (1981), p. 281
3. Boulton, *Letters*, Vol 4, p. 351
4. Mabel Dodge Luhan, *Intimate Memoirs*, Vol 3, p. 141
5. ibid, p. 233
6. ibid, Vol 4, p. 215
7. Boulton, *Letters*, Vol 4, p. 304
8. ibid, p. 313
9. Luhan, *Lorenzo in Taos*, p. 72

10. ibid, p. 94
11. Tedlock, *Frieda Lawrence*, p. 238
12. Boulton, *Letters*, Vol 4, p. 337
13. ibid, p. 363
14. *The Tales of D. H. Lawrence* (1951), p. 645
15. ibid, p. 777
16. *Collected Poems*, pp. 399–400
17. O'Sullivan and Scott, *Mansfield Letters*, Vol 2, p. 229
18. Quoted in Tomalin, *Katherine Mansfield*, p. 190
19. Boulton, *Letters*, Vol 4, p. 375
20. ibid

Chapter Seventeen: Old Mexico

1. Witter Bynner, *Journey with Genius* (1951), p. 23
2. ibid, p. 31
3. ibid, p. 32
4. Nehls, *Composite Biography*, Vol 2, pp. 229–30
5. Bynner, *Journey with Genius*, p. 61
6. Nehls, *Composite Biography*, Vol 2, p. 247
7. Boulton, *Letters*, Vol 4, p. 426
8. Carswell, *Savage Pilgrimage*, p. 199
9. Boulton, *Letters*, Vol 4, p. 487
10. ibid, p. 529

Chapter Eighteen: Frieda and Murry

1. Nehls, *Composite Biography*, Vol 3, p. 266
2. ibid
3. Quoted in F. E. Lea, *The Life of John Middleton Murry* (1959), pp. 117–18
4. Carswell, *Savage Pilgrimage*, p. 202
5. Quoted in Lea, pp. 117–18
6. Tedlock, *Frieda Lawrence*, p. 303
7. ibid, p. 340
8. ibid, p. 353
9. ibid
10. Boulton, *Letters*, Vol 4, p. 532
11. ibid, p. 596
12. Tedlock, *Frieda Lawrence*, p. 223
13. Boulton, *Letters*, Vol 4, p. 578
14. ibid
15. ibid, p. 528
16. ibid, p. 546

17. Brett, *Lawrence and Brett*, p. 31
18. Boulton, *Letters*, Vol 4, p. 578
19. Quoted in Lea, p. 120
20. Carswell, *Savage Pilgrimage*, p. 222

Chapter Nineteen: Once Again in the New World

1. Brett, *Lawrence and Brett*, p. 63
2. Luhan, *Lorenzo in Taos*, p. 191
3. Boulton, *Letters*, Vol 5, p. 52
4. Quoted in Meyers, *D. H. Lawrence*, p. 313
5. Boulton, *Letters*, Vol 5, p. 192
6. ibid, pp. 203–4
7. ibid, p. 203
8. *The Plumed Serpent*, p. 463
9. ibid
10. *Aaron's Rod*, pp. 288–9
11. Frieda Lawrence, *Not I, But the Wind*, p. 141
12. ibid, pp. 149–50

Chapter Twenty: The Return

1. Nehls, *Composite Biography*, Vol 3, p. 8
2. ibid, p. 9
3. ibid, p. 12
4. Frieda Lawrence, *Not I, But the Wind*, p. 33
5. Boulton, *Letters*, Vol 5, p. 350
6. Nehls, *Composite Biography*, Vol 3, p. 21
7. ibid
8. Brett, *Lawrence and Brett*, p. 279
9. ibid, p. 283
10. Quoted in Meyers, *D. H. Lawrence*, p. 315
11. Brett, *Lawrence and Brett*, p. 279
12. Boulton, *Letters*, Vol 5, p. 421

Chapter Twenty-One: The Villa Mirenda

1. Boulton, *Letters*, Vol 5, p. 380
2. ibid
3. Harry Moore (ed.), *Collected Letters of D. H. Lawrence* (1962), p. 1172
4. Nehls, *Composite Biography*, Vol 3, p. 180
5. *Lady Chatterley's Lover*, p. 8
6. ibid, p. 18

7. ibid, p. 57
8. ibid, p. 47
9. ibid, p. 210
10. ibid
11. ibid
12. ibid, p. 170

Chapter Twenty-Two: Last Things

1. Frieda Lawrence, *Not I, But the Wind*, p. 182
2. Quoted in Moore, *Priest of Love*, p. 547
3. Boulton, *Letters*, Vol 6, p. 535
4. ibid, p. 409
5. Aldington, *Portrait of a Genius But . . .*, p. 111
6. ibid
7. Boulton, *Letters*, Vol 6, p. 616
8. Quoted in Moore, *Priest of Love*
9. Quoted in Seymour, forthcoming biography of Ottoline Morrell
10. Quoted in Moore, *Priest of Love*
11. Aldous Huxley (ed.), *The Letters of D. H. Lawrence* (1932), p. 364
12. Quoted in Moore, *Priest of Love*
13. ibid, p. 592
14. *Collected Poems*, p. 603
15. Quoted in Meyers, *D. H. Lawrence*, p. 371
16. Moore, *Letters*, p. 1164
17. Huxley (ed.), *Letters*, p. 792
18. ibid, p. 781
19. Ibid, p. 364
20. *Collected Poems*, p. 721
21. ibid, p. 697
22. ibid, p. 701
23. Moore, *Letters*, p. 975
24. *Collected Poems*, p. 716
25. Frieda Lawrence, *Not I, But the Wind*, p. 274
26. ibid
27. ibid, p. 273
28. ibid, p. 275

Chapter Twenty-Three: Aftermaths

1. Frieda Lawrence, *Not I, But the Wind*, p. 275
2. E. M. Forster, 'D. H. Lawrence', *Listener*, 30 April 1930
3. Bynner, *Journey with Genius*, p. 347
4. Quoted in Seymour, forthcoming biography of Ottoline Morrell

5. ibid
6. ibid
7. *Frieda Lawrence and her Circle*, pp. 43–50
8. Tedlock, *Frieda Lawrence*, p. 255
9. Letter from Dorothy Brett to Edward Nehls, quoted in Meyers, *D. H. Lawrence*
10. John Middleton Murry, *Son of Woman* (1931), p. 51
11. ibid, p. 66
12. ibid
13. Frieda Lawrence, *Not I, But the Wind*, p. 33
14. ibid
15. Huxley (ed.), *Letters*, pp. 769–70
16. Quoted in Corke, *D. H. Lawrence's Princess*, pp. 38–46
17. ibid, p. 39
18. ibid, p. 40
19. ibid
20. Luhan, *Lorenzo in Taos*, p. 274
21. Tedlock, *Frieda Lawrence*, p. 246
22. ibid, p. 248
23. Quoted in Lisle, *Portrait of an Artist*, p. 281
24. Tedlock, *Frieda Lawrence*, p. 412

SELECT BIBLIOGRAPHY

Aldington, Richard, *Portrait of a Genius But ...* (London, 1951)

Asquith, Lady Cynthia, *Remember and be Glad* (London, 1952)

Beauman, Nicola, *Lady Cynthia Asquith* (London, 1987)

Boulton, James T. (ed.), *Lawrence in Love: Letters from D. H. Lawrence to Louie Burrows* (Nottingham, 1968)

Boulton, James T. et al (ed.), *The Letters of D. H. Lawrence* (6 volumes, Cambridge, 1979–91)

Brett, Dorothy, *Lawrence and Brett* (Philadelphia, 1933)

Bynner, Witter, *Journey with Genius* (New York, 1951)

Callow, Philip, *Son and Lover* (London, 1951)

Carswell, Catherine, *The Savage Pilgrimage* (New York, 1932)

Chambers, Jessie ('E. T.'), *D. H. Lawrence: A Personal Record* (1935)

Corke, Helen, *D. H. Lawrence's Princess* (Surrey, 1951)

Corke, Helen, *In Our Infancy* (Cambridge, 1975)

Delavenay, Emile (trans. Katherine Delavenay), *D. H. Lawrence: The Man and his Work* (London, 1972)

Garnett, Richard, *Constant Garnett: A Heroic Life* (London, 1991)

Gathorne-Hardy, Robert (ed.), *Ottoline at Garsington 1915–18* (London, 1974)

Green, Martin, *The Von Richthofen Sisters: The Triumphant and the Tragic Modes of Love* (New York, 1974)

Hankin, C. A. (ed.), *The Letters of John Middleton Murry to Katherine Mansfield* (London, 1983)

Holroyd, Michael, *Lytton Strachey* (London, 1970; revised 1979)

Huxley, Aldous (ed.), *The Letters of D. H. Lawrence* (London, 1932)

Lawrence, Ada and Gelber, Stuart, *Young Lorenzo* (1931)

Lawrence, Frieda, *Not I, But the Wind* (New York, 1934)

Lea, F. E., *The Life of John Middleton Murry* (London, 1959)

Lucas, Robert (trans. Geoffrey Skelton), *Frieda Lawrence* (New York, 1973)

Luhan, Mabel Dodge, *Lorenzo in Taos* (New York, 1932)

Luhan, Mabel Dodge, *Intimate Memoirs*, Vol 4 (New York, 1937)

McDonald, Edward (ed.), *Phoenix: The Posthumous Papers of D. H. Lawrence* (London, 1936)

Meyers, Jeffrey, *D. H. Lawrence* (London, 1990)

Millett, Kate, *Sexual Politics* (New York, 1972)

Moore, Harry, *The Priest of Love: A Life of D. H. Lawrence* (London, 1974)

Moore, Harry and Roberts, Warren (eds.), *Phoenix II: More Uncollected Writings of D. H. Lawrence* (London, 1968)

Murry, John Middleton, *Son of Woman* (London, 1931)

Murry, John Middleton, *Reminiscences of D. H. Lawrence* (London, 1933)

Murry, John Middleton, *Between Two Worlds* (London, 1935)

Nehls, Edward (ed.), *D. H. Lawrence: A Composite Biography* (3 volumes, Madison, 1957–59)

Sagar, Keith, *The Life of D. H. Lawrence: An Illustrated Biography* (London, 1980)

Stevens, J. C., *Lawrence at Tregerthen* (New York, 1988)

Tedlock, E. W. (ed.), *Frieda Lawrence: Memoirs and Correspondence* (New York, 1964)

Tomalin, Claire, *Katherine Mansfield: A Secret Life* (London, 1987)

Worthen, John, *D. H. Lawrence: The Early Years, 1885–1912* (Cambridge, 1991)

INDEX

Aaron's Rod 132, 159, 165–6, 190, 211, 225
Adelphi 197, 201, 214, 220
'Adolphe' 162
Aga Khan 233, 234, 238
Albert Street School, Eastwood 33
Aldington, Richard 109, 116, 137, 150, 159, 216, 222, 229, 232, 234
'All Souls' Day' 235
Almgren, Antonia 101
Alvarez, Al 241
Amores 155
Andrews, Esther 147, 151
Anna Karenina (Tolstoy) 91
Antic Hay (Huxley) 150
Aphrodite 232
'Argument' 83
Arlen, Michael *see* Kouzoumdjian, Dikran
Arno Vale Farm 56
Asquith, Lady Cynthia 107–10, 111, 134, 159, 174, 249–50
Asquith, Herbert ('Beb') 107, 108, 109
Asquith, John 110
Asquith, Michael 110
Athenaeum 98, 162, 171, 201

'Baby Movements' 46
Balzac, Honoré de 39
Barr, Barbara Weekley 68, 76, 97, 137, 138, 196, 202, 213, 215–16, 217, 218, 221, 227, 237, 238, 240, 241–2, 243
Barr, Ursula 242
Barrie, J. M. 116
Baudelaire, Charles 47
'Bavarian Gentians' 235
Beach, Sylvia 230
Beardsall family 13, 23
Beardsall, George 14

Beardsall, Lettie 36
Beauvale Board School, Eastwood 22
Bendall, Edith 121
Bennett, Joan 251
Bentinck, Lt-General Arthur 110
Berenson, Bernard 181
Beresford, J. D. 137
Bernhardt, Sarah 53–4
'Bibbles' 189
Bid Me To Live (H.D.) 150
Birds, Beasts and Flowers 163
Black Sun Press 231
Blackwood, Lord Basil 108–9
Blake, William 170
'Blessed are the Powerful' 220
'Blind Man, The' 115
'Borderline, The' 201
Bottomley, Horatio 171, 229
Bowden, George 99
Boy in the Bush, The 118, 175, 200
Brett, Dorothy 100, 117–18, 124, 135, 196, 202, 203, 204–9, 212, 215, 217–18, 231, 244, 246, 248
Brewster, Achsah 169, 173–4, 183, 194, 217, 227, 228, 229, 237, 240
Brewster, Earl 169, 172, 173–4, 184, 194, 217, 227, 228, 229, 230, 233, 235, 237
Brontë, Emily 35
Burrows, Louie 45, 64–9, 71, 84, 94, 131, 248
Bynner, Witter 182, 191–4, 199, 201

Cannan, Gilbert 116, 120, 125, 132
Cannan, Mary 106, 116, 120, 132, 161, 171, 203
Carco, Francis 99, 132, 133

Carossa, Dr Hans 227
Carrington, Dora 125
Carswell, Catherine 103, 106, 114–16, 121, 125, 135–6, 146, 147, 149, 152, 155, 159, 160, 167, 171, 187, 195, 196, 197, 198, 201, 203, 214, 220, 249
Carswell, Donald 114–15, 121, 171, 196, 203, 249
Carswell, John 160
Carter, Angela 149
Carter, Frederick 206
Castaneda, Carlos 193
Cézanne, Paul 233
Chambers family 26, 29–33, 38, 40, 45, 56, 71
Chambers, Alan 31, 43
Chambers, Ann 29, 30
Chambers, David 32, 37, 247
Chambers, Edmund 29, 34
Chambers, Jessie 10–12, 23, 28, 235
    early friendship with Lawrence 29–43, 130
    character 30, 32–3, 53, 58, 92
    education 32, 34, 39
    relationship with Lawrence's mother 33, 35–6, 39, 56, 62, 70, 247
    influence on Lawrence's writing career 33–4, 39, 41, 45–6, 49, 50, 55, 57–8, 62, 69–70, 77, 95, 225
    discussions of marriage 35–6, 38, 40, 58
    sexual relationship with Lawrence 34–5, 37, 38–9, 47–8, 49–52, 55–7, 64–5, 70–1, 81, 83, 85, 88, 158
    Lawrence's criticism of 36–8, 51, 57
    and Alice Dax 42, 43, 50, 56

269

Chambers, Jessie – *cont'd.*
  correspondence with
    Lawrence 44, 94–5
  relationship with Helen
    Corke 48–9, 61, 66, 68,
    94–5, 246–8
  views on Louie Burrows
    66–7, 68
  views on Frieda 94–5
  life after Lawrence 246–8
  memoirs 247–8, 249
Chambers, May 23, 30, 32, 33,
    62, 70, 95
Chekhov, Anton 100, 125
Chesterton, G. K. 45, 58
'Child-Who-Was-Tired, The-'
    100
Churchill, Randolph 107
Churchill, Winston 117
Clarke, Eddie 71
'Coldness in Love' 54
Collier's Friday Night, A 18
Collinshaw, Mabel 19, 22, 25,
    30, 232
Conrad, Joseph 58, 67
Cooper, Gertrude 22
Coriolanus (Shakespeare) 34
Corke, Helen 45, 48–9, 52–7,
    58, 61, 64, 66, 67, 68, 69,
    85, 92, 94–5, 108, 131,
    149, 184, 225, 246–8
'Corot' 55
Cowper, William 13
Crime and Punishment
    (Dostoevsky) 95
Crome Yellow (Huxley) 111,
    156
Crosby, Caresse 230, 231
Crosby, Harry 230–1, 235
'Crown, The' 133

Daily Chronicle 66
Daily News 45, 133
'Dangers to Civilisation, The'
    (Russell) 123
Davidson Road School,
    Croydon 44, 46, 48, 50,
    68
Dax, Alice 11, 40–3, 46, 50,
    53, 55, 56, 57, 71, 77, 81,
    98, 228, 249
Day-Lewis, Cecil 251
de la Mare, Walter 80, 99, 124
Death of a Hero (Aldington)
    229
Delavenay, Emile 57, 247
Delius, Frederick 134, 173
Dennis, Gypsy 25, 35
D. H. Lawrence: Novelist
    (Leavis) 250, 251
D. H. Lawrence's Princess
    (Corke) 248

'Discipline' 46
'Discord in Childhood' 21
Dodge, Edwin 181
Doolittle, Hilda ('H.D.') 117,
    150–1
Dostoevsky, Fedor 11, 95,
    101, 125, 144, 146
Douglas, James 134
Douglas, Norman 161, 166–7,
    168, 222
Dowson, Will 75, 78, 80, 91
'Dreams Old and Nascent' 46
Duckworth 67, 90, 99, 177
Duncan, Isadora 166, 181

Eastwood 13, 16–17, 18, 25,
    27, 35, 40, 42, 45, 50, 60,
    64, 98
Eastwood Debating Society
    40
Eder, Dr David 105, 148, 169
Eliot, T. S. 198
Eliot, Vivien 198
English Review 45, 46, 58, 65,
    66, 87, 114, 149
Esher, Viscount 117, 206
Eunice Temple (Chambers) 247
Evans, John 187
Evans, Karl 181
Evening Standard 233
'Excursion Train' 53

Fantasia of the Unconscious 20,
    28, 169, 170
'Fantasy' (Corke) 54
Fiascherino, Italy 103
Fight for Barbara 93
First Lady Chatterley, The 236
'First Morning' 83
'Flying Fish, The' 211
Ford, Ford Madox *see* Hueffer,
    Ford Madox
Forrester, Arthur Dennis 180
Forster, E. M. 121, 240, 251
Four Winds of Love, The
    (Mackenzie) 120
'Fragment of Stained Glass, A'
    45
Frederick III, Kaiser 167
Freud, Sigmund 76, 91–2,
    169, 170
*Frieda Lawrence: The Memoirs
    and Correspondence*
    (Tedlock) 246
Friedan, Betty 252

Galsworthy, John 58, 67
Gamble, Mary 198, 199
Gardiner, Rolf 220
Gardner, Helen 251
Garnett, Constance 101–2,
    105, 107

Garnett, David 87, 88–9, 98,
    101–2, 105, 116, 119, 133
Garnett, Edward 25, 54, 67,
    78, 80, 87, 91, 92, 93, 97,
    101–2, 105, 107, 124, 134
Garsington 111–14, 125, 134,
    143, 144, 156, 228, 232
Georgian Poetry (Marsh) 102,
    107
Gerhardie, William 214, 229
Gertler, Mark 104, 118, 124,
    132, 139, 155, 202, 203,
    230, 237
Gill, Eric 238
Glasgow Herald 66, 114, 135
'Gloire de Dijon' 85, 223
Gotsche, Kai 189, 197, 201
Gray, Cecil 141, 150–1, 154
Greer, Germaine 252
Greiffenhagen, Maurice 114
Gross, Freidel 76
Gross, Dr Otto 75–6, 77, 78, 80,
    84–5, 87, 91, 162, 223, 241

Haggs Farm 29, 36, 50, 61,
    148, 246
Haply I May Remember
    (Asquith) 107
Hardy, Thomas 29, 58, 66
Harpers 126
Haywood's Surgical Garments
    26
Heinemann 58, 62, 66, 237
Heinemann, William 58, 67,
    124, 177
Heseltine, Philip (Peter
    Warlock) 113, 134, 138,
    171
Hilton, Enid 40–1, 98, 220,
    228
Hite, Shere 252
Hobson, Harold 88–9, 93–4
Hocking family 148, 154
Hocking, William Henry
    147–50, 155, 178
Hoggart, Richard 251
Holroyd, Michael 111
Holt, Agnes 46–7, 49, 50, 88
Hopkin, Sallie 9, 41–2, 86, 93,
    98
Hopkin, Willie 16, 25, 40, 41,
    95, 228
Howards End (Forster) 122
Hueffer, Ford Madox (later
    Ford Madox Ford) 45–6,
    57, 58, 67, 162
Hunt, Violet 58
Huxley, Aldous 89, 109, 111,
    150, 156, 198, 221, 227–8,
    229, 230, 234, 238, 240, 245
Huxley, Maria 221, 227–8,
    230, 234, 238–9, 240

Ilkeston Pupil–Teacher
  Centre 64
In a German Pension
  (Mansfield) 99
'Indiscreet Journey, An'
  (Mansfield) 133
Intimate Memoirs (Luhan) 183,
  184, 248

Jackson, Herbert 114
Jaffe, Dr Edgar 73
Jaffe, Else (*née* von
  Richthofen) 73, 75, 76,
  79, 81, 87, 92, 124
James, Henry 58
James Tait Black Prize 173
'Je ne parle pas Français'
  (Mansfield) 133
Jeanne d'Arc (Garnett) 92
Jenkins, Mrs 173, 174, 175
Jennings, Blanche 35, 41, 42
'Jimmy and the Desperate
  Woman' 19
John, Augustus 107, 111, 157,
  233
John Bull 171, 229
Johnson, Willard 'Spud' 182,
  191–3
Jones, Ernest 170
Jones, Mr and Mrs 44, 66
Jong, Erica 252
Journey with Genius (Bynner)
  191, 194
Joyce, James 230, 231
Joynson-Hicks, William 222
Juta, Jan 173

Kangaroo 145, 147, 160, 161,
  173, 176–9, 180, 210, 211
Kapp, Yvonne 214
Karavas, Saki 234, 243
Kennedy, Margaret 214
Kennerley, Mitchell 117
Keynes, John Maynard 123,
  142
Kipping, Professor 75
Knopf, Alfred A. 236
Koteliansky, Samuel S. ('Kot')
  125–6, 131–2, 138, 140,
  143, 149, 155, 159, 176,
  190, 196, 198, 200, 201,
  202, 203, 222
Kouzoumdjian, Dikran
  (Michael Arlen) 113, 223
Krenkow, Ada (*née* Beardsall)
  14, 72, 80, 88
Krenkow, Professor Fritz 14,
  72, 80, 88

Lady Chatterley's Lover (initially
  called 'Tenderness') 10,
  11, 178, 210, 221–6, 229,

230, 231, 232, 233, 234,
  242, 250, 251
'Ladybird, The' 108
'Laetitia' *see The White Peacock*
Last Poems 232
Lawrence, Ada (sister) 65, 67,
  71, 160, 213
  early life at home 16, 18,
    21, 23
  and Jessie Chambers 30, 35
  holidays with Lawrence 55,
    66, 69
  correspondence with
    Lawrence 94, 98
  in Italy 216–17
  visits dying Lawrence 230
  Lawrence's estate 240–1
Lawrence, Arthur (father) 33,
  37, 63, 71
  character 15–17, 24, 25, 29
  marriage 14–20
  drinking 18
  isolation from family 18–19
  death of Ernest 27
  death of wife 63
Lawrence, David Herbert
  9–12
  feminist attacks on 11,
    251–2
  and homosexuality 10, 11,
    31, 121, 123, 133, 142,
    148–50, 161, 166, 176,
    178, 207
  family background 13–17
  birth 17
  relationship with father
    17–20, 23, 63, 141, 167,
    170, 174
  relationship with mother
    18–22, 23, 24, 25, 28, 31,
    34, 39, 61, 82, 84, 141,
    170, 174, 179
  illnesses 21, 27–8, 32, 33,
    67, 69, 92, 119, 137, 140,
    142, 145, 154, 192, 201,
    207, 208, 211–12, 214,
    216, 221, 226, 227–31
  childhood 21–8
  education 22, 24–6, 30
  love of animals 23–4
  work at Haywood's factory
    26–7
  death of brother Ernest
    26–7
  visits to Chambers family
    29–32, 38, 56, 148
  early friendship with Jessie
    Chambers 29–43
  temper 32–3, 93, 94, 137,
    162, 163–4, 182, 187, 205
  early writings 33–4, 45–6,
    49

teaches at Albert Road
    school, Eastwood 33
  mother's views on writings
    34, 39, 62
  sexual relationship with
    Jessie Chambers 34–5,
    37, 38–9, 47–8, 49–52,
    53, 55–7, 64–5, 70, 81, 83,
    85, 88, 158, 246–8
  relationship with Alice Dax
    40–3, 46, 50, 53, 55, 56,
    57, 71, 77, 81, 98, 228, 249
  early sexual experiences
    40–3, 46, 49–50
  teaches at Davidson Road
    School, Croydon 44
  relationship with Helen
    Corke 45, 48–9, 52–7,
    58, 66, 67, 85, 108, 184,
    246–7
  relationship with Louie
    Burrows 45, 64–9, 71,
    84, 94, 248
  relationship with Agnes
    Holt 46–7, 49, 50, 88
  fear of powerful women
    53–4, 94, 158, 165, 180
  entry into London literary
    world 45–6, 57–9
  mother's death 60–4, 69, 92
  first meetings with Frieda
    Weekley 71, 72, 76–8
  relationship with Ernest
    Weekley 72, 80
  relationship with Frieda's
    children 77, 93, 95, 213–14
  elopement with Frieda to
    Germany 77–87, 124
  domesticity 81–2, 90, 121,
    141, 165, 184, 214
  quarrels with Frieda 10, 20,
    81, 84, 89, 101–2, 112,
    120, 126, 128, 133, 138,
    139, 140, 141, 146, 162–3,
    170, 186, 189, 191–5, 202,
    205, 214, 215–16, 245
  sexual relationship with
    Frieda 83–6, 87–9, 106,
    126–30, 141, 143, 146,
    150, 162, 163, 165, 188,
    209, 210, 216, 217, 221,
    222, 224–5
  in Gargnano, Italy 90–5
  return to England 95–8
  friendship with Middleton
    Murry and Katherine
    Mansfield 99–105, 120–1,
    130–3, 138–44, 149, 152,
    153, 155, 158, 162–3, 165,
    171, 190, 194, 201–3, 209,
    214, 219–20, 223–4, 231,
    245

Lawrence, David Herbert –
   cont'd.
   return to Italy 102–5
   attitude to the aristocracy
      103, 106, 108, 157, 206
   marriage to Frieda 105, 136,
      138, 178, 179, 186, 187,
      199
   and Lady Cynthia Asquith
      107–10, 111, 159, 174,
      249–50
   and Lady Ottoline Morrell
      10, 106, 110–14, 121,
      122–3, 134, 135, 138, 145,
      155–8, 171, 228, 234,
      242–3
   and Catherine Carswell
      114–16, 121, 125, 135–6,
      146, 149, 152, 155, 159,
      160, 167, 171, 184, 187,
      195, 203, 220, 248–9
   and Mary Cannan 116, 132,
      171, 203
   and Amy Lowell 116–17,
      143, 145, 160, 162, 167,
      177, 181, 194
   financial situation 117, 120,
      145, 159, 160, 161, 162,
      166–8, 172, 194–5, 208,
      213, 219, 240
   and Dorothy Brett 117–18,
      135, 196, 202, 203, 204–9,
      212, 217–18, 231, 246
   First World War 119–20,
      123–4, 145, 154–5, 160,
      161
   and E. M. Forster 121–2
   and Bertrand Russell
      121–4
   views on fascism 123–4,
      126, 177, 220
   anti-Semitism 124–6, 177,
      220
   Rainbow obscenity charge
      134–5, 137, 138, 222
   in Cornwall 137–59
   theories on blood
      brotherhood 142–3, 153
   call-up for military service
      145, 154, 160, 178
   and Esther Andrews 147
   and William Hocking
      147–50, 178
   visits Capri and Taormina
      161–8, 171
   visits Baden-Baden 169–70,
      214, 220, 236
   visits Sardinia 172–3
   visits Ceylon 173–5
   in Australia 175–80
   in New Mexico 172–3,
      180–90

   relationship with Mabel
      Luhan 172–3, 180–8,
      194, 200, 204–9, 211, 248
   and female sexuality
      188–90, 210–11, 222–3,
      224–6
   in Mexico 191–4, 208–12
   separations from Frieda
      194–7, 199, 216–18
   Murry's affair with Frieda
      196–203
   return to England 200–2
   reconciliation with Frieda
      202–3
   return to New Mexico
      202–11
   father's death 207
   return to Europe 212–14
   in Italy 214–27
   Frieda's affair with Angelo
      Ravagli 215–18, 221,
      222, 224, 229
   in Majorca 231–2
   paintings 232–4, 239, 250
   enters sanatorium 237–8
   death 68, 186, 199, 211,
      215, 220, 223, 230, 231,
      234–9
   burial 240
   obituaries 240, 242
   estate 240–1, 244
   ashes taken to New Mexico
      244
   accounts of his life and
      work 244–52
Lawrence, Emily (sister)
   early life at home 17, 21, 23
   Lawrence's views on 213
   visits Lawrence in
      Switzerland 228
   Lawrence's estate 240–1
Lawrence, Ernest (brother)
   early life at home 17, 21,
      24, 179
   and Gypsy Dennis 25, 35
   death 26–7, 33, 64, 69
Lawrence, Frieda 10–12
   quarrels with Lawrence 10,
      20, 81, 84, 89, 101–2, 112,
      120, 126, 133, 138, 139,
      140, 141, 146, 162–3, 170,
      186, 189, 191–5, 202, 205,
      214, 215–16, 245
   and Alice Dax 42–3, 249
   influence on Lawrence's
      writings 55, 91–2, 152,
      153, 223
   first meetings with
      Lawrence 71, 72, 76–8
   character 72, 92, 101
   family background 72–3,
      124, 161, 230

   meeting and marriage to
      Ernest Weekley 74–5
   writings 75, 92, 121–2,
      245–6
   extramarital affairs 75–6,
      78, 81, 88–9, 91, 94, 95,
      150–1, 230
   children 77, 78, 80–1, 82,
      86, 91, 92–4, 95, 97–8,
      100, 101–2, 105, 113, 120,
      126, 127, 131, 137–8, 176,
      194, 195, 196, 213–14,
      215–18, 220
   elopement with Lawrence to
      Germany 77–87, 124
   divorce from Weekley 80,
      86, 92–3, 99, 103, 105,
      120, 137
   domesticity 81–2, 90, 184,
      214, 219
   sexual relationship with
      Lawrence 83–6, 87–9,
      106, 126–30, 141, 143,
      146, 150, 162, 163, 165,
      188, 209, 210, 216, 217,
      221, 222, 224–5
   in Gargnano, Italy 90–5
   return to England 95–7
   friendship with Middleton
      Murry and Katherine
      Mansfield 99–105, 120–1,
      128, 130–3, 138–44, 146,
      190, 194
   jealousy 101, 104, 110, 112,
      113, 121
   return to Italy 102–5
   marriage to Lawrence 105,
      136, 138, 178, 179, 186,
      187, 199
   and Lady Cynthia Asquith
      107–10, 249
   and Lady Ottoline Morrell
      110–13, 138, 145, 156,
      158, 216, 242–3
   and Catherine Carswell
      114, 116, 146, 220
   financial situation 117, 120,
      145, 161, 172, 194–5, 208,
      219, 240, 243
   and Dorothy Brett 118,
      196, 206–8, 212, 215, 244
   First World War 119–20,
      154–5
   and Lawrence's
      anti-Semitism 124, 126
   in Cornwall 137–59
   illnesses 147, 208
   visits Capri and Taormina
      161–8, 171
   visits mother in
      Baden-Baden 169, 198,
      202, 236–7

visits Sardinia 172–3
visits Ceylon 173–5
in Australia 175–80
in New Mexico 172–3,
    180–90
relationship with Mabel
    Luhan 172, 181–3, 185,
    186–7, 202, 204–9, 248
in Mexico 191–4, 208–12
separations from Lawrence
    194–7, 216–18
affair with Middleton Murry
    196–203, 214, 241, 242
reconciliation with
    Lawrence 202–3
return to New Mexico
    202–11
return to Europe 212–14
in Italy 214–27
affair and marriage to
    Angelo Ravagli 215–18,
    221, 222, 224, 229, 241–4,
    250
Lawrence's illness and
    death 227–30, 234–9
in Majorca 231–2
Lawrence's paintings 232–4
death 234, 250–1
Lawrence, George (brother)
    64, 66, 98
early life at home 17, 21,
    22, 23, 24, 25
Lawrence's estate 240–1
Lawrence, Lydia (née
    Beardsall) (mother) 9,
    157
family background 13–14
marriage 13–20, 71
relationship with children
    16, 21, 24, 179
household management 16,
    22
death of Ernest 27
opinion of Jessie Chambers
    33, 35–7, 39, 56, 70, 247
views on Lawrence's
    writings 34, 39, 61–3
illness and death 60–4, 67
Lawrence, Walter (uncle) 26
Lawrence and Brett (Brett) 246
'Lawrence and the Apocalypse'
    (Corke) 247
le Maistre, Violet 214
Lea, Frank 142
Leavis, F. R. 250, 251
Leighton, Frederick 192
Letters of a V.A.D. (Skinner)
    175
Lewis, Wyndham 58
'Lilies in the Fire' 51–2
Listener, The 240
Literary Society 33

Literature in My Time
    (Mackenzie) 162
Litvinoff, Maxim 104
Look! We Have Come Through!
    82, 83, 86, 159
Lorenzo in Taos (Luhan) 183,
    185, 248
Lost Girl, The 167, 173, 201,
    249
Love Poems and Others 95
Low, Barbara 105, 148, 169
Low, Ivy 103–5, 114
Lowell, Amy 116–17, 120,
    143, 145, 160, 162, 167,
    177, 181, 194
Lucas, Robert 104
Luhan, Antonio 181–4, 185,
    187, 194, 205, 206, 207
Luhan, Mabel (Mabel Dodge
    Sterne) 10, 147, 172–3,
    174, 180–8, 194, 200, 202,
    204–9, 211, 224, 244, 248
Lynd, Robert 133

MacCarthy, Desmond 134
MacCartney, Herbert 48, 52
Mackenzie, Compton 31, 120,
    161–2, 224, 237
Mackenzie, Faith 217
McLeod, Arthur 61, 64, 93
Magnus, Maurice 166–8
Mailer, Norman 252
'Man Who Died, The' 235
'Man Who Loved Islands,
    The' 162, 237
Mandrake Press 232
Mansfield, Katherine 125, 165,
    206, 229
early friendship with
    Lawrences 98, 99–105
writings 99, 100, 194, 198
marriage to Murry 103, 130,
    131, 141, 143, 152, 153,
    159
illness 118, 155, 163
with Lawrences at
    Chesham 120–1, 130–3
death of brother 138
with Lawrences in
    Cornwall 139–44
death 190, 196
Mansfield, Leslie 138
Marsh, Edward 102, 107, 117,
    119
Mason, Agnes 48
Maugham, Somerset 208
Memoirs of the Foreign Legion
    (Magnus) 166, 168
Mencken, H. L. 169
Mendel (Gertler) 125
Merrild, Knud 189, 193
Merrivale, Lord 241

Methuen 126, 134–5, 177
Methuen, Algernon 135
Meynell, Alice 104
Meynell, Viola 104, 108, 121,
    132, 133
'Michelangelo' 55
Middleton, Richard Barnham
    149
Miller, Henry 252
Millett, Kate 11, 61, 188, 252
'Modern Lover, A' 49
Moore, Harry 10, 26, 32, 98,
    177, 244
Moore, Henry 232
'More Pansies' 232
Morland, Andrew 237
Mornings in Mexico 209
Morrell, Lady Ottoline 10,
    106, 110–14, 121, 122–3,
    134, 135, 138, 142, 143,
    144, 145, 146, 155–8, 171,
    185, 216, 228, 230, 232,
    234, 242–3
Morrell, Philip 110, 135, 157,
    158
Morrison, Nelly 171
Mountsier, Robert 147, 174,
    177, 180
Mr Noon 75, 80, 83–4, 88, 89,
    252
Murry, John Middleton 155,
    165, 223–4
early friendship with
    Lawrences 99–105, 118
literary career 101, 102,
    105, 125, 162–3, 201
marriage to Katherine
    Mansfield 103, 130, 131,
    141, 143, 152, 153, 158
and Lady Cynthia Asquith
    108
with Lawrences at
    Chesham 120–1, 130–3
discussion with Lawrence on
    sex 128
views on Lawrence's
    writings 135, 171, 245,
    249
with Lawrences in
    Cornwall 138–44, 146,
    149
writings 144, 146, 244
correspondences 150
Katherine's death 190, 196
exploitation of Katherine's
    work 194, 198
affair with Frieda Lawrence
    196–202, 241, 242
invited to join Lawrences in
    New Mexico 203
and Dorothy Brett 209
remarriage 214

Murry, John Middleton – cont'd.
Lawrence ends friendship
with 219–20, 231
My Life and Times (Mackenzie)
31

Nation & Athenaeum 169
'Nethermere' 45, 46, 49
Neutral Ground (Corke) 48, 52,
248
Neville, George 25, 26, 35, 51,
66
New Age 169–70
Newton family 13, 23
Newton, Ernest 23
Newton, John 13
Nietzsche, Friedrich 44–5, 126
Not I, But the Wind (Frieda
Lawrence) 42, 86, 87,
245–6, 249
Nottingham High School 25,
26, 30
Nottingham University
College 34, 44, 64, 74
Nottinghamshire Guardian 45, 64
Nys, Maria 123

Obscene Publications Act
(1857) 135; (1959) 251
'Odour of Chrysanthemums'
57, 65
O'Keeffe, Georgia 182, 250
Orioli, Pino 222, 234

*Paintings of D. H. Lawrence,
The* 232
Palms in Chapala 192
Pansies 230
Passionate Years, The (Crosby)
231
Patmore, Brigit 229
'Paul Morel' *see Sons and Lovers*
Pawling, Sidney 58
'Pax' 235
PEN Club, Mexico City 208
Penguin Books 251
Personal Record, A (Chambers)
247, 248
Pilley, W. Charles 171
Pinker, J. B. 134, 145, 167
Plumed Serpent, The 10, 193,
208, 209–10, 219
Point Counter Point (Huxley)
198, 229
'Pomegranates' 164
Portland, Duke of 110
'Portraits from Memory'
(Russell) 123
Pound, Ezra 58, 88, 90, 117,
134
'Prelude, A' 45
'Princess, The' 209

Principles of Social Reconstruction
(Russell) 123
'Prussian Officer, The' 119
'Psychoanalysis and the
Unconscious' 169

Radford, Dollie 140, 160
Radford, Dr Maitland 140, 160
Rainbow, The (initially called
'The Sisters') 44, 91, 105,
112, 114, 115, 121,
126–31, 148, 151, 158,
167, 175, 186, 245
obscenity charges 133–5,
137, 138, 222, 233
Ravagli, Angelo 215–18, 221,
222, 224, 229, 234, 240,
241–4, 250–1
Read, Sir Herbert 68
Reed, John 181, 183
'Reflections on the Death of a
Porcupine' 220
Remember and be Glad
(Asquith) 250
'Repulsed' 53
'Return, The' 53
Rhys, Ernest 65
Rhythm 99, 102, 105, 132
Richards, Grant 233
Rickards, Padre Edward 208
Rivera, Diego 191
'Rocking Horse Winner, The'
110
Royal Literary Fund 120,
159
'Ruby Glass' 45
Russell, Ada 177
Russell, Bertrand 113, 121–4,
126, 142, 157, 242

'Saga of Siegmund, The' *see
Trespasser, The*
'St Mawr' 187–8, 206, 245,
246
Sargent, John Singer 107
Saturday Review 87, 98
Savage, Henry 149
Savage Pilgrimage, The
(Carswell) 115, 146, 249
'Scent of Irises' 51
Schopenhauer, Arthur 35
Scrutiny 251
Sea and Sardinia 172–3, 248
Secker, Martin 167, 171, 215,
221, 236
Seltzer, Thomas 158, 169, 177,
194, 204, 213
Sexual Politics (Millett) 61, 252
Seymour, Miranda 112
Shaw, George Bernard 45
'She Looks Back' 82
Shelley, Percy Bysshe 38, 140

'Ship of Death, The' 236
Shorter, Clement 134
'Sigh No More' 56
Signature 133
'Sisters, The' *see Rainbow, The*
Skinner, Mollie 175, 200
'Snap-Dragon' 65, 107
Sobieniowski, Floryan 100
Society of Authors 134
Son of Woman (Murry)
244–5
'Song of the Man Who is
Loved' 85–6
Sons and Lovers (initially 'Paul
Morel') 15, 19–20, 25,
30, 36–7, 38, 42, 51, 55,
57, 60, 63, 69, 70–1, 77,
91–2, 95, 98–9, 101, 103,
107, 125, 126–7, 135, 149,
156, 173, 186, 204
'Sorrow' 60
Soule, George 169
Sphere 134
Star 134
Stein, Gertrude 181
Stephenson, P. R. 232
Sterne, Mabel Dodge *see
Luhan, Mabel*
Sterne, Maurice 181
'Still Afternoon' 46
Still Life (Murry) 144
Stone, Idella Purnell 192–3
Strachey, Lytton 111
'Sun' 231

Taylor, Rachel Annand 28, 65
Ten Days that Shook the World
(Reed) 181
Thompson, Clarence 207
Times, The 159
Times Literary Supplement, The
159
Titus, Edward 230
Tolstoy, Leo 11, 125, 151
Tomalin, Claire 155
Trespasser, The (initially called
'The Saga of Siegmund')
48, 52, 55, 62, 67, 69, 87,
90, 108, 117, 124, 184
Trinidad 209
Twilight in Italy 247

Uhlfelder, Dr Sidney 211
Ulysses (Joyce) 230, 231
Untermeyer, Louis 220

'Virgin and the Gypsy, The'
97
Volkhovsky, Vera 105
von Henning, Udo 81
von Marbahr, Lieutenant Karl
73–4

von Richthofen family 119
von Richthofen, Baroness 73,
    169, 198, 202, 214, 220,
    230, 237
von Richtofen, Frieda *see*
    Lawrence, Frieda
von Richthofen, Friedrich 72,
    73, 79–80
von Richthofen, Kurt 73
von Schreibershofen, Johanna
    ('Nusch') (*née* von
    Richthofen, later Frau
    Krug) 73, 75, 79, 171,
    227
von Schreibershofen, Max 75

Wagner, Richard 44–5
Warlock, Peter *see* Heseltine,
    Philip
Warren, Dorothy 232, 233
Warren Gallery 232–3

Waterfield, Aubrey and Lina
    63
Weber, Professor Max 73
'Wedding Ring, The' *see*
    Rainbow, The
Wedekind, Franz 75
Weekley, Elsa 97, 196,
    216–17, 218
Weekley, Ernest 71, 72,
    74–80, 91, 92–3, 97,
    100, 105, 120, 137, 138,
    205
Weekley, Frieda *see* Lawrence,
    Frieda
Weekley, Montague 76, 97,
    98, 196, 220
Wells, H. G. 45, 58, 238
Wemyss, Earl of 107
West, Dame Rebecca 251
Westminster Gazette 80, 99
Westminster Review 105

White Peacock, The (initially
    called 'Laetitia') 31, 34,
    39, 41, 50, 59, 62, 66, 69,
    95, 114, 149, 179
Wickham, Anna 133
Wilkinson, Arthur 218, 219
'Woman Who Rode Away, The'
    188, 206, 207, 211, 245
Women in Love 10, 56, 91, 125,
    130–1, 142, 143, 144, 146,
    148, 151–4, 155–8, 171,
    178, 187, 201, 210, 228,
    247
Women's Co-operative Guild
    18
Wood, John R. 246
Woolf, Leonard 125
Woolwich, Bishop of 251

Yeats, W. B. 88
Yorke, Dorothy 160, 229